I0606440

Praise for

UNSETTLED GROUND

"Jeffrey Katz has found a way to add something revelatory and powerful to the vast literature of the Holocaust: With a reporter's eye for detail and a passionate drive for stories that tell larger truths, he has produced a heart-rending history of his Jewish family's journey in and out of acceptance in pre-war Germany. He has returned to the homeland that rejected—and murdered—so many of his kinsmen, not so much to revisit the scars of genocide, but to understand those who have dedicated themselves to breaking their fellow Germans' silence about the Shoah. In the endless battle between the quest to remember and the human need to forget, Katz pushes to find what really drives people to dig among the shadows of a past that still hides so much pain."

MARC FISHER, author of *After the Wall: Germany, the Germans and the Burdens of History*

"Jeffrey Katz has given us an engaging and sensitive account of two worlds moving hesitantly toward each other via the past of his Jewish ancestors from two villages and two cities in Germany. As he belatedly uncovers their history, descendants of their persecutors try to face up to it, too. This is a remarkably balanced and human portrait of the benefits and limits of reconciliation over time and space."

PETER HAYES, author of the bestselling *Why? Explaining the Holocaust*

"Who are the German 'memory activists' who resurrect the stories of Jews the Nazis murdered, and do so not out of collective guilt, but a kind of righteous shame? Jeffrey Katz finds in the unsettled ground of the book's title a common ground with these truth-tellers, who just might reclaim the phrase 'ordinary Germans.' At the same time, Katz deftly takes up larger, knottier questions of public history and collective remembrance in this courageous, nuanced, and generous book. And he shares enough of himself to deliver that richest of hybrids—a reported memoir with the sweep of historical saga."

ALEXANDER WOLFF, author of *Endpapers: A Family Story of Books, War, Escape, and Home*

"If we mean it when we say, 'Never again!' we have to remember what happened to German Jews. The numbers—6 million—convey the enormity of the slaughter, but only the stories of individuals move us. They remind us that we offspring of German Jews who survived have a particular obligation to stand up today when tyrants threaten other peoples. Jeffrey Katz tells his family's story with detail and passion and eloquently celebrates the efforts of many Germans who are helping Jews recover the stories of our ancestors and labor to make sure that Germany never forgets."

DAVID WESSEL, senior fellow at The Brookings Institution

"Jeffrey Katz has used his journalistic skills of digging into the past to write *Unsettled Ground*. He's created a fascinating glimpse of what it was like to live in small towns in Germany as a Jew before and during World War II and put Holocaust history into perspective in our tumultuous present day. Bravo! I could not put it down."

JOAN NATHAN, author of *My Life in Recipes: Food, Family, and Memories*

"This is a moving journey to discover how generations of German citizens have tried to accept and make sense of the lasting damage done to their country by the dozen years of National Socialism that is both timely and timeless. The term *Vergangenheitsaufarbeitung* (coming to terms with the past) may not rip off the tongue, but it holds badly needed lessons for us all."

MARTIN GOLDSMITH, author of *The Inextinguishable Symphony: A True Story of Music and Love in Nazi Germany*

UNSETTLED GROUND

JEFFREY L. KATZ

UNSETTLED GROUND

REFLECTIONS *on* GERMANY'S ATTEMPTS *to* MAKE AMENDS

www.mascotbooks.com

Unsettled Ground: Reflections on Germany's Attempts to Make Amends

Portions of this book's introduction and chapter 20 first appeared, in different form, in *Moment Magazine*, as "In Praise of Germany's Flawed 'Culture of Remembrance.'"

Excerpt from *In the End, It Was All About Love* by Musa Okwonga, copyright © 2021 by Musa Okwonga. Reprinted by permission of Rough Trade Books.

For more information, please contact:
Mascot Books, an imprint of Amplify Publishing Group
620 Herndon Parkway, Suite 220
Herndon, VA 20170
info@mascotbooks.com

Library of Congress Control Number: 2025919094

CPSIA Code: PRV1025A

ISBN-13: 979-8-89138-809-3

Printed in the United States

For Mollie

And for Dad, Mom, John, Omi, Emily,
Ben—and Elisabeth

That wherever a right arm is extended and raised aloft,
The surrounding atmosphere cannot remain soft;
That trauma daily drifts up from the streets,
And exists in the mists and clouds around us.
In this way, history is forever among us,
Seething, teeming—
And maybe, if we heed its weight,
Even teaching.

—*From* In the End, It Was All About Love *by Musa Okwonga, a British author with Ugandan roots who lives in Berlin*

Contents

An Introduction

"WHEN OUR PATHS CROSSED"

The German village of Lembeck cherishes its history, which you might expect in a place that recently celebrated its first one thousand years. Tourists are drawn to a moated castle that originated in the twelfth century. Residents are proud of a Catholic church that's only about a century younger than that. But their collective memories skipped right past Lembeck's darkest chapter soon after it ended, when villagers persecuted their Jewish neighbors during the Nazi era, then watched as the Jews were hauled away to be murdered.

Elisabeth Schulte-Huxel, who grew up there in the 1960s and early '70s, had a simple answer when I asked what she learned about the Holocaust as a youngster. "*Nicht viel*," she said. Not much. The subject was discussed only briefly during her later years in school.

Elisabeth's interest was piqued in the early 1980s when she started to realize villagers were hiding something important. She soon joined forces with a small group of her peers from the area—now incorporated into the town of Dorsten—who shared her annoying habit of asking rude questions about the Nazi period. Their elders' discomfort only deepened their resolve. Dirk

Hartwich was one of those pesky activists, having learned in his twenties that his father's family included many active Nazi supporters. Now that he was a member of the city council, he had a public platform to ask whether Jews had ever lived there and what became of the town's leading Nazis. His determination stiffened when his inquiries were ruled out of order.

Thus began Germany's slow reckoning about a time it had worked so hard to erase, as what was happening in this small western corner of the country was being repeated elsewhere by the children and grandchildren of Nazi perpetrators and bystanders. They could have easily excused themselves from responsibility for crimes committed before they were born. Instead, they got busy documenting painful, hidden truths. They felt ashamed at what they learned, channeling their emotions into a powerful remembrance movement that came to fruition four decades after the war. They were determined to educate others about a Jewish presence in Germany that had existed for more than a millennium and to do what they could to prevent another genocide. This process of "working through the past" became known by the unwieldy name of *Vergangenheitsaufarbeitung*.

Around the time these young Germans were taking responsibility for atrocities their country committed during the Nazi era, I was belatedly expressing interest in my family's roots there. This book, in a sense, is what happened when our paths crossed.

I grew up in America only vaguely familiar with my heritage. I didn't know that my father's family had lived in the area around Lembeck and Dorsten for at least two centuries before most of them were killed. I didn't know that my mother's family had lived in Bavaria for a similar amount of time until they fled. And I hardly knew anything about the circumstances surrounding my parents' flight to freedom. My parents weren't interested in talking about what they had gone through until I was old enough and curious enough to ask. Even then, they were reluctant witnesses. They weren't enthusiastic about reliving the trauma they endured at an early age, nor subjecting my brother and me to it.

Whatever success I've had in reconstructing where my relatives lived for centuries—until escape was the only means of survival—is because I was helped by contemporary Germans, most of them born after the Hitler regime.

The bonds are tight between Germans at the forefront of this remembrance movement and descendants of Holocaust survivors, at least those of us who are open to it. I'm appreciative of the Germans I've met who've dedicated much of their lives to this cause. Some of them made it their career.

But I'm also keenly aware of the challenges when people commemorate a religious and cultural heritage that they were never part of. Their work can betray inauthenticity. There's also a performative aspect to the memory movement. Jews can feel relegated to the role of perpetual victims, assigned to vouch that a newly redeemed Germany bears no relation to a nation that once embraced Nazism.

More importantly, Germany has not fully eradicated its long-standing anti-Semitism, despite an earnest reckoning with the past. No nation has done so, though Germany might have been different. Goodwill built up over four decades buckled against the onslaught of anti-Semitism soon after Israel's destructive invasion of Gaza followed Hamas' murders and hostage-taking in October 2023. This wave of hate threatens the small but burgeoning Jewish community in Germany and shocks those who devoted much of their adult lives to extolling tolerance and diversity.

Still, I've been touched by the personal commitment that postwar, non-Jewish Germans have made to try to overcome their country's long-standing denial and apathy about the Holocaust. No, they aren't "righteous gentiles," akin to those who protected Jews from Nazi barbarians. They didn't save lives, and they didn't end racial and religious hatred. But they did save *memories*: uncovering artifacts and traces of a Jewish past, restoring synagogues and cemeteries, building memorials and museums, and educating members of subsequent generations who approached with open minds. These achievements are worth honoring, too. They've made history by helping those who were willing to remember history more accurately. Their actions in the "culture of remembrance," or *Erinnerungskultur*, ought to be preserved in any telling of the Holocaust and what came after. I've become as interested in their personal journeys as much as those of my relatives.

The pages that follow largely focus on a nation's remembrance culture, the stories told about a country's history that help shape what its citizens stand for today. In this way, "working through the past" is also rooted in the present. A psychological theory suggests that groups of people tend to cite history in a way that serves their current interests. The primary goal isn't accuracy; it's burnishing the group's image. Historical figures and events that don't fit the prevailing viewpoint get discounted. That's how the U.S. ended up with an executive order from the White House in 2025 decrying cultural institutions that promote "national shame" and "divisive narratives." It directed federal institutions to "remove improper ideology" and become "solemn and uplifting public monuments."

The problem is, if you believe as Rev. Martin Luther King Jr. did that "the arc of the moral universe is long, but it bends toward justice," you can't pretend that the arc is actually a straight line.

The German remembrance movement sought to bend the country toward historical justice. Activists shattered the relative silence about the Holocaust (also referred to as the *Shoah*, the Hebrew word for catastrophe), challenged the nation's collective memory, and achieved progress despite imperfect results. Most impressive is that this initiative began as a loose coalition of local efforts. Average citizens—not trained historians or elected officials, by and large—felt personally responsible for finding out what had happened in their hometowns and for seeking reconciliation with Jewish descendants, like me.

This book examines the movement through a wide lens, from its origins to its impact four decades later. But it provides personal stories, too. I write about my family's long history in Germany, how my relatives embraced their native land despite having to contend with centuries of restrictions on Jews, and how the lucky ones survived the Nazi era only by fleeing or hiding when they had the chance. I took too long to appreciate the relevance of their lives, wasting opportunities to capture more firsthand memories. I then agonized over whether I had the right to embrace my German roots, given my family's fate. I finally did so with my father's encouragement, as well as friendships I formed with German contemporaries. I seek to tell their stories, too, to understand what compelled them to respond to heinous acts they had nothing to do with. We'll meet people (most of them not Jewish) who live where my family once did and restored synagogues and Jewish cemeteries, created Jewish museums, and sponsored memorials that now dot the land.

Are there lessons for an America still wrestling with the legacy of crimes committed during this country's racist past? I think so. "What brought change and had made the German approach to commemoration into one that is seen by many as a model to be emulated," wrote historian Jenny Wüstenberg, "was not a sudden epiphany, but the tireless work of activists—Holocaust survivors, initiatives for reconciliation, and citizens' groups. This, indeed, is a lesson for us all."

But this book isn't a lesson plan for America. Focusing mainly on Germany's memorials neglects the hard work it took to get there, as well as its imperfections and the difficulty of changing hearts and minds.

Besides, there's no need to compare tragedies, to weigh the ravages of the Holocaust with the ravages of slavery and the century-plus of discrimination, segregation, and racism against African Americans that came after. For one thing, Jews weren't brought to Germany in chains. Though they endured centuries of discrimination regarding where they could live, work, or even be buried, Jews were in many ways more integrated into German society in the years just before Hitler's ascendance than they had ever been. And largely gone soon afterward.

Not only is this not a contest to see which group suffered most; I am also not an impartial umpire and don't pretend to be one. I come to this project unable to shake my background as a Jewish person living in America. African Americans, Native Americans, and others with their own history of persecution will look at Germany's memory movement and come away with their own perspectives.

The Nazis drew inspiration from slavery and America's eugenics movement (which sought to breed the perfect human race) to pursue their own program of racial hatred. But the Germans who followed in their wake years later, determined to take collective responsibility for the evils of the Hitler regime, didn't work from another country's blueprint to figure out how to make amends. They found their own way. My life is enriched by friendships that overcome the hate that motivated prior generations of their ancestors to terrorize mine.

Retracing My Family's German Heritage

This contemporary map of Germany and its neighbors includes places important to my family. The group of places in the northwest, around Essen, is where my father's family lived for centuries. My mother's family was from the area in and around Augsburg. I met with members of the local remembrance movement in both regions.

Map credit: David E. Chandler

CONFRONTATIONS WITH HISTORY

Chapter 1

VIEW FROM THE RHINE

"You shouldn't know from it."

The train I was on raced north along Germany's Rhine River even as my mind retreated deeper into the past.

By all appearances I was an American traveler, just turned thirty, out to see some of the world. I had spent several days with friends in historic Mainz and was now headed off the beaten path to the town of Dorsten. The train mostly hugged the banks of the Rhine, each town presenting a different face to the river. I saw castles built atop hills, one of them coincidentally named *Burg Katz* (Castle Katz). I admired the architecture of Cologne and Düsseldorf, cities I mostly associated with their connections to my family. Once the train reached Düsseldorf, I grabbed my suitcase and stepped off, bracing for what might come next.

I was less confident I belonged there than when I had boarded the train some two hours earlier. What had I been thinking? Did I have the right to *enjoy* a trip to Germany? *Germany?* Both of my parents fled during the Nazi regime—one with her immediate family, the other totally on his own. Relatives who didn't leave early enough perished. "This is not meant for me to enjoy," I wrote in my notebook that day in 1986. This wasn't my home. Why had I thought it was a good place to take a vacation?

My mother, Margot, was born in Augsburg in 1933, the same month Adolf Hitler became chancellor. We have a family tree, through her father's side of the family, that stretches across seven generations in Germany. It starts with my grandfather's great-great-great-grandfather, born around 1700.

My mother holds a doll for this family portrait in Cali, Colombia, with her brother, Gerd, and parents, Julius and Else Landauer.

My father, Rudy, was born in Essen in 1920. We have a family tree, through his mother's side of the family, that stretches back to my great-great-great-grandfather, born in 1769.

My father with his younger brothers, Karl-Heinz and Manfred, and mother, Rosalie Katz

Both of these family trees show dense branches in Germany, staying close to their roots. A contemporary car trip would take only an hour or two between the various towns where my father's family lived for two centuries in the North Rhine-Westphalia area or where my mother's family lived, farther south, in Bavaria.

My relatives were German patriots; a great-uncle died defending the country in World War I. That didn't matter to the Nazis and their many sympathizers and enablers—some of whom were my family's friends and neighbors. All that mattered was that my relatives were Jewish.

Practically the only survivors in either family were those who fled when they could. My mother's family recognized that oppression was looming and had enough resources to leave. She was five when they sailed to South America in 1938, making a new home in Colombia among a small group of German Jewish exiles.

My father's family stayed in Essen. Yes, there had been a history of Jewish persecution in Germany, as there was in many countries. But there were also periods of acceptance that lulled people like my grandfather into thinking this threat would pass, that Hitler and his henchmen wouldn't last. It was a mistake with fatal consequences. My dad survived only because his parents arranged for his escape. He was smuggled into a refugee camp in Belgium, then left shortly before the Germans overran it.

Exactly how he managed to get to the United States was something of a mystery to me as a youngster. Actually, *mystery* isn't the right word because I didn't think too much about solving it. I write that sentence now with shame that I could have been so naive to just leave it at that. I guess I thought that however he got here, I was an American, growing up in Philadelphia and then suburban Chicago, acculturated to all this country had to offer (even if, as a child of the 1960s, I rebelled against some of it).

My parents weren't eager to talk about their experiences. I think their attitude about the Holocaust was best characterized by the expression, "You shouldn't know from it." They were here to make a better life for themselves and their children—my younger brother, Mike, and me. There was no need to dwell on how they got here. Life began anew when they did.

Besides, why talk about the past and the sorrow it represented, especially for my dad? His goodbye to his parents and younger brothers needed to be quick and whispered, with a final hug they knew would have to last a lifetime.

The Nazis left few traces of my family's history in Germany. Even some Jewish cemeteries were desecrated, including those that held the remains of generations of my ancestors who had died by the 1930s. There weren't many burials after that. Most of the subsequent deaths came after they were deported and murdered, usually in lands to the east, their remains cremated or dumped in mass, unmarked graves. Why speak of that, of a government and people who saw Jews as an enemy? No, you shouldn't know from it, not in America, an imperfect place, to be sure, but one that offered a sense of hope, a new start.

My interest finally piqued when I was a young reporter based in Little Rock, working for a Memphis newspaper. I spent some of 1980 and 1981 writing about thousands of Cuban refugees temporarily housed in Fort Chaffee, a military training facility in Northwest Arkansas. I was telling my dad one day that I was moved by stories the refugees told me, about their quest for freedom and a better life. That's when he casually mentioned that he, too, had been a refugee.

I was stunned. And embarrassed. Here I was in my mid-twenties and had only just learned my father was a refugee. How could I have been so clueless? Okay, I told him, you *have* to tell me about your escape from Germany. And you *have* to let me write about it for *The Commercial Appeal*, the newspaper I was working for in Memphis, where he then lived. He refused at first. He didn't want to make a big deal of having been a Jewish refugee to so many people who didn't know about his past. He agreed only after I offered to not use his full name.

I now know the first task for many children and grandchildren of Holocaust survivors who become curious about their family's origins is one of discovery. What secrets did those survivors live with? Can we sift through newly discovered evidence to piece together the puzzle of what happened to those who perished eight decades ago, as well as those who lived through the nightmare years? How does this newfound knowledge color our thinking of the children and grandchildren of those who perpetrated the crimes or were complicit in their silence? And how does that calculation change when those offspring take the initiative to remember the past and memorialize what was lost?

My particular journey of discovery was paved by the children of some of my family's German neighbors. Around the time I first asked my father about his escape, they were an ocean away, asking uncomfortable questions like, "What happened to the Jews who used to live here?" That's how, eventually, my father and I befriended a group of people in the town where his mother was from. That's where I was headed on the train in November 1986, along the Rhine River. I had underestimated the anguish I would feel once I arrived. Was I disgracing my ancestors by enjoying a visit to the country that had taken their lives?

My soul-searching surfaced again a few days later. My new German friends took me to a railroad station shortly before midnight, where I boarded a train to visit what was then known as West Berlin. I noticed the train would continue on to Warsaw and Moscow. Several decades earlier, my dad's parents and brothers were rounded up and herded onto another eastbound train, perhaps on the very same tracks. It was to be their final destination in every sense.

Here I was, just one generation later, freely moving about the country as if none of this had happened. How could I have been so callous?

Then I realized, once and for all, there was no need to second-guess myself. I wasn't ignoring my heritage. My father had actually encouraged me to make the trip. I was guided in part by his handwritten notes on places that were meaningful to his life. More importantly, I was about to meet a group of people—most of them non-Jews—who took personal responsibility to restore the history of Jews who lived in the small town where my grandmother lived.

Elisabeth Schulte-Huxel pictured in 2011 in the Jewish Museum of Westphalia that she helped start

My appreciation for their work has only deepened over the years. That's why I've returned to Germany again and again. I wanted my wife and children to also walk where their relatives once did. And I wanted to meet more of the people who've been at the vanguard of a generation of Germans who acknowledge their country's horrific past of anti-Semitism and genocide. They wanted to understand how neighbors turned on one another, to memorialize the many Jews who were murdered, and to commemorate how they had lived.

In that way, Germany has been much more forthcoming about its ugly past than, say, America has been in acknowledging its own racism and history of slavery. You won't find Nazi statues and landmarks in Germany (though there have always been a minority of people who still embrace that hateful past). No one has carried a swastika into the Reichstag the way one protester waved a Confederate flag while storming the U.S. Capitol on January 6, 2021. That attack prompted my mother—who has never forgiven Germany for what it did to her family and the Jewish people—to text me from suburban Chicago, two days shy of her eighty-eighth birthday: "I am scared, it is incredible, looks like Germany."

These Stolpersteine adjoin the property line where the Lebenstein family house once stood and where my family members were deported.

But you will find one hundred thousand *Stolpersteine*, or stumbling stones, throughout Germany and the rest of Europe. These small bronze memorials, embedded in the ground, mark the last residence of choice of those who were deported during the Holocaust.

The names of some of my relatives are on those *Stolpersteine*, along with their birth date, the day they were deported, and where they were taken. The memorials exist because a group of Germans were determined that memories of a Jewish heritage not be erased as their lives once were.

Which is not to say that Germany's response is beyond reproach. Its success is more nuanced than it's often been portrayed. Recriminations for the Nazi era didn't cleanse the country of present-day anti-Semitism and nationalism. They also didn't inoculate Germany against the wave of anti-Jewish hate touched off by the Israel–Gaza war in October 2023.

Grassroots groups at the vanguard of Jewish museums and memorials in Germany occasionally display the limitations of non-Jews presenting Jewish history to other non-Jews. Contemporary terms like "Holocaust tourism" and "theater of memory" suggest the risks of historical inauthenticity and role-playing. Some non-Jews and Jews alike wonder if hyperfocusing on the Holocaust has created a sense of perpetual victimhood and left German schoolchildren with the impression that Judaism is essentially extinct.

I know that Germany can be overly solicitous in embracing Jews as a way of turning the corner on its violent past and have us vouch for a new, modern Germany. I've seen it. I've felt it. But I've also been deeply impressed by the many Germans who tirelessly sought to uncover the atrocities committed by a prior generation and atone for them.

Here are some of their stories. About places where many of my relatives lived for generations. About family members whose lives were taken from them—and those who escaped and survived to create new lives in America. And about a generation of Germans who owned up to their country's past and set a standard that the U.S. has yet to meet, however imperfect that standard might be.

On May 8, 1985, West German President Richard von Weizsäcker urged Germans to take responsibility for what their country had done. His speech before the German Bundestag, or parliament, marked forty years since the country's official surrender ended World War II in Europe. "*Es Versöhnung ohne Erinnerung gar nicht geben kann*," he said. "There can be no reconciliation without remembrance."

I recently learned that my maternal grandmother visited Augsburg in 1988, just three years after Weizsäcker's speech. She told a newspaper reporter that she was still haunted by memories that forced her family to flee fifty years earlier. But she used similar language as Weizsäcker to explain why she had returned. "*Ich bin mit Augsburg versöhnt,*" she said. "I'm reconciled with Augsburg."

Here are the first people who helped me reconcile with Germany and welcomed me to a home I never knew.

Chapter 2

FRESH FLOWERS ON A GRAVE

"Follow these traces."

Hildegard Scheunert always seemed energetic, so I imagine her walking purposely after hearing a knock on the door of her Düsseldorf apartment. The timing was curious. It was lunchtime that day in June 1985, and she wasn't expecting visitors.

She was startled when she opened the door. A stranger introduced herself and said she had questions about Franz Stutzinger, Hildegard's deceased partner. Hildegard was seventy-three at the time and more than a little intimidated by Elisabeth Schulte-Huxel, who was taller and less than half her age. Why was this woman asking about her dear friend who died four years earlier? Sorry, she said. Not interested.

Elisabeth had a lot riding on the conversation. The person she actually wanted to know more about was Franz's late wife, Malli, who had preceded him in death and was buried next to him. Elisabeth had been researching the Jewish history in her hometown of Lembeck, a history that ended abruptly with the Holocaust. That's how she knew of Malli Stutzinger, a member of the Lebenstein family, and why she had visited her gravesite. Elisabeth noticed that fresh flowers kept appearing on the Stutzinger graves. Perhaps whoever was responsible for the flowers knew something about the Lebensteins. Maybe one of the Lebensteins was still alive.

It wasn't Elisabeth's job to research local Jewish history. Far from it. She was a secretary at an energy company in Düsseldorf. But this was her passion. Her friends described it as more of an obsession, and an odd one at that. "Elisabeth is back on the 'Jewish Rally,'" one of them teased about her new-found interest in what happened in Lembeck and Dorsten during the Nazi era.

Her interest began during a trip to Israel in 1980 with her husband, Paul, her sister, and a friend. Paul's parents had given them the name and address of Josef Moises, who used to live in the nearby village of Wulfen. Moises had been taken into police custody during the *Kristallnacht* attacks on Jews on November 9–10, 1938, beaten, and forced to sell his house and textile business. Moises and his wife, Senta, soon emigrated to what is now Israel, where he happily greeted Elisabeth and her traveling companions and proudly showed them his orange grove. His home in Israel was filled with souvenirs from his hometown in Germany. He spoke warmly of his native land and encouraged Elisabeth to correspond with him, which she did.

Two years later, Elisabeth noticed that Moises was mentioned in an article written by a Dorsten journalist. She spotted some errors and contacted the writer, Wolf Stegemann. She learned that he was working with Dirk Hartwich, a member of Dorsten's town council, researching the fate of Jews who had lived in the area from 1933 to 1945. Elisabeth was intrigued by their efforts and joined them. Neither Schulte-Huxel, Stegemann, nor Hartwich is Jewish, nor are they trained historians. But they shared a mission.

Once Elisabeth learned about the Lebensteins' fate, she began asking questions of her parents and grandmother, who supported her efforts, and former neighbors of the family, who had mixed reactions. She quickly realized that many people in her small village didn't share her enthusiasm for digging up the past. They were hostile to anyone wondering what they had done—or not done—during an era now cloaked in shame. "Some indicated they didn't know anything about it, others attacked myself personally," she recalled. "To be quite frank, at the beginning I was shocked about these reactions."

She couldn't understand neighbors saying they didn't notice anything unusual going on as the Nazi persecutions began: "You should know that in Lembeck, being a very small town, you live on top of each other. Which means everybody sees exactly what's going on—and everybody is interested in what is going on in the neighborhood."

Yes, word travels fast in a small town. That includes when a group of people breaks a code of silence and asks leading questions about a time others prefer to forget. Soon Elisabeth and her colleagues were considered troublemakers.

She discovered that most Germans had short memories and little curiosity about what had happened during the Nazi era. It was as if they had followed my parents' admonition to their children: You shouldn't know from it. Except my parents were protecting their children from the horrors they had lived through; Germany was in denial. Nazi perpetrators had been caught and prosecuted, the thinking went. In reality, the number of those held accountable for Nazi-era crimes was a small fraction of those responsible. But a mythology developed that no one else who lived in postwar Germany did anything, because nobody saw anything, so nobody needed to feel too bad about anything. The new constitution banned Nazis and displaying anything having to do with that era, including swastikas. End of story.

As author Ruth Ellen Gruber put it, "Public anti-Semitism became officially taboo, but so, informally, did open reflection about the war, the Nazis, and German complicity in the Final Solution. An embarrassed and deliberate 'wall of silence' grew up about the 'Nazi Time.'" That's why Elisabeth responded "not much" when I asked what she had learned about the Holocaust as a youngster.

Two events in particular helped spark the German public's interest in learning more. One was the publication in the 1950s of *The Diary of Anne Frank*, a revealing portrait of a teenage girl hiding in Amsterdam, desperately clinging to her idealism even as she and her family were being hunted and betrayed. The other was the American TV miniseries *Holocaust*, which was shown in West Germany in 1979. It was the first time a major mainstream drama focused less on the perpetrators and more on the lives of Adolf Hitler's victims.

The television show was a turning point, Stegemann later wrote as part of the burgeoning *Dorsten unterm Hakenkreuz*, or *Dorsten Under the Swastika*, book and project. In a forward to the first book in the series about

Dorsten, Stegemann said the show prompted Germans to ask one another, "How could Germans commit such atrocities against people simply because they were Jews?"

The country provided few answers then. "Schools and teachers did not address this issue at the time," he continued. "It was only when the generation of teachers who were active in the Nazi regime and the war had retired that schools here and there began to answer questions about National Socialism and the persecution of the Jews."

The tide turned in the 1980s in many places across the country as a postwar generation of West Germans began questioning their parents, grandparents, and neighbors about what they did or didn't do in the Nazi era. These were not historians, by and large, and few of them were Jewish, the Jews having largely been wiped from the German map. These "memory activists" came from all walks of life. Some were inspired by taking part in broader left-wing protests against the established order in the late 1960s. All of them were now curious about what *wasn't* being talked about as the country began to mark major forty-year and fifty-year milestones of events after Hitler came to power.

They came together determined to get at the truth of why rank-and-file Germans closed ranks behind the Nazis and why neighbor turned on neighbor. This was a grassroots movement that formed organically in many parts of the country, without a national organization or leader. Each local group was united in the belief that their work needed to focus on what happened in the places where they now lived. They were inspired by the expression "*grabe wo du stehst*," or "dig where you stand."

The Dorsten group published the first of several volumes under the name *Dorsten unterm Hakenkreuz* in 1983. One chapter had condensed histories of Jewish families from the immediate area, including the Lebensteins of Lembeck. But little was known of the few survivors. It said my dad, whose mother's maiden name was Rosalie Lebenstein, had left via Belgium in 1939 on his way to America. That was all they knew. Elisabeth made her first appearance as an author for the project in May 1985.

There were plenty of detractors of these early efforts. One reader insisted Elisabeth got everything wrong. "He stated that I had not reported correctly the story of the Jewish family Lebenstein, since nothing happened to Jewish families in Lembeck," Elisabeth recalled. "Furthermore, he wanted to make believe that Lembeck and its inhabitants had passed the Nazi era with dignity and that Lembeck was an immaculate spot on the map during the time of the Nazi regime."

Elisabeth knew that one of Rosalie's sisters, Amalie (better known as Malli) Lebenstein, had married Franz Stutzinger, and that they were buried in Düsseldorf. The fresh flowers on Franz's grave were a clue that someone still cared deeply about them. So she asked the cemetery administrator and nursery responsible for its upkeep to tell her who was providing the flowers. They said it was a woman named Hildegard Scheunert and gave Elisabeth her address on Zietenstraße, which happened to be an easy ten-minute walk from her job.

Aunt Malli and Uncle Franz Stutzinger

Things got off to a rocky start after Elisabeth knocked on her door that day in June 1985. Hildegard was not only suspicious but actually frightened. She finally agreed to talk with Elisabeth, but only if they sat outside on her balcony despite the unusually chilly weather. That way a neighbor could listen to their conversation from an upstairs balcony, ensuring Hildegard's safety.

Tante Malli (seated left), friends Cläre and Anton Mies (standing), and an unidentified woman are gathered on the balcony on Zietenstraße in Düsseldorf in 1941. Four decades later, Hildegard Scheunert sat on that balcony and hesitatingly began to tell Elisabeth Schulte-Huxel about my family.

Elisabeth eventually convinced Hildegard that her motives were pure. The older woman softened, telling her about Franz and Malli. She also connected Elisabeth to my dad, who was living in Memphis, and to me, living in Washington, D.C. Elisabeth and Paul's first visit with us was during the fall of 1985 with my dad, who was vacationing in Asheville, North Carolina, at the time, and then with me in D.C.

My father and I were immediately struck by Elisabeth's deep humility, the intensity of her interest in what happened to the Jews in her village, and her desire to know more. My dad provided details about his life that he hadn't told me about, because I hadn't thought to ask. I was simply a repository of her knowledge then and, frankly, kind of befuddled that she was so interested in the subject.

In hindsight, as I contemplate recent critiques of the remembrance movement for being performative, it's worth noting that Elisabeth didn't approach us with an apology. She was doing the hard work of finding out what happened to the Jewish families in her hometown at a time when her parents' and grandparents' generations didn't want to talk about it. Her interest in our family wasn't confined only to what happened during the Holocaust. And she wasn't, by any means, patronizing. We weren't abstractions. She was eager to meet us, get to know us, ask questions, and share what she had learned.

Elisabeth's making contact with Hildegard and then my dad was a critical first step. It connected two people with personal knowledge of the Lebensteins with someone deeply researching what happened in the village my family was from. It typified inquiries being made across Germany then, stirring new interest in the Holocaust.

Elisabeth and the other members of her research group had no *need* to research the Jewish families who once lived in the area around Dorsten, the town that annexed the small village of Lembeck in 1975. They had nothing personally to atone for regarding events that occurred before their birth. Yet they wholeheartedly devoted themselves to this project not only with their minds, as an intellectual exercise, but also with their hearts, as they met with me and other descendants of survivors. And they asked questions early on that some of us had not even thought to ask.

"Through my research work, I have learned much about the sorrow and fate of Jewish families and I learned as well of the injustice towards prisoners of war, foreign workers, civilians," Elisabeth wrote in a letter to me soon after we met in 1985, concerned that she hadn't been able to express herself fully in English when we met.

"Very often I had restless nights after interviewing people and learning more and more horrible facts. I feel deeply ashamed that there was a generation before mine that acted worse than barbarians in medieval times," she said. "My visit to Auschwitz in springtime this year showed me even more clearly how horrible and inhumanly people acted. This remains a fact that I shall never comprehend ever in my life. For all these reasons, more and more I have the desire to point out to my generation and the following ones of what happened so that this shall never ever happen again—anywhere."

The memory activists were determined, even in these early days, as Elisabeth put it, to accurately depict the Nazi era to as many people as possible. "Young Jewish people, especially of my generation, are open and unprejudiced towards us," she wrote. "But this, however, is only possible as long as the events of the years 1933–1945 shall not be concealed and played down, but being recognized and coped with."

My father was impressed by his initial conversations with Elisabeth. "You and your colleagues will certainly be criticized a lot," he wrote to her in German. "Young people like you make me proud that my roots are German, and my culture and the culture of my children will remain German. The criminals of the old government were convicted by the judges. I have a lot of hope for the new generation, and now even more that I know from your reports, I wish you good luck!" He added at the end, "It seems that we know each other already for years!"

By now, my friendship with Elisabeth and Paul has endured over many decades. And though my connection to Germany is obviously more tenuous than my dad's was, the dedication of Elisabeth's research group has brought me much closer to my ancestral home.

Within weeks of returning from my first trip to Germany in the late fall of 1986, I got engaged to Mollie Fromstein, a young woman I had met earlier that year after joining *The Milwaukee Journal* as its political reporter. Elisabeth and Hildegard were among the guests at our wedding in Milwaukee the following year.

Elisabeth and Hildegard while in Milwaukee for our wedding in 1987

Like Tante Malli, Hildegard didn't speak English, so it was hard for us to communicate. I remember her as being full of pep, with an easy smile that let anyone who saw her know how joyful she was to be there. Neither Hildegard nor Elisabeth was family, but it certainly felt like they were, though we hadn't known each other long. Back then, I knew less about my family's history in Germany than I do now. But I knew enough to know these two people connected me to my roots in a way that time and distance and the Holocaust could not erase.

Our wedding presents from Elisabeth were two items that have become family heirlooms. One was a commemorative plate depicting the house in Lembeck that my family had owned for a full century before the Holocaust—a home I never knew in a country where my ancestors had long lived. The plate sits in a prominent place in our living room, a reminder of generations of relatives who called that house a home and the friend who gave us the memento.

The other item was Elisabeth's typewritten, sixteen-page, two-thousand-word history of my father's family, from 1800 to the birth of my brother and me in the 1950s. The final page was the first representation I'd ever seen of my father's family tree.

The narrative ends by describing the Jewish cemetery outside of Lembeck, which at the time had only a single tombstone and a memorial stone placed there by the Dorsten research group. Elisabeth wrote that my Jewish ancestors left behind "*eine vielzahl von spuren*," or "a multitude of traces," that they once lived there. It concludes, "If you follow these traces, they give a clear picture of the life and death of the Jews who used to live in Lembeck."

The greatest gift I received from Elisabeth and others like her was enabling me to piece together my own family narrative. These traces have taken on greater value as the years have gone by, whether they come in the form of documents, photographs, family histories—or, most moving of all, as guides to help me stand where my relatives once did. Each artifact, each moment, now takes on almost a sacred aura in my mind, representing my ancestors' hope and religious faith when faced with anti-Semitism and evil no matter when they lived in Germany. They are also irrefutable, enduring proof of how my relatives lived and how they died.

I can see more clearly why they felt safe in Germany longer than they should have and how they ultimately fell victim to a long-running pattern of anti-Semitism. To be a minority requires being wary. Even as a youngster in America, well before I learned the details of my family's experiences, the expression "it couldn't happen here" never felt right to me. How could we be so sure? Events of the last several years underscore that the environment is still ripe for hate and violence and despots.

Not long after the Gaza war began in 2023, Elisabeth and I shared regret that both Israelis and Palestinians had suffered and that hatred of Jews quickly followed in its wake. "We can only keep saying, 'No,' clearly when antisemitism, hatred and exclusion spread from the left and the right: in politics, in schools, in families and in clubs," she wrote me. She said it was important for her as an individual and for the regional Jewish museum she helped start to emphasize "respect, humanity and dialogue."

Those were some of the values that enabled the children and grandchildren of a generation of oppressors to reach out to the descendants of victims. Their initiatives enabled me to stand where my family's house did for a century, at the spot where some of them were deported, and place roses on memorial stones that honor them. To visit a synagogue where my father had his bar mitzvah and stand in wonder while my daughter danced at an interactive musical display there. To pay homage to Jewish cemeteries where some of my ancestors were buried, joining my son in placing a stone on the tombstone for the family matriarch. To follow my wife's lead in reciting the Hebrew prayer for thanks, the *Shehecheyanu*, at the miracle of standing on a new street named for the Lebensteins. To be in awe in the splendid, restored synagogue in Augsburg that one of my mother's relatives had designed.

Of course, nothing can replace the losses suffered by my family and many others like ours. Most of the survivors who directly felt the searing pain of the Holocaust have since passed on. The work that some present-day Germans have done to restore at least remnants of a Jewish heritage is for the rest of us. They are reminders that a proud, ancient religion once took root there. That even seemingly "good" people can be corrupted and succumb to their most base emotions, including to longtime friends and neighbors. That diversity of all kinds is a strength. And that some measure of reconciliation is possible even after one of history's most brutal chapters.

ORIGINS

Chapter 3

A VILLAGE IN GERMANY

"I don't know what we have done that the Germans would do this to us."

The Lebensteins were woven so tightly into the social fabric of their remote German village it was easy to forget they were outsiders. After all, they had lived in the small town of Lembeck for at least 150 years. Their house stood in the shadow of the town's Catholic church.

Various family members worked as farmers, traders, butchers, and stocking weavers, jobs that required them to constantly interact with other townsfolk. Most importantly, they were reliable. That was a critical trait in a village so poor and isolated that a popular saying was, "*Ein guter Nachbar ist besser als ein weiter Freund,*" or "A good neighbor is better than a distant friend."

Even in this digital age, with a firm emphasis on what's happening right now, standing in Lembeck today still lets you easily summon another time and place. You see an old town square that remains the town's centerpiece. A centrally located church where almost everyone belonged. A street grid based on the ancient flow of pedestrians, horses, and cattle. A traditional marketplace.

It's a village of about 5,100 people in western Germany, about thirty miles from the Dutch border. These days it's a part of Dorsten, itself a town of some 76,500 inhabitants, north of the old industrial city of Essen.

Lembeck emerges from nearby fields, meadows, and pastureland, much as it did a millennium ago. It was first mentioned as a place in 1017, when Holy Roman Emperor Heinrich II donated property in the area to the church. The name Adolf von Lembeck appeared in the documents of the Episcopal bishop of Münster several decades later.

The pastoral setting has plenty of forests, juniper bushes, streams, and farmland, as well as clay deposits that were used to build early houses. Most of those houses were grouped around the St. Laurentius Catholic Church, which officially dates to 1217. But in a village that happily traces its origins to medieval times, local historians note that this date is only when the church was first mentioned in documents that are now available. They like to say it was actually founded as early as the ninth century.

Lembeck's name lives on not only in the village that bears it but also on a moated castle, still a must-see attraction for tourists as the ancestral home of the knights of Lembeck. Schloss Lembeck originated in the twelfth century and, as *The New York Times* put it, has "stood in its present sandstone Baroque splendor since its last reconstruction and expansion was finished in 1692." The Count and Countess von Merveldt live in the castle that has been privately owned by his family for more than three hundred years.

Local residents take pride in the village, having recently celebrated a year's worth of events commemorating its first one thousand years. Their collective memories can be selective. There was a nine-year gap in the official online chronology from the parish church expansion in 1936 until "the village and castle suffer from bombs, shelling and looting" in 1945.

Wars and economic calamities did occasionally infringe on village life. But in many ways, Lembeck stood apart from outside influences. Much of it was a matter of geography. Today, it's an easy forty-minute drive from Essen. But throughout much of its long history before cars and modern roadways, it was removed from major trade routes and town centers.

Isolation was a defining aspect of life, so residents depended heavily on one another for help. Families designated a "first neighbor" as well as six additional neighbors they could turn to in a time of need. These designated neighbors summoned a midwife when a birth was near. They took care of guests at a wedding. And they let others know when a neighbor died, including notifying the pastor and gravedigger, and arranged to transport the body (sometimes having to do so themselves).

The village relied on agriculture. Its remoteness contributed to widespread misery and poverty. A report from about 1800 concluded that its residents would never prosper, despite their simple lives and frugality. In 1838, the mayor described its citizens in decidedly unglamorous terms. "Their way of life was simple, more dirty than clean, and they were not particularly industrious," he wrote. "A religious sense and a deep sense of morality were a major trait of their character, as were feigned humility, bitterness and mistrust of their rulers."

Power was generally held for centuries by knights, according to long-standing German laws. The Age of Enlightenment and French Revolution eventually changed that, as noblemen were forced to give up their privileges and the status of lowly farmers improved. The local economy began to diversify as crafts grew in popularity. Some people started working in areas such as spinning flax and weaving linen.

But there was no such diversity of religious beliefs. Almost everyone in the village of slightly more than two thousand people was Catholic, according to an 1840 census. There were twenty Jews.

And there was no particular reason for Jews to want to settle there. While it was common for castle owners to give some protection to the Jewish people in their midst, they didn't have the same rights as anyone else. Jews existed "without land ownership, without civil rights, mostly tolerated only for a short time, objects of exploitation and dispute between emperors, princes and cities, feared and hated by the guilds, viewed with the utmost suspicion by the church. The Jews lived almost exclusively from money-lending, which was as risky as it was despised."

Again, some of that changed at the end of the eighteenth century, when the effects of the French Revolution were felt in the region. And it was amplified when Jews obtained citizenship and equality under the law under the Prussia Emancipation Edict of 1812.

The name Lebenstein first appears in local documents around 1800. Mendel Lebenstein (also spelled as Loewenstein for a time) was born in 1769 and died in Lembeck in 1863, at the age of ninety-four. He and his wife Sara were my great-great-great-grandparents.

Lembeck's two Jewish families were generally integrated into village life. They attended the same festivals and celebrations as everyone else, taking part in choirs and local history and cultural associations. Jewish children joined their friends in decorating streets for Christian processions.

Similarly, no distinction was made between Jews and Catholics when Lembeck got its hands on its first fire engine, a prized possession in 1837. Bendix Landau and Nathan Lebenstein (one of Mendel and Sara's five sons) were among the many names listed in a publication two years later as being allowed to use it.

While agriculture was the main source of income in the village, handicrafts—from spinning flax to weaving linen—were becoming more popular in the 1800s. Salomon Lebenstein, the eldest son, was the only stocking weaver in the village. His oldest son, Alexander, eventually took over the business.

As time went on, the Jewish families made a living from trading in livestock, hides, skins, and other farm products, as well as grain, wool, honey, and haberdashery. "Alexander Lebenstein in Lembeck works as a stocking weaver," according to an account from 1853 that now resides in the Jewish museum in Dorsten, "eats well and sets a good example for his fellow believers."

Another of Mendel and Sara's sons, Nathan, started as a tradesman, became a butcher after cattle breeding grew in importance, and by 1855 was the village's only master butcher. Nathan married twice. He had three children with his first wife, Nette Spier, before she died in 1838.

A year later, he married Regine (or Regina) Salmon. They were my great-great-grandparents. In 1850, they bought a plot of land in the center of town, diagonally opposite the church. That's where they built a large home, at an address then known as Lembeck No. 15. They also owned small plots for gardening and livestock.

Together, Nathan and Regine had eight children. One of them was Isaac Lebenstein, my great-grandfather, born on July 10, 1847, in Lembeck.

The Lebensteins were Orthodox, the most traditional Jewish denomination, and belonged to the synagogue in Dorsten. The synagogue building was a simple apartment or house, so plain that it easily fit into the center of Dorsten.

The Lebenstein family appear in synagogue documents in 1858, which four of the brothers all signed by marking XXX. That doesn't necessarily mean they were illiterate. While they spoke German, they could only read and write in Hebrew. One of the family members was elected to the synagogue's board of directors in 1861 but turned it down because he said the eight-mile walk from his house in Lembeck was too far. His son was also elected but soon resigned because he was frequently late paying his dues.

For anyone living in Lembeck, getting a Jewish education meant making the long trek to the Dorsten synagogue on Sundays, for lessons that took place from nine to eleven o'clock in the morning and four to six o'clock in the afternoon. At one point, Isaac refused to send his children there, saying it was too far to walk and he couldn't afford to pay for the religious teacher or for a ride. So he asked if a Sunday school teacher could provide the lessons in Lembeck, expenses to be paid for by the royal government. He got a response from the government dated September 11, 1903, saying he was responsible for his children's religious education.

Isaac Lebenstein traded in manufactured goods, including haberdashery, cattle, furs, and honey. His trade was confined to areas immediately nearby because he had no ability to travel anywhere else, leading to an "insignificant business" and a "poor financial situation." His 1908 trading license described him as having a small stature, brown eyes, dark hair, and a full beard. Indeed, that carefully groomed beard is the most distinguishing feature in a photo that survives today, balancing a receding hairline. He stares into the camera intently, a formal appearance that matched his attire.

Isaac's first wife, Helene, died as she gave birth to their daughter, Regina, in 1887. A year later he married Sara Sophie Elkan (usually referred to as Sophie), my great-grandmother, in the nearby town of Raesfeld. Together they had seven children over fifteen years: Moritz, Rosalie (my grandmother), Amalie (or Malli), Selma, Bertha, Paula, and Hugo.

The Lebensteins of Lembeck (from left to right): Regina, Paula, Amalie, Sophie, Rosalie, Hugo, Moritz, Isaac, Selma, and Bertha

There's a photo of all of them, including Regina, in front of their house. Everyone is standing except for Sophie and Isaac, who are seated on wooden chairs placed on the cobblestones. It's undated, but given the height of the children, it was probably taken just a few years before Isaac died in 1918. They're wearing varying stages of formal attire, with expressions to match. Only Malli and Moritz (who's almost a head taller than anyone else) have a relaxed expression. Selma and Bertha look particularly uneasy, and Paula has a hand on her mother's wrist, perhaps for reassurance. Little Hugo, in the middle of the picture, seems to be proudly wearing a uniform of some type.

Isaac's death was noted throughout the village. Elisabeth says her grandmother told her that many of the village's residents accompanied Isaac's funeral procession. Sophie Lebenstein became the center of her large, extended family after that.

Pictures still exist of the house that once stood at the address now known as Wulfener Straße 16. Most noticeable was its long, steep, gabled roof. The side of the house faced the street, with four windows on the first and second floors and two more on a third floor under the gables, confirming my dad's recollection of its large size. The house appeared to be turned ninety degrees so that the front entrance was actually on the side, perpendicular to the street. I recently found a small photo in my dad's papers, marked on the back

"Malli's Haus—Lembeck" and dated 1929. It shows a young boy walking along the street as three women pass underneath two large trees, about to enter the front door. Just to their left stands another young boy holding his own umbrella. Given his size and the date, perhaps that's Manfred, the oldest of my father's younger brothers.

In another picture taken a year later, a band marches in front of the house. It looks like flutists are playing when the picture is taken, while musicians holding brass instruments follow close behind. They're followed by a long procession of well-dressed men, walking three abreast, some of them carrying placards that are not legible in the photo. It looks like a rainy day. The sidewalks are lined with people watching them parade by, some holding umbrellas.

Look closely and you'll see a young boy near the open door to the Lebenstein house, staring at the procession. At least a couple of women stand near him, doing the same. Two more women peer from the doorpost. One has white hair and dark clothing, perhaps my great-grandmother Sophie.

I've stared intently at these photos, looking for details, trying to imagine the moment when each one was taken. They briefly transport me to that time and place. Seeing that house, that town, makes my family's history more real.

A former neighbor, Josef Langenhorst, often visited the house around 1941–42, when he was about six years old. "There was a pear tree in front of the house that had very tasty fruit," Langenhorst recalled years later. "You had to walk down a bit to get to the entrance of the house. First you entered a very large room, where a beautifully curved staircase went up at the back. A balustrade ran around the top, from where you could reach the individual rooms above—at least three—and look down. At the bottom of the entrance area on the right was a huge cupboard that was very beautiful to look at. In front of the staircase was a seven-branched chandelier. Everything was always twinkling. Towards the back was the stable, where there were several stalls for horses and cows."

Sophie Lebenstein "was always dressed in dark clothes and wore long skirts or dresses," Langenhorst said. "She often had a scarf wrapped around her head. I always liked it there. I received lots of presents. My mother was also once given a vase as a present which I still fondly remember."

My great-grandparents Sophie and Isaac Lebenstein

A portrait of Sophie Lebenstein shows her staring at the camera, with perhaps slightly less intensity than a comparable portrait of her husband. Her hair had waves, and she wore an outfit with a high collar, her mouth set in what looks to be almost a rigidly straight line. She continued the family's manufacturing business with the help of her children. The cattle trade also grew with the help of sons Moritz and Hugo and the construction of a new slaughterhouse in the 1930s.

Relations between the Jews and non-Jews in Lembeck were relatively good until then. After education became compulsory in what was then Prussia, Jewish children attended the Catholic elementary school. Authorities noted that the Jewish and Catholic students happily played together. Isaac Lebenstein's grandson from his first marriage, Bernard Bendix, who was born in nearby Dülmen in 1917, loved his time in Lembeck.

"In 1919, my parents went to Lembeck to visit," Bendix said. "Grandmother Sophie wanted me there for a few days longer. My father became ill and died in 1921. Those few days turned into a few years. When I was six years old, I went to school in Lembeck. I went to elementary school until the fourth grade, but I had to go back to Dülmen to live with my mother. I was always homesick for my grandma in Lembeck. Then I was allowed to go there during my school holidays."

Celebrating religious holidays was no cause for dissension between Lembeck's few Jews and its overwhelming Catholic majority. The Lebensteins set up an altar at the annual Corpus Christi procession, which commemorates Jesus' Last Supper. One of my father's brothers, Karl-Heinz Katz, who also attended school in Lembeck for several years in the 1930s, fit in so easily that he was chosen to play Jesus in a Christmas nativity play. It was said he exchanged Passover matzah for ham sandwiches with his school friends, an unorthodox trade in every sense of the word.

The Lebenstein house was long considered the family's go-to place for large family gatherings. The many siblings, aunts, uncles, and cousins who had moved to nearby cities welcomed the chance to visit their relatives in the countryside.

"We used to have a good number of family get-togethers, usually in Lembeck, at my grandmother's house," my father told me, gatherings that could easily include fourteen to sixteen people or more. "Of course, she was the one who could not do much traveling. So we always used to converge for different occasions, usually birthdays, family occasions, holidays, whatever. I would spend a lot of summer vacations there." He would travel twenty-five miles north from his home in Essen alongside his parents, and his younger brothers, once they were born. Even in his sixties, my dad still fondly remembered being friends with many families in Lembeck, mentioning several of them by name.

They didn't have to venture far from Essen for the landscape to turn from factories and industrial buildings to green pastureland. I imagine the children in particular showing great anticipation as they approached this house they knew intimately. It was a home they had known their whole life, a place of comfort and warmth that welcomed them even as conditions around them deteriorated. A knock on the door would yield a chorus of loud greetings, open arms, and kisses. They'd step into the house and immediately inhale the enticing smells of a supper that had been planned for days. Bertha and Selma, two of my dad's unmarried aunts who lived with his oma, did much of the cooking and baking. "It was too rich," he said of the food, "and too good."

This was not only a big family but also a close-knit one. "That had to be, really," my dad said. "For one thing, as things got rougher, there was less chance for having contacts with the outside world. You spent more time within the family group. You had to be closer within the family."

By then, the storm clouds gathering over Germany cast large shadows in Lembeck in the years after Hitler came to power as chancellor in 1933. The little village was swept up by the same vicious anti-Semitism that was becoming prevalent throughout the country.

There's a receipt from 1931 showing the Lebensteins' annual membership to the *Heimatbund der Herrlichkeit Lembeck*, the village's home association that promoted local history and housed some of its cultural assets. But that same organization in 1934 included an essay in its annual publication titled "*Warum Rassenkunde*," or "Why Racial Studies?" It was written the year before by a local elementary school teacher who quoted Hitler extensively and warned that "racial cross-breeding lowers the level of the higher race and causes mental and physical decline." Stegemann, writing about the region's history in the Nazi era, described the essay as "nonsense about the Nordic master race, the de-normalization and re-normalization of culture and morals, but also the thesis that sick and weak life is a criminal disgrace that must be wiped out by the state."

Hitler was obsessed with racial purity and made anti-Semitism and racism a basic tenet of Nazi ideology. The Nazis considered the so-called "Jewish race" to be inferior and dangerous and needed to be purged from Germany.

The official persecution of Jews began on April 1, 1933, when Nazis boycotted Jewish businesses. It quickly intensified. Soon, Jews were banned from civil service. By 1935, they were stripped of their citizenship through the Nuremberg Race Laws, which restricted citizenship to those of "German or kindred blood." Jewish families like mine were excluded, no matter how many centuries they had lived in the country or how many wars they fought to defend it.

The pace of ostracism accelerated. Jews were banned from public facilities. In 1933, Jewish businesses were encouraged to Aryanize—to sell their businesses to non-Jews, usually for dramatically less than their worth. By 1938, Aryanization was mandatory. Jewish workers were dismissed. Jewish physicians were forbidden to treat non-Jews. Jewish lawyers had to abandon their practice.

These edicts were enforced in Dorsten and Lembeck as they were throughout the country. In March 1933, swastika flags first flew at Dorsten's town hall, post office, and train station. The following month, uniformed SA and SS paramilitary troops were posted outside Jewish-owned businesses with signs like, "*Kauft nicht in jüdischen Geschäften*," or "Don't buy in Jewish stores." Residents were ordered to perform a Hitler *Sieg Heil* salute during subsequent Nazi parades.

So perhaps it's no coincidence that my family's house appears buttoned-up in a picture taken on May 18, 1937, as a torchlight procession passes directly in front of it. The parade honors the bishop of Münster, who was attending the inauguration of the newly rebuilt church across the street.

The large Lebenstein family, so well entrenched for so many decades, had become the enemy. Some residents still secretly traded with the

Lebensteins, even when forbidden to do so. But most neighbors shunned them, reporting to authorities anyone who was still in contact with them. At one point, members of the *Hitlerjugend*, or Hitler Youth, screamed Nazi songs outside the Lebenstein house, smashed the windows, and poured manure through them. There was no going back after that. Townspeople avoided the Lebensteins when they could and insulted them when they could not. Survival became the watchword of the day for this once proud family. In order to make ends meet, the Lebensteins sold a large part of their belongings at well less than what they were worth.

Sophie Lebenstein was devastated that the family was now an outcast. She was eventually deported from the family's longtime home on January 24, 1942, along with the two daughters who still lived with her.

It's hard to imagine what that must have felt like for the matriarch of a large family rooted in Lembeck for one and a half centuries, much of it living in a house that was practically in the shadow of the church. To be part of a growing family—with eight children (including one from her husband's first wife) and nine grandchildren—that had branched out throughout much of the North Rhine-Westphalia region. To be part of a small religious minority that had generally been accepted in this overwhelmingly Catholic village.

What we do know is that she said something as she was about to be deported, a comment that has become a part of local lore, one hopes with shame. There are slight variations in precisely what she said, as her words were handed down through generations and translated to English. I've chosen to repeat them here as I first heard them, from Elisabeth's father, during my first trip to Germany.

The variations amount to the same thing. The meaning of the words is clear. They were undoubtedly thought and said, in one way or another, throughout history by previous generations of German Jews who were periodically persecuted and banished from their homes. They also reflect the pain and anguish of millions of people who were persecuted by the Nazi regime throughout Europe, regardless of their religion. In this case, they represent the shock of a woman, not quite eighty, entrenched in a rural village that had long depended on the goodwill of neighbors from birth through death, and who now viciously turned on her family. They also reveal a belated recognition that even friends and neighbors had turned their back on them, no longer identifying the Lebensteins as one of their own, no longer thinking of them as being German.

"I don't know what we have done," she said, after being cursed at, humiliated, isolated, and about to be deported, "that the Germans would do this to us."

Chapter 4

A MOTHER'S TOUCH

"She tried to be lighthearted during the darkest hours."

The door that closed on my great-grandmother's house for the last time in 1942 used to frequently swing open for large family gatherings. My relatives routinely sought one another's company even after most of them had moved away from Lembeck, looking for more opportunities than the small village could offer. The family's urban migration typified what was happening throughout Germany and to its Jewish population, as restrictions eased on where Jews could live. Although German Jews lived almost exclusively in villages and small towns in 1800, they steadily migrated to urban settings. By 1933, more than 70 percent of German Jews resided in urban areas.

As much as Lembeck represented Germany's rural heritage, Essen was an essential part of its industrial backbone. It was the longtime home of the Krupp family ironworks, a major supplier of steel, artillery, and ammunition, the country's premier weapons manufacturer for both world wars. Essen was also home to the huge Zollverein Coal Mine Industrial Complex, a major local employer and coal producer for 150 years, familiar to readers of Anthony Doerr's historical novel *All the Light We Cannot See*. "Essen benefited from the nearby coal mines of the Ruhr, the technological advances of the steam engine, and the entrepreneurial ingenuity of its most famous family, the Krupps," historian Michael Meng wrote. The city became known as "Armorer of the Reich."

My dad was born in Essen on December 15, 1920. He was given the name Rudi Katz, though he never told me that his first name originally ended with an *i* instead of a *y*. I learned that only after he died, while going through papers that showed he changed his name after coming to America. It was a startling discovery and a disappointing one, because I would have liked to have heard it directly from him. Perhaps he thought of it as a blip given the traumatic events in his life, if he thought of it at all.

His father, Leopold Katz, originally from Cologne, was a textile salesman who occasionally traveled across Germany representing a men's clothing manufacturer. The Katz side of my father's family was small compared to his mother's large and sprawling Lebenstein contingent. My father's paternal grandparents both died before he was born. His father's brother, Carl, fought for Germany in World War I and was killed on a French battlefield. About the only relative he met from his father's side of the family was an aunt who still lived in Cologne (and who later became instrumental in his escape).

My dad recalled his father as a "very lighthearted man most of the time" whose personality darkened as conditions worsened. "I mean anybody who was very lighthearted and the life of the party, so to speak, once all these things started to take place, you started to live with fear. It changes everybody. But my father, he had a lot of personality. He was a talkative sort of a guy. He was not the quiet type."

It turned out to be a difficult time and place for my dad to come of age as a Jewish youngster, but he remembered his home as a loving one. He fell under two strong maternal influences—his grandmother Sara Sophie Lebenstein and his mother, Rosalie Lebenstein Katz. He easily recalled his mother's influence when I asked him about it years later.

"I feel certain that she was most influential in endowing me with her personality traits, her kind of lifestyle and in teaching me early how to distinguish right and wrong, good and bad, to be frugal and yet to enjoy the nice things in life, providing they were in my grasp," he wrote to me when I asked about her. "She also taught me kindness and compassion, and that it took very little effort to act as a *Mensch* whenever possible," he wrote, using the Yiddish word for a person of dignity and good character.

Rosalie Lebenstein was born on February 7, 1899, in Lembeck, where she attended the Catholic elementary school and received her Jewish education in Dorsten. She worked as a saleswoman in the city of Mönchengladbach, near the border with the Netherlands, where she met my grandfather. They moved to Essen after getting married, first in an apartment at Sachsenstraße 16, then at Sachsenstraße 13.

Rosalie stopped working after being married, and her formal education was minimal, even for the standards of the time. But, my dad said, it was "more than compensated in her perception, her total character and the self-acquired knowledge in dealing with people, circumstances and her resourcefulness later when fate and disaster knocked on her door and the effect it had on all our lives. My father, too, possessed most of these qualities, but his severe heart ailment allowed him only passive participation in these activities."

She had a great sense of humor, loved to be with friends, and had the wisdom to deal with people as individuals. She was perceptive in recognizing character traits in friends and foes.

Rosalie Katz, née Lebenstein

Rosalie was a gracious and resourceful host, preparing gatherings that often involved her large, extended family. Her wit always came through. As people left a party, her standard goodbye was to say, "Too bad you can't be with us at the highlight of this evening!" When a departing guest was foolish enough to ask what she meant, my dad said, she replied, "That will be right after you leave and we will talk about you!"

My grandmother relied on all sorts of sayings and proverbs, no matter whether the occasion fit her quotation. If she forgot where she put an item before rediscovering it, she would say, "One has to lose something sometimes in order to experience the joy of finding it again." When things weren't going well, her favorite saying was, "Nothing will be eaten as hot as it gets to the table!"

She remained close to her two brothers, four sisters, and half sister. My dad said the whole family would meet three to four times a year at his oma's house in Lembeck (oma being another German word for grandmother).

Rosalie was not particularly religious, though my dad's family observed major Jewish holidays and attended synagogue throughout the year. They didn't keep a kosher kitchen, meaning they didn't follow the strict dietary laws of many Orthodox Jews, but they did try to maintain appearances for their grandmother. "Whenever Oma came to visit us," my dad said, "we purged all non-kosher items vigorously. I don't think our purging fooled my oma at all, and she used to kid us about our hiding game."

Rosalie didn't have any musical ability, nor did she play an instrument, but she loved listening to music (traits my dad and I both inherited). She preferred her music on the lighter side, such as operettas and show tunes. Some of her favorite composers were Richard Strauss, Franz Lehár, Emmerich Kálmán, and Jacques Offenbach, whose music she played on the family's wind-up His Master's Voice gramophone. The memories would come rushing back to my dad, some six decades later, when he would occasionally hear what he still thought of as one of "her" tunes.

My dad said his mother wasn't a strict disciplinarian and didn't like punishing her children, even when they deserved it. "However, when thoroughly provoked," he recalled, "she did not limit herself to scolding and made liberal use of her ring-bearing hand. I was the recipient on more occasions than I like to admit."

But she didn't carry a grudge. Once the punishment was administered, all was forgiven. On rare occasions, she would defer punishment and say, "I think we should wait until your father comes home." My dad described this as "music to my ears, because my father was definitely more of a softie and usually my punishment was a lecture and his standard phrase after his lecture was, 'I will not hit you now because it will hurt me more than it will hurt you!' Since I was the oldest of the three boys, my guilt usually was a foregone conclusion—since I should have used better judgment!"

My father had two brothers: Manfred, born on March 3, 1927, and Karl-Heinz, born on November 11, 1925. Karl-Heinz, by the way, was named after his uncle Carl who died in World War I.

As the economy tightened and political conditions worsened, my grandparents sent Karl-Heinz to Lembeck to live with his grandmother Sophie and two of her daughters. "The sadness of the situation, Karl-Heinz's separation from the rest of us, was a direct result of my father's inability to provide for us as an entire family," my dad recalled. Still, it worked out okay for a few years, as Karl-Heinz was generally accepted despite being just about the only Jew in an otherwise Catholic public school. "As a matter of fact, in one of the earlier years he was invited to the annual Christmas play," my dad said. "According to local lore, which made the rounds long after World War II ended, his curly hair and peaceful disposition made him a natural choice to play the main character."

Back in Essen, weekday afternoons were a good time for Rosalie to get dressed up, head to the city center, and visit a favorite *Caféhaus* for *Kaffee und Kuchen*, a midday German tradition of catching up with friends or family over coffee and cake. "Or she would take me to a nearby park for a leisurely walk and refreshments," my dad said. "Our lives were uncomplicated, filled with simple pleasures. There was not much traveling or opportunity for vacation trips. Being together with the family was usually at the center of our existence."

When the political climate still allowed it, she would invite friends to come over on Election Day, to sit near the radio and listen as the results came in, enjoying *Kaffee und Kuchen*. These gatherings usually lasted past midnight and were "a mixture of politics and *Gemütlichkeit*," my dad said, invoking the German word for good cheer and coziness.

"Above all, she was caring and loving to us, untiring in her efforts to make life better for us, protective and concerned," my dad said. "She tried to be lighthearted during the darkest hours and never gave up a good measure of humor to make the worst things a little more acceptable."

But the hours were getting darker, and good humor was soon in short supply.

Chapter 5

THE TEXTILE ENTREPRENEUR

"It took a lot of belief in the future."

Moses Samuel Landauer wasn't going to use his family's modest means as an excuse for why he couldn't get ahead in life. He was born in 1808, when Jews had few rights, the youngest of six children in a household where the breadwinner was a small-town Bavarian grocer. He started working at age thirteen as an apprentice in a weaving factory. He was still working more than five decades later, blessed with a long life when the average life expectancy was thirty-eight. By then, he was modest no more. The textile business he started continued long enough to celebrate its centennial and be managed by four generations of my mother's family.

He was known as M. S. Landauer, as was the company that bore his name, and he remains the dominant personality in the long history of my mother's family. Gernot Römer, who wrote authoritative books on the region's Jewish community and its impact on the local cultural, economic, and political life, characterized Landauer as "*ein erstaunlicher Mann*"—"an amazing man."

This early family history is bound up with Hürben, a formerly independent village that became part of adjacent Krumbach in 1902. M. S. Landauer's life is a useful measuring stick for the limitations placed on Jews and how those limitations could be overcome with a lot of work.

The earliest known ancestor of my mother's family was Raphael ben Iser, who was born in the last years of the eighteenth century, and his wife, Lea, born in 1813. It's not clear if they took the name Landauer, but subsequent generations did. Their hometown of Hürben typified the kind of small Bavarian village where Jews took some refuge from the many restrictions on their life. Documents confirm the existence of four Jewish families there in 1504. More Jewish residents followed over the next few centuries after they were expelled from nearby towns.

Jews had limited options as to where they could live in those days and what jobs they could hold. Even Bavarian towns like Hürben that permitted Jewish residents forced them to live in specific areas and limited how many could do so. They were subject to the notorious *Matrikel*, or "register," restrictions in Bavaria that sought to limit the number of Jews from 1813 until 1861. Every Jew was required to register with the local Matrikel, and the only way to obtain a *Matrikel* number was when one became vacant, such as by death of the previous holder.

Jews were also severely restricted in their occupations. Guilds prohibited membership to Jewish handicraftsmen, so they were prevented from many trades. Exceptions were made for occupations that the Jews needed to sustain themselves, such as baker and butcher. Because the Catholic and Orthodox churches banned their own members from lending money at interest, some Jews also filled the role of moneylenders for the Christian majority, then suffered the consequences of the stereotypes that went with it. Other occupations filled by Jews included weavers, cattle brokers, and peddlers who bought finished goods in town and sold them in the countryside.

Over time, Jews benefited from more freedoms granted to citizens throughout Europe. By 1808, the year M. S. Landauer was born, a report by a district court in nearby Ursberg described better living conditions: "Their physical condition in terms of their wealth has improved extraordinarily since the beginning of the French war, in that every traveler immediately notices the partly good and solid and almost mostly newly built houses as Jewish houses." It said even the few poor people don't starve "because they are treated without further ado by the rich Jews, and in this single piece they also deserve their praise, since they shame many a Christian community that lets their truly poor people languish."

Jews accounted for nearly half of all residents in Hürben throughout much of the 1800s, when the total population fluctuated at about one thousand people. A synagogue built in 1675 was expanded multiple times, as the outlook for its Jewish residents began to brighten.

The Jewish publication *Allgemeine Zeitung des Judentums* wrote about a Christian-Jewish Harvest Festival at the synagogue in 1847. "All the inhabitants of the village went to the Israelite house of worship and the rabbi gave a sermon that spoke to all hearts, deeply moved all minds and won him the love of all listeners," it reported. "In the evening, a meal was served, to which the district court assessors were also invited, and many heartfelt toasts were offered to the Israelite clergyman."

A history of the Landauer firm, written for its centennial by Otto Landauer, one of the founder's grandsons, described Moses Samuel's rags-to-riches story. He was top of his class in elementary school before being sent to work for three years as an apprentice in a weaving factory. He worked as a journeyman in at least two other such businesses, where he continued to learn about the textile trade. Because he didn't want to work on the Sabbath, he persuaded his employers that he could accomplish as much in five days as other workers could do in six.

One of his jobs was located about forty miles away in the city of Augsburg. Visiting his parents in Hürben, Römer wrote, required two twelve-hour walks.

In 1833, he got permission from local authorities to start his own company in Hürben. This was not an auspicious time or place to start a business, grandson Otto wrote one hundred years later. "The stagecoach was still the fastest means of transportation on poor country roads, there was no cable to convey messages, and a multitude of countries, mints, measures, etc., made business life in Germany difficult. The '*Schlagbaum*' [toll barrier] still prevailed and hindered traffic and the exchange of goods. It took a lot of faith in the future and good health to produce on one's own responsibility, a great daring to pursue the goal of expanding a small business."

M. S. Landauer set up his first handloom in his parents' house and sold textiles at local fairs. He added two more looms in a neighbor's home, employed several hand weavers, and started selling fabrics from a front-room store. He bought his own house soon thereafter and installed twelve machines in the basement. The business kept growing and expanding over the years, moving to larger quarters, as machines replaced hand weaving, churning out cotton fabrics, bedding, calico, linen, furniture, and sackcloth. Its customer base expanded, too, reaching as far as Berlin.

In 1835, he married the former Klara Guggenheimer. Between 1838 and 1858, she gave birth to fifteen children, of whom eight survived early childhood illness. And yet, "she worked every free minute in the company until her death in 1858," Römer wrote. M. S. remarried six years later to a woman also named Klara.

M. S. was even more successful as the family's progenitor than he was in his business. Years ago, my mom handed me a professionally published family tree dating from 1934. It consists of fourteen pages of high-quality paper, now yellow with age, kept inside a cardboard box that displays the names of M. S. and Klara Landauer. It associates the couple with 142 offspring (equally divided between men and women) across four generations, as of April 12, 1934. Each of their eight children who lived past age two reached adulthood, married, and had children and grandchildren of their own. Almost all of them lived in the area known as Bavarian Swabia, one of seven administrative regions in the southeast German state of Bavaria. My mother—one of their nineteen great-great-grandchildren at the time—was one of the last entries.

Formal portraits of M. S. and Klara Landauer from the family tree prepared in 1934

I knew this family tree was valuable but paid it scant attention until diving into research for this book. I would look at it occasionally, put off by its complex, multipage annotation as to who's who and how they were related.

Now I stare at the stately depictions of M. S. and Klara Landauer included in this keepsake and try to glean what I can from them. Her portrait appears to be a painting cast in dark hues, preserved in an oval frame. They're both wearing formal attire. She's outfitted in a black dress accented with white lace at the neck. A headscarf is draped over dark hair that's carefully parted in the middle and drawn back, earrings dangling at her side. She looks posed and a little uneasy. Her body faces toward the right on the page, her head turned a little to face the artist, the right side of her lips in a slight upturn.

Their portraits, printed on separate pages, look unmatched when placed next to one another. He was obviously depicted later in his life and in what looks like a photograph. His strong facial features are readily apparent—a prominent, straight nose; full lips; pointy chin. His hair has turned white and receded but continues in close-cropped fashion from sideburn to sideburn under his chin in what we would now think of as a Lincoln-style beard. He's dressed in a dark suit and white shirt with a black, crossover string necktie. While his torso faces the camera, his head turns to the right side of the page as he gazes into the distance. His facial expression is more at ease than Klara's, which seems to also match the lighter tone of his profile. While her name is printed under her portrait, his is distinguished by his signature, "MS Landauer" with no periods after his initials and a dramatic, eye-catching flourish underneath.

He gets top billing in everything, including the title on the cover. "*Die Nachfahren des M. S. Landauer,*" referring to his descendants, is about twice of the size of the words "*und seiner Ehefrau Klara*" that follow. Yes, it was a patriarchal society. But surely the woman who gave birth every year but two between 1838 and 1854, then died four years later, deserved equal billing for the generations of Landauers who followed.

Their portraits are also accompanied by smaller depictions of the houses in Hürben where he was born and later lived, as well as the company's head office. M. S. Landauer made his first venture into mechanical weaving in 1847 and was now selling cloth across Germany. But he needed a steady supply of water to grow the business further, to power machines instead of relying on hand-operated models. There were only a few mechanical textile companies then operating in southern Germany. In 1854 he obtained the rights to use water from the Kammel River, bought land nearby, and built his first full-fledged factory with modern machines powered by hydroelectric power. He got permission from the king to own a factory and, in a turnabout from his early religious practices, got the local rabbi's approval to run the machines on Saturdays.

The company took care of its employees, starting a progressive initiative in 1858 requiring workers to contribute to a health care plan that covered their medical treatment and medication. A fire destroyed the weaving mill in 1862, but the firm quickly recovered and by 1871 owned two hundred looms in a newly built factory.

Bavarian Jews were incrementally given more freedoms starting in the mid-1800s, which also gave the Jews of Hürben more options to emigrate, including to America. One of the most prominent émigrés was Lazarus Morgenthau, whose grandson, Henry Morgenthau Jr., served as treasury secretary under President Franklin D. Roosevelt, and great-grandson, Robert Morgenthau, was the longtime Manhattan district attorney.

Still, Jews continued to maintain a presence in Hürben. When the synagogue was totally renovated and reinaugurated in 1908, the *Allgemeine Zeitung des Judentums* wrote, "May the beautiful church be consecrated to its noble purpose and the service have an ennobling effect on heart and mind!"

By then, the Landauer firm had cast its eyes outside of rural Hürben to Augsburg, which offered better sales opportunities and improved transportation. This hadn't been an option before. For centuries, Jews were allowed to enter the city only through its Gögginer Gate and only to carry out their business affairs during the day, not to live there. In 1861, the discriminatory restrictions against Jews were abolished, and they were permitted to engage in all occupations, though they weren't granted complete equality until 1872.

In 1868, the company's headquarters moved to the town of Oberhausen, just outside of Augsburg, which became part of the city in 1911, and built an additional, larger factory there. In doing so, Römer writes, Landauer harnessed power from the Mühlbach and Hettenbach streams, an important ingredient in early industrialization efforts. The firm also benefited from many working-class families who lived in the immediate area.

M. S. Landauer ran the company that bore his name until retiring in 1874. He died in 1893 at the age of eighty-five, choosing his birthplace of Hürben as his final resting place.

The firm kept growing, becoming one of the largest textile factories in an area that was home to many of them. Augsburg was a center of Europe's textile industry long before the industrial revolution, according to the city's Textile and Industry Museum. The city's first cotton manufacturer opened in 1759, and by 1870 Augsburg had nineteen spinning mills, weavings, and bleach plants. An entire textile district developed around these manufacturing sites, employing more than thirty thousand workers as the twentieth century began.

The local industry declined during World War II, largely due to globalization. When Mollie and I visited Augsburg in 2022, there was but one remaining locally based textile company still manufacturing and marketing textiles in significant quantities. At the city's textile museum dedicated to this once-flourishing industry, I asked if Bavaria had grown its own cotton because I sure didn't see any growing now. No, said the museum's director, Karl Borromäus Murr. It was shipped there, usually via the port in Liverpool, England. "The availability of cheap cotton from the U.S.," he said, "was the basis of the economic success in the nineteenth century."

His words landed with a sickening thud. I understood the implications. Until then, I thought my family was about as far removed from the evils of slavery as any family could be. Now came the realization that the company my ancestors owned took advantage of enslaved people some five thousand miles away. I read later in Otto Landauer's history of the firm that the American Civil War dramatically raised cotton prices in 1863–64.

Murr also pointed us to a paper he had written on Augsburg's cotton imports and global trade. It notes that the regional chamber of commerce was concerned about the future of cotton production in the American South following slavery's abolition. "No evidence has survived of what spinners in Augsburg thought about the connection between cotton production and slavery," he wrote.

Even after the Civil War, no matter how well the Landauers treated their own employees, much of the American cotton at the heart of their business was produced at a time when white and Black sharecroppers were exploited by white landowners. "Although slavery had now been abolished," Murr wrote, "cotton production remained reliant on African American laborers, who still lacked full rights and independence."

Hürben remained a production facility for the company until the factory located there was set on fire by an arsonist in 1906. The house where M. S. Landauer had lived was sold to someone out of the family a few years later. "With this, the relationship with the ancestral homeland of Hürben expires," Otto Landauer wrote.

By then the Landauers considered themselves fully and comfortably ensconced in Augsburg, active in civic life and the Jewish community, and optimistic about the future.

NIGHTMARE YEARS AND NEW BEGINNINGS

Chapter 6

DARING ESCAPE

"I was pretty sure that I wouldn't see my parents again."

My dad began in a surprising place after I asked when he first realized he was no longer safe in Germany. He started not with any sort of dramatic development but with a short, simple phone call from his mother while he was at work. "I want you to come home immediately," she said, before quickly hanging up.

It was Thursday afternoon, November 10, 1938. My father had already been thrown out of school not because of anything he had done, but because he was Jewish. And he lost his previous job because he was Jewish. Now, a month before his eighteenth birthday, he was a wanted man.

A few years earlier, he'd been a student at Essen's *Humboldtschule,* a boys-only school that had existed since 1864. My dad left sometime after the German government began restricting Jews from attending schools in 1933. He tried to get an apprenticeship at a local department store. But at thirteen years of age, was told he was too young.

My dad (circled) in an undated school photo

There was nothing new about persecuting Jews in Essen. They were first mentioned in municipal records in 1291, then expelled during the next century, falsely blamed for an outbreak of the plague known as the Black Death. Several hundred years passed before there were enough Jews to formally establish a Jewish community in 1858. The most striking symbol of their presence was the 121-foot-high *Alte Synagogue* built in 1913 on Steeler Straße, smack in the city center. The Byzantine-style synagogue was built from limestone and topped by a green copper dome. It was one of Germany's largest and the pride of the roughly 4,500 Jews who lived in Essen by 1933, representing less than 1 percent of the city's population.

The consecration of the synagogue marked a high point in relations between the Jews and their neighbors. "The new building incorporates not only the advances made in the rise of the Jewish community," Mayor Wilhelm Holle said at a ceremony marking its opening on September 25, 1913. "It also demonstrates the tremendous development and upswing in the fortunes of our dear fatherland. Hand-in-hand the gifted artist and the Jewish community have produced a majestic building, and for this they have earned the gratitude of the city." The structure received wide praise for its innovative, modern style, which one reviewer termed the "beginning of the twentieth century."

Essen wasn't considered a hotbed of support for the Nazis when Hitler came to power twenty years later, but it quickly fell into line. Storm troopers stood outside of the city's Jewish-owned shops and businesses when a boycott began in 1933, preventing customers from entering. Hitler Youth took over a Jewish youth center—which included a café, lounges, and gymnasium—and emptied its contents.

With few options, my dad entered a newly opened "holiday home" for Jewish young people called Haus Berta that was created in response to Jews being excluded by much of society. About 250 boys and girls from the Rhineland and Westphalia region lived in barracks in the outskirts of Dorsten for parts of 1934–35. They were about the same age—somewhere between fifteen and twenty, my dad later recalled—tossed out of school, unable to find jobs. It was a camp of sorts, in the best meaning of the word, with days spent playing sports, singing, attending religious services, hiking, making crafts, and taking part in agricultural activities.

My dad was there for about six months, until it became the springboard for his next endeavor. The camp was visited one day by a sponsor, Gustav Blum, owner of a large Essen clothing store that bore his name. Blum had a conversation with my dad, who told him he had applied for an apprenticeship. My father must have made a good impression because he joined the store in 1935. That's also where Tante Paula—one of my grandmother's sisters—was a longtime employee. My dad worked there until September 1, 1938, when German authorities forced Jewish owners like Blum to sell his store and the Jewish employees were let go.

It was time to look again for work. "There was a small hardware store in one of the suburbs of Essen, still owned by Jewish people," my dad said, a store small enough to have avoided being shut down by the authorities to that point. "And they had given me a temporary job."

In hindsight, an obvious question comes to mind. Why not leave Germany by any means and as soon as possible? Jews were rapidly being stripped of their rights. It would have been hard to imagine even then that this would end well.

Hitler himself visited Essen a number of times over the years. He spoke to thousands of Krupp munition plant workers at a massive factory in 1936. "We are once again capable of accomplishing anything in Germany!" he shouted. "What great tasks we have once more! In these three years we have proven that we are a *Volk* [a people] with nothing to be ashamed of before the other peoples." Video shows him on a raised walkway with adoring crowds on either side, applauding and saluting. Other scenes show massive crowds in streets and town squares, swastika flags draped from the side of buildings.

The problem for Jews seeking to leave was they needed proper resources. They needed money and connections elsewhere to make a safe passage. They needed a country that would accept them at a time when many restricted Jewish immigration. And they needed to set aside, once and for all, any hope that their family's long-standing German heritage was going to matter to people who now saw Jews as a threat.

That last one was a particular sticking point.

"My father was of the opinion, having three young children and having some roots in Germany, we considered ourselves as German as anybody else," my dad told me, speaking slowly, carefully considering each word. After all, documents showed they were no less than fifth-generation Germans. "He felt that a lot of Hitler's extermination threats and wanting to rule the world were the threats of a maniac, that the German people sooner or later would get fed up and he wouldn't be the leader for long."

My grandfather should have known better, my dad said, especially after he had lost his job as a clothing salesman, then started a radio repair shop that was confiscated, ending the family's main source of income. He must have been scrambling to make ends meet any way he could. I was recently shown a pdf, now online, of the Essen synagogue's community newspaper, dated November 27, 1936. It includes a small ad with the headline, "The wise woman remembers the title of 'Alba,' the proven remedy!!" It touts Alba as a soap, dishwashing powder, and bleach, represented through the "distribution warehouse" of Leo Katz at Sachsenstraße 13—in reality, the address of the family's apartment. (An unrelated ad at the bottom of the page is for a record store, the address of which was the newly renamed Adolf Hitler Strasse.)

"I think he was just an optimist," my dad said of my grandfather, "at least until November 1938, when the pogroms started. And then it was too late."

November 9, 1938, was a fateful day for Jews across Germany. Nazi leaders unleashed a series of violent attacks against them that Wednesday night. *Kristallnacht*, the Night of Broken Glass, was so named because of the shattered glass strewn across the streets after Jewish-owned businesses, synagogues, and homes were vandalized and destroyed.

In Essen, National Socialists had changed the name of Burgplatz to Adolf-Hitler-Platz and used the square, which had been the city's central meeting place for two centuries, for their rallies and meetings. That night, they swore in volunteer units of the *Schutzstaffel*, or SS, the elite "Protection Squad" entrusted by Hitler to remove and eventually murder enemies of the Reich, like the Jewish population. They were joined by members of the paramilitary *Sturmabteilung*, or SA.

The iconic synagogue in the city center was a particularly inviting target. First the Nazis destroyed the iron gate that surrounded the building. Then they rousted Albert Heidt, the rabbi's assistant (sometimes referred to as a *shamash* or *gabbai*), and his son Ernst from the adjacent house they lived in. They forced the Heidts to open the synagogue doors, turn on all the lights, and retrieve the sacred Torah scrolls. Father and son watched in horror as the mob doused the holy books with gasoline, set the books on fire, then set fire to the building itself. The nearby fire brigade was called in late, with orders to protect only the surrounding residential buildings. Essen's Jewish youth homes were also set ablaze, as were Jewish-owned restaurants, shops, and homes.

But the Nazis weren't done yet. When Thursday morning dawned, the Gestapo checked for other Jewish shops in Essen that hadn't yet been destroyed and ordered that they be ruined, too. What did the residents of Essen make of all this? How did they respond? There's a photo from that Thursday showing smoke still pouring from the synagogue. What most draws my eye is the group of men in the foreground, wearing fashionable hats, passively taking in the scene. I wonder how many of them were the "good people" who had remained silent in the face of growing hatred, anti-Semitism, and fascism until it was too late.

A crowd outside the Essen synagogue on November 10, 1938
(Photo credit: Fotoarchiv Ruhr Museum)

About thirty thousand Jewish men were rounded up during these attacks nationwide and taken to concentration camps. It marked the first time Nazis conducted large-scale arrests of Jews solely because of their religion.

My father went to work at the hardware store as usual that Thursday, or as usual as he could under the circumstances, until his mother abruptly told him to come home at midday. I don't know what direction my dad was coming from on his way home, so I don't know if he saw the synagogue. His family's apartment was only about one and a half miles away, so he almost certainly noticed the smoke.

I do know what he heard once he got home and safely closed the front door. "My mother said that two people from the SS had been there, at our apartment," my father recalled. "They specifically had looked for my father and for me. They wanted to know where we are. My mother said she didn't know. She really didn't know where my father was. He had gone out that morning. She knew where I was. I said, 'What do you think I ought to do?' So she said, 'I really don't know what to tell you. But it's best that you leave as quickly as possible. Maybe you ought to go and visit Aunt Malli.'"

After everything he had endured for the past five years—being barred from attending schools, the boycotts and forced closing of Jewish-owned businesses, his parents' dwindling sources of income—it was only then, my father said, that he began to fear for his safety. And now the options were few.

One of Rosalie's sisters, Amalie (better known as Malli), lived in Duisburg at the time, about fifteen miles west of Essen. Malli, a saleswoman in a cigar store, was married to Franz Stutzinger, a lawyer. Uncle Franz wasn't Jewish, which gave him certain protections other relatives lacked. But it didn't immunize him from discrimination and eventually led to his being forced to stop practicing law. A file on him from 1939 says, "It is most regrettable that as a result of his marriage to a non-Aryan the very hard-working civil servant is limited in the fields of his work and is excluded from any sort of promotion."

So while it was better for my father to be out of the house and stay temporarily with his aunt and non-Jewish uncle, it wasn't a foolproof hideout. Just getting to them was risky. One of my dad's neighbors could spot him and notify the Gestapo, the political police force of Nazi Germany.

"I thought rather than take the train—you know, they're more apt to check things in a train station," my dad said, "you could also go from Essen to Duisburg by trolley car, but you had to make a couple of changes. So, I figured I'd take a trolley to Duisburg, which took longer, then see what I do from there." I can imagine him on crowded trollies that day, avoiding eye contact and any sudden movements that would attract attention. Subtly keeping his distance from the police and anyone who might recognize him. Suddenly wary of the familiar sounds and rhythms of the industrialized city. Knowing the risk that anyone who sat next to him, anyone who noticed him, could call him out as a Jew who was suspected of avoiding authorities. At that moment, his life depended on being a stranger in a place that had always been his home.

He stayed in Duisburg briefly, following Uncle Franz's advice to lie low. "I didn't venture out or anything for about a day or two, just kept myself concealed." He then traveled about forty-four miles north to the town of Südlohn, not far from the Dutch border. Moritz, one of Rosalie's brothers, had married a woman from there and took over his father-in-law's butcher shop. "I wanted to find out if there was a chance of being smuggled over the border, from there to Holland," my dad said.

Turns out that wasn't an option. "They weren't too happy. I mean, they were nice, and I could stay there. But they were concerned about themselves, and they didn't want anybody else who wasn't part of their family being there." Moritz and his wife, Antonia, were already preoccupied caring for their three young children.

"Then I went back to Duisburg," my dad continued. "So, I actually traveled for about five or six days. Which wasn't such a bad thing. It was probably safer to do than to stay in one place."

He stayed with his aunt Malli and uncle Franz until threats against Jews seemed to briefly subside. "We heard some people who had been rounded up and sent to concentration camps were being sent back or somewhere. So that's when I went back home, to see what was going on. I went back at night." But by then it was obvious that any respite in the Nazis' war on Jews would be brief.

Soon thereafter my grandparents made a gut-wrenching decision, made time and again by people throughout history who are oppressed and persecuted, with no end in sight. They now realized it was too late for all of them to leave the country safely and no place for them all to go. So they acted to save their eldest child from the Nazis' grasp, on the assumption he was the one most likely to make it on his own and most endangered if he stayed put. "I was the only one who was old enough," he told me, "to just try something that was little more daring."

My father had just turned eighteen. "People my age were their prime target," my dad said. "So there really wasn't any choice. My parents felt the same way."

My grandfather contacted his sister, Erna Rodenbusch, in Cologne, who was in touch with outfits that smuggled people across the Belgian border. "She told him someone was leaving in January," my dad said. "And he arranged things for me." He stuffed a few belongings in a satchel and prepared to say goodbye. He described the moment for me in a sentence as heartbreaking as it is straightforward: "I was pretty sure that I wouldn't see my parents again."

He hugged them one last time, then set off for the unknown. I think how ill-prepared he was for the journey. Nothing in his experience prepared him for what lay ahead. I don't think he had ever been out of the country at that point or even traveled beyond the immediate area. I'm not sure he knew anyone but Germans. On the other hand, he had to grow up fast as a teenager once the government-imposed layers of restrictions on his schooling and his work. Signs of anti-Semitism and hatred of Jews were everywhere. The best chance for survival required escaping and being on his own, whatever the risk. He had to leave behind everybody and everything he knew, hoping he could eventually make it to safety and save them all.

He boarded a train to Cologne and spent the night at his aunt's apartment. He was off again in the morning, this time traveling with smugglers and a small group of refugees, hiding in farmhouses on the journey west to Belgium. They arrived at the border near the German city of Aachen, on what my dad said was "some cold dark night in January 1939." Given that description, it was probably on or around the new moon phase of the 20th. He jumped out of the car and was taken by his rescuers to hide in the basement of a restaurant, along with several other refugees. A few days later, they were driven to Brussels.

Belgium's economy was suffering, and it no longer wanted refugees. So he looked for help from HIAS, the Hebrew Immigration Aid Service, which had formed in 1881 to help Jews fleeing pogroms in Russia and Eastern Europe. Its mission has broadened considerably since then, first to include Jewish refugees no matter where they came from, then to aid refugees of all nationalities, religions, and ethnic origins.

With HIAS' help, my father entered the Merksplas refugee center in northern Belgium, not far from Antwerp and along the Dutch border. He was legally able to stay in Belgium as long as he remained with about nine hundred other Jewish refugees from Austria, Hungary, Poland, and Germany at part of a huge prison farm sectioned off from other refugees. His cousin Herbert Rodenbusch from Cologne was among them.

Life there was bearable, my dad recalled. The refugees did a good job administering their part of the camp themselves. They were thrown together from different backgrounds and cultures. Most had left their families behind, and they were edgy. Sporadic fistfights occurred, but there were no large-scale disturbances.

The food was bad, though recreational activities were adequate. Refugees took intensive courses in English and trained in skills such as welding, "in the hope of getting an entry visa into the United States," my dad said.

Although he left home doubtful he would see his family again, my dad did visit a few times with his brother Manfred, who had arrived in Antwerp on a *Kindertransport*. The children's transport formed after *Kristallnacht* to rescue children from Nazi-controlled territories. The most well-known effort was in Great Britain, where immigration restrictions were eased for some children under the age of seventeen, allowing them to enter the country from Germany and German-annexed territories. The Belgian government organized a similar effort, which let about one thousand Jewish children temporarily find safety there. That's how Manfred was able to shelter in Antwerp with a Jewish family named Bochner.

Suddenly, a lifeline appeared for my dad. Rolf Braude, who recently married my dad's aunt Paula, had a brother in New York who could sponsor him. This was no easy task. Filing an affidavit of support, necessary to get a permanent visa into the United States, was like putting up a bond. The American would offer a certain amount of money to guarantee that a refugee would not pose a burden to society.

I have the blue duplicate and pink triplicate copies of my dad's notarized affidavit of support, dated November 8, 1939, one day short of a year since *Kristallnacht*. I can easily imagine the clicks and clacks of a typewriter as the keys repeatedly hit the ink ribbon and struck paper, providing the necessary information in all capital letters. Then the notary used a clamping device to emboss the seal. These papers are thin, fragile artifacts now. But they meant the world to my dad when they were sent to the American consulate in Antwerp, where he picked them up.

His sponsor, Edward Braude, had lived in New York only since February of that year. He listed my dad's financial status as "MODERATE," which was a stretch no matter what the criteria. And he listed my dad's occupation as "WELDING," which was also a stretch since it was simply the trade he and other refugees were taught for several months in Belgium.

Braude described himself in the affidavit as a salesman for the Mercantile Metal & Ore Corp. of New York, earning $150 a month. He listed his only assets as $5,657.36 in a bank. He said my dad, still referred to as Rudi Katz, would stay with him until he was self-sufficient.

Having an acceptable affidavit of support was only part of the requirement to sponsor a refugee. You also needed a favorable quota number.

Luckily, my grandfather had applied for a number long before he knew anyone in his family would have a chance to use it.

Quotas were part of America's strict immigration laws enacted after World War I, as the country became more isolationist. The economic recession and fallout from the 1918 worldwide flu pandemic prompted the U.S. to set limits for the first time on how many immigrants could enter the country. A succession of laws in the 1920s created an immigration cap based on the "national origins" of those already in the country. The numbers bore little resemblance to those desperate to flee Nazi persecution in the late 1930s.

Fortunately, my dad's quota number was called about three months after his father sent it to him. He went to the American consulate in Antwerp and confronted a line of people four blocks long, waiting for their number to be called or for an affidavit of support.

N° 173

Nr van het dossier O. V. / N° du dossier S. P. 704.

Naam / Nom Katz

Voornamen / Prénoms Rudi

Geboren te / Né Essen

Den / Le 15. Dez. 1920.

Nationaliteit / Nationalité Deutscher

Handteekening des houders - Signature du titulaire. Rudi Katz

30F

Zegel communal. / Sceau communal.

MODEL B

N° 173

Burgerlijke staat / État civil 1. Ongehuwd

Beroep / Profession 2. Handelsagent

MODEL B

Ingeschreven onder Nr / Inscrit sous le N° 173

rue n°

Afgeleverd te / Délivré à Merksplas

den / le 30 NOV. 1939

Dit attest, dat te allen tijde door den Dienst der Openbare Veiligheid kan worden ingetrokken, is geldig tot :

Ce certificat, révocable en tout temps par l'Administration de la Sûreté publique, est valable jusqu'au :

30 MEI 1940

De Burgemeester (of zijn gemachtigde). — Le Bourgmestre, (ou son délégué).

VERLENGINGEN — PROROGATIONS — N°

De geldigheidsduur van dit bewijs is verlengd tot : / La durée de validité de ce certificat est prorogée jusqu'au : 19

Te / A den / le

De Burgemeester (of zijn gemachtigde). — Le Bourgmestre (ou son délégué).

MODEL B

Ieder vreemdeling moet, alvorens een betrekking in België te vervullen, in het bezit zijn van een arbeidsvergunning.

Avant d'occuper un emploi en Belgique, tout étranger doit être en possession d'un permis de travail.

I have a couple of documents he must have had with him that day. One is a copy of his birth certificate, freshly provided on December 7, 1939, stamped and certified by the city of Essen. Given the date, his parents must have sent it to him after he left home. Another is his Belgian proof of registration, effective for six months beginning on November 30. The basic information is filled in with black ink, with dramatic penmanship and flourishes that don't look at all like my dad's handwriting. A small black-and-white headshot is stapled to it. He's wearing a tie and jacket, neatly coiffed. His mouth is in the same straight line I'd seen in photos of other family members over the years. It betrays nothing.

He showed the documents to a clerk, who approved them and gave my dad a three-by-five-inch card that became his lifeline—an entry visa, issued by the U.S. Department of State. On one side, with a green mesh background, was his immigration quota number, 14434, and the stamped signature of the U.S. consul; on the other side, a green immigrant identification card to be completed upon his arrival in the U.S.

I hold the card in my hands now, as he must have on that day, December 27, 1939. But I do so from the comfort of my home. He held it in a crowded American consulate, bound for a country he'd never set foot in, where he hardly knew a soul, fearful of what might be in store for the family he had to leave behind.

As the tumultuous year came to a close, he had most of what he needed to come to America. He just needed a way to get there. Short of cash, HIAS stepped in again, paying for the trip. That's how he was able to be aboard the SS *Westernland* as it set sail from Antwerp on March 1, 1940, to New York.

The ship already had several lives by then. It was built in 1917 as the steamer *Regina*, used mainly to ferry troops between Liverpool and Boston during World War I. Then it was retrofitted as a passenger carrier, mostly sailing between Liverpool and North America. It was sold twice, renamed the *Westernland*, and used by Holland America beginning in 1939 on an Antwerp–Southampton, U.K.–New York run.

What was my dad thinking as the ship navigated west out of the Scheldt River, then turned southwest, out of the North Sea, past the English Channel, and across the North Atlantic for ten days? He'd escaped the horrors of Europe, the Nazi jackboots, the increasingly harsh edicts, and the sense of foreboding that had long since overwhelmed even optimists like his own father. But what of all those family members left behind? And what would he do, where would he go, in America?

Perhaps seeing the Statue of Liberty, that iconic, 305-foot statue that was supposed to represent freedom, gave him some hope. Yet the words of Emma Lazarus, engraved on a bronze plaque in 1903, seventeen years after the statue was dedicated—"Give me your tired, your poor, your huddled masses yearning to breathe free"—represented an idealized view of America's openness to refugees that hardly reflected its policies.

The SS *Westernland* arrived in the Port of New York on Tuesday, March 12, 1940, a seasonably cold day. A document now in the National Archives lists Rudi Katz as one of the "alien passengers" who disembarked that day. He was nineteen years old. He was one of several Jews who listed Merksplas as being their last place of residence. It described his occupation as a merchant and said he spoke both German and English, a language skill he probably got from the refugee center.

The immigration inspector put a checkmark next to each name on the sheet and signed it at 10:30 a.m. Once my dad's entry was approved, an immigration officer flipped over the green card that had allowed him to leave Belgium for America. The other side had a copy of his black-and-white headshot stapled to it, as well as his name, birthdate, nationality, and eye color. The inspector signed it, then took stamp pads to mark the ship my dad had sailed on, his entry point, and the date. I can imagine the authoritative sound of the rubber stamps, loudly pressed against a wet ink pad, then held tightly against his ID card before being handed to my father.

IMMIGRANT IDENTIFICATION CARD
UNITED STATES
DEPARTMENT OF LABOR

3 19878

KATZ
SURNAME

Rudi
GIVEN NAME

Germany — COUNTRY OF BIRTH
Dec. 15, 1920 — DATE OF BIRTH

German — NATIONALITY
blue-grey — COLOR OF EYES

PORT OF ARRIVAL
STEAMSHIP

DATE ADMITTED
STATUS OF ADMISSION

Rudi Katz
IMMIGRANT'S SIGNATURE

IMMIGRANT INSPECTOR

ORIGINAL

And with that bureaucratic flourish, he legally entered the United States. He met Edward Braude, identifying him with the help of a photograph.

But any relief he felt must have been tempered by concern for his family. In fact, he made it out of Europe just in time. Germany captured both Holland and Belgium within two months of my dad's arrival in the U.S. and "they obviously deported all the people who were left in those refugee camps." My dad was among the no more than ninety of the nine hundred

Jewish refugees at the Merksplas refugee camp who had left. Those who stayed behind were destined for concentration camps.

German troops also captured youngsters who were part of the Belgian *Kindertransport.* My dad's brother Manfred was forced to leave the family he was living with in Antwerp and returned home to Essen.

My dad's voyage was the penultimate for the SS *Westernland* as a passenger ship. It sailed once more from Antwerp to New York in April before again being pressed into duty for a world war. It was used as the home of the Dutch Government in Exile at Falmouth, England, then as a troop transport, a repair ship, and finally a destroyer depot. There's a photograph of French General Charles de Gaulle and British General Edward Spears aboard the ship on route to Dakar in what's now Senegal, in September 1940.

It only took my father a couple of weeks to decide that he should get out of New York. The city was teeming with other freshly arrived immigrants. Jobs were extremely hard to find, and my dad didn't have a useful trade to fall back on. He never had much of an opportunity to figure out just what kind of career he wanted while growing up in Germany, having spent his teenage years reacting to the Nazis' harsh restrictions on Jews.

So he borrowed money for a bus trip to Philadelphia. He soon ran into a boyhood friend from Essen who was staying as a boarder with a family and working at Climax Dental, a laboratory and supply company for the local dental industry. Identical arrangements were soon made for my father. He moved into the home of Abraham and Carrie Schulmann in Philadelphia's Nicetown-Tioga neighborhood. My parents remained lifelong friends with one of their sons and daughter-in-law, Irv and Jean Schulmann.

My dad's declaration of intent to become a U.S. citizen was approved on December 3, 1940. He was described as having blue eyes; brown hair; a height of five feet, ten inches; and a weight of 140 pounds. He looks only slightly older in his newest black-and-white headshot than he had in one from the year before.

Now that he began to get settled, he tried to get the rest of his immediate family to join him. His new employer and friends helped scrape together enough money to get the necessary affidavits of support and pay for their passage to America. To complete the deal, he was asked to send a telegram to his parents to make sure they were still in Essen and verify they could receive exit visas when he sent them. He had exchanged letters with them periodically since he left (letters that unfortunately got lost in a move many years later).

The telegram was sent on December 6, 1941. "I never got a reply," he said, "because the next day Japan bombed Pearl Harbor, and there was no more communication between America and Germany."

Determined not to leave his family stranded, he enlisted in the military, hoping to return to Germany and find them. The goal, he later told me, was to be a parachutist. He was approved for training and services on September 25, 1942, and inducted into the Army on December 7. A document describes him as a dental laboratory technician—a more justifiable occupation than welder and an industry that would sustain his employment for a half century.

He never made it back to Germany before the war ended, getting no closer than the Hampton Roads area of Virginia. He was assigned to the medical detachment at Camp Patrick Henry in Newport News, a troop staging ground for deployment to Western Europe. That's also where he became a U.S. citizen on July 1, 1943. A black-and-white headshot attached to the paperwork shows him in a tan Army uniform with a tie and a cap worn at a slight tilt. Again, his mouth set in what looks to be a perfectly straight line.

He kept looking for ways to save the rest of his family. My recent online search turned up a letter dated November 29, 1944, from the Justice Department's Immigration and Naturalization Service to the War Refugee Board. It says the request by Sgt. Rudy Katz of Fort Patrick Henry, Virginia, for an immigration visa for his parents was approved. It provides his parents' names, birth dates, birthplaces, and last known address.

If only they could have been provided a visa much, much earlier.

World War II ended in 1945, marked by a series of tumultuous events. Hitler committed suicide on April 30. A week later, Germany gave its unconditional surrender. In August, the U.S. dropped two atomic bombs with devastating effects on Japan, which surrendered soon thereafter.

The war was over. Now it was time to see whether anyone else from his family had survived.

Chapter 7

MARCHING IN THE STREETS

"Julius, this is the last moment."

Unlike my father, my mother left Germany with her immediate family intact, though they, too, left under dire circumstances. The Landauers probably benefited from some combination of foresight, resources, connections, and luck, much of which my father's family lacked.

The way my maternal grandmother told the story, she had no illusions about what would have happened if they didn't hightail it out of there. She could scarcely believe her eyes as she watched brown-shirted Nazi storm troopers marching in the streets in the 1930s. They sang a song popular among their kind, words that haunted her for the rest of her life. "*Wenn das Judenblut vom Messer spritzt, Dann geht's noch mal so gut,*" they sang. "When Jewish blood drips from the knife, it is twice as good."

This was Augsburg, after all. *Her Augsburg.* A place where the large and thriving Landauer family had been successful in business, German patriots, and pillars of a Jewish community that considered the long history of anti-Semitism to be, well, mostly confined to history.

My grandmother, whose maiden name was Else Morgenthau, married into the family in 1928, a few days shy of her twentieth birthday. Her husband was

Julius Fritz Landauer, who became the fourth generation to run the family textile business when he joined the management team in 1929. Whatever the broader economic conditions, the mill endured. By 1933, the factory operated about 1,000 looms, employed about 430 people, handled the pensions of 45 former employees, and provided 40 flats at reduced rents for some of the workers.

The Landauers took their civic and religious responsibilities seriously, as embodied by one of M. S. Landauer's sons, Heinrich (1838–1917). Heinrich not only ran the textile business with his three brothers, but he also was "the synagogue and cemetery commissioner for over a generation and did outstanding work in this capacity," according to a chronicle by a subsequent commissioner, Albert Dann. "His upright, sincere character, his charity, his entire personality made him a worthy representative. Not only was he always open-minded about all Jewish affairs, he also worked in the city administration for decades, successfully handling the departments of municipal construction and human resources. He was awarded the extraordinary honor of the Golden Citizen's Medal."

The Landauers were patriots who served their country when it was at war, which was not an uncommon circumstance. The company supplied uniforms for the military during European wars of the late nineteenth century and during World War I. Otto Landauer (1882–1974), part of the third generation to run the firm, was awarded an Iron Cross for distinguished service during World War I.

My great-grandfather Hugo (1867–1929) was, like his father, Heinrich, a member of the synagogue's building committee. Cousin Fritz Landauer was one of the architects of the magnificent new synagogue built in 1917 on Halderstraße, near the city's center.

So my grandfather had every reason to feel comfortable when he settled into his usual seat, forty-two, in the synagogue's sanctuary on the High Holidays. "The name Landauer had a good reputation in Augsburg," wrote Gernot Römer, who included profiles of both M. S. and Heinrich Landauer in one of his many books about the local Jewish community. "The Landauers were very respected citizens of Augsburg until the Nazi seizure of power," said Karl Borromäus Murr of Augsburg's textile museum.

Hitler's shadow had loomed over Augsburg for years. The city was only about forty miles from his adopted home of Munich. His first documented appearance in Augsburg may have been in March 1920, helped by a local entrepreneur and benefactor. He returned often, his ideals having found fertile ground. A noncomprehensive list of his public speeches shows that he spoke there at least thirteen times, all but one of them before being sworn in as chancellor. Topics of his first two speeches, in 1921, were "The worker in a future Germany" and "Versailles: Germany's destruction." A local chapter of the *Sturmabteilung*, or SA, a paramilitary organization associated with the Nazi Party whose members enjoyed singing the vile song that alarmed my grandmother, was founded in Augsburg in November 1922. It suffered a brief setback a year later when it was temporarily banned after the Nazis' failed overthrow of the Weimar Republic, an effort known as the Beer Hall Putsch.

But a local group soon formed again. Hitler returned triumphantly to Augsburg on July 31, 1926, accompanied by two notorious collaborators, Rudolf Hess and Joseph Goebbels. The website TracesOfEvil.com mentions many more times Hitler came to Augsburg to speak, attend Nazi rallies, and even appear in court because of a traffic accident. Hitler's ideology influenced the Augsburg citizenry well before it spread throughout the rest of Germany. By 1932, Nazis were Augsburg's second largest local party. Hardly a day went by without one of their public meetings or demonstrations.

This would have posed a real threat to the Jews of Augsburg, who had lived in the city for hundreds of years despite periodically being banished. Archaeologists found an oil lamp and a menorah dating from the fourth century. Records from the thirteenth century document the presence of a synagogue, cemetery, ritual bathhouse, and "dance house" for weddings. But once Jews were blamed for the Black Death of 1348–49, they were either killed or expelled from Augsburg, much as they were in Essen.

Some Jews eventually returned to Augsburg, though anti-Semitism persisted. By 1434–35 they were forced to wear a yellow badge, then expelled again. An organized Jewish community wasn't reestablished until 1803. A synagogue opened in 1865, and the congregation continued to grow, eventually outstripping its home. A larger synagogue, built in Art Nouveau style, opened in 1917. Seating was available for nearly 800 people, representing most of the 1,000 Jews who lived there in 1933, still a small fraction of the overall population of about 176,000.

My mom was oblivious to worsening political conditions in Germany as a toddler. But my grandparents weren't. Hitler was appointed chancellor and assumed control of Germany just twenty-two days after my mother was born. Conditions spiraled out of control during the next few months and years, with the creation of the first concentration camps, book burnings, ban on Jews in public schools, and enactment of the Nuremberg Race Laws in 1935.

One of my grandmother's relatives in Augsburg, Oscar Rosenau, was prescient enough to sell his businesses—a china factory, as well as a cheese and dairy wholesale business. My grandparents were not as proactive.

By 1938, my omi was convinced that there was no time to waste, that the family needed to leave the country as soon as possible. My grandfather resisted, she said, because he wanted to sell the textile company first. "I had a feeling that this would not lead to a happy ending," she told an Augsburg newspaper during her visit fifty years later. She finally set a deadline of June 30. "I told him, 'Julius, this is the last moment. Otherwise you won't be alive much longer.'"

I know about some of the circumstances surrounding my family's departure from Augsburg but not, alas, because I ever asked my grandmother about it. I have instead been aided by documents and the recollections of others. One of the most valuable sources of information was an interview my grandmother gave to the *Augsburger Allgemeine* newspaper. Its long-standing interest in the topic came directly from veteran editor Gernot Römer, one of the most influential people in local efforts to remember and memorialize the Jewish heritage.

My mom remembered hearing that it was her father who insisted on leaving as quickly as possible, not her mother. Regardless, they left. The sale of the M. S. Landauer company was ultimately part of the aforementioned process known as "Aryanization," where Jews were forced to sell property to non-Jews at well below market value. Sometimes Jewish owners preempted official orders to divest their holdings by selling to a trusted business associate instead, though that didn't necessarily help them avoid major losses. Thus, the cotton weaving mill M. S. Landauer was sold under duress to the C.F. Ploucquet company, on March 21, 1938, for much less than it was worth.

"We would like to take this opportunity to thank you most sincerely for the trust you have placed in us," a memo confirming the sale concluded, in a total misdirection of what had just happened.

My mother was five when she left Augsburg on June 28, 1938, with her parents, older brother Gerd, and three surviving grandparents. But not before a final indignity. A uniformed German who was there as they prepared to depart suddenly snatched a small bag from her hand. "I will never forget the child's tears when the man opened the bag and confiscated ten individual pfennigs (pennies)," my grandmother said years later.

My mom forgot that incident and almost everything else about her early years in Germany, beyond having a couple of turtles that she fed lettuce to. But she never forgot or forgave the hatred that forced her family to flee.

They left Augsburg in 1938 with little time to spare, about four months before Nazis wreaked more havoc on whatever remained of the Jewish community. The Sabbath service on November 4 began on a particularly somber note at Augsburg's central synagogue, with Rabbi Ernst Jacob urging congregants to emigrate if they still could. By then, it was quite late. That became more obvious five nights later, when *Kristallnacht* left in ashes whatever optimism lingered among Augsburg's Jews, thirty-one years after the synagogue opened.

Sofie Dann, the daughter of an Augsburg synagogue board member, later described the destruction. She said twenty to thirty young men forcibly entered the synagogue armed with spears, axes, and clubs. They cut the telephone line, destroyed documents, smashed candlesticks, and vandalized Torah scrolls and other sacred objects. Then they set the synagogue on fire.

That the building visibly expressed the congregants' devotion to their country as well as their religion couldn't have been less relevant. The only thing that saved it from being completely destroyed was its close proximity to homes on Halderstraße, homes owned by non-Jews. The presence of a gas station directly across the street raised the stakes, increasing the risk that the fire could flare out of control and engulf the entire neighborhood.

Even so, witness Henry Landman said it appeared firefighters were more interested in confining the blaze to the synagogue rather than fully extinguishing it. His son, Rick Landman, later wrote, "He saw all of the lines of fire hoses on the ground. The fire engines were watering down the surrounding buildings and were letting the synagogue burn in a rather controlled and strange fashion." The blaze finally ended by four o'clock the next morning.

Some of my grandmother's relatives in Augsburg had left by then, but not all. Three Rosenau cousins fled to Philadelphia (some of them via Brazil), though their parents remained behind. On *Kristallnacht*, Paul Rosenau recalled, "They tried to get father, but mother convinced the Gestapo agent that wanted to get him that he had malaria. Father slept with his mouth open and looked awful. And that saved father's life; he would have been in Dachau."

About thirty miles west of Augsburg, the long Jewish presence in Hürben and Krumbach was coming to a fiery end. Members of the SA, SS, and Gestapo broke into the synagogue on November 11. They forced its remaining members to throw their Torah scrolls, other religious books, and Torah ornaments onto trucks, which hauled them away to be destroyed. A report in the *Krumbacher Bote* newspaper reflected the hatred of the times. "Yesterday evening, the Jews of Krumbach were rounded up to clear out their synagogue," it said. "The rare opportunity to see Jews sweating from their work was seized by many of their fellow citizens."

A story by Krumbach's history association in 1988 described the scene: "On entering the synagogue, the Jews were shouted at and mobbed by the Nazis. The abuse and maltreatment as well as the looting and destruction continued over the next few days." What did their friends and neighbors make of this? The story said, "The fatalistic attitude of not wanting to see anything more, out of the feeling that there was nothing they could do about it, emerged in the statements of various eyewitnesses, as did the fear of possibly being killed themselves."

The synagogue building was later used to store hay, then burned down by arsonists on November 26, 1939. The few Jews who remained in Krumbach in 1942 were deported to the Jewish ghetto in Piaski, Poland, where they were murdered. Four centuries of Jewish presence in the town was over. And there were no more Landauers in Bavaria.

Chapter 8

BROKEN BRANCHES FROM THE FAMILY TREE

"Nobody said a word."

For my dad, as for many people whose families had been torn apart during a nightmare that lasted more than a decade, a fundamental question after the war was—did anyone else make it out alive? And if so, where were they?

He was honorably discharged from the Army as a staff sergeant, paid $247.49, and provided a Good Conduct Medal, American Theater Ribbon, and World War II Victory Ribbon. He returned to Philadelphia and began working again at Climax Dental. He attended night school for veterans, seeking to continue an education that was disrupted by Nazi edicts.

The only relative he knew was alive when the war ended was his aunt Paula. She made it out of Germany a few months after my dad did and was living with her husband, Rolf, in Patterson, New Jersey. But what of the others?

My dad continued to hold out hope throughout the long war that his parents and brothers might still be alive, four years after they'd last been in touch. He turned to a German-language newspaper, the *Aufbau*, based in New York and read by German-speaking Jews worldwide. One of *Aufbau's* regular features was publishing lists of Jewish survivors in Europe, as well as some of the victims. It also became a popular place to take out classified ads in hopes of finding someone, anyone, who might know the whereabouts of the missing.

It was only while researching for this book that I discovered one such ad in the issue dated November 16, 1945. I found it during an online search, amid a sea of ads and lists of names, all desperately seeking signs of life from family members and friends. It reminded me of similar, heartbreaking queries placed at the World Trade Center in the days after September 11, 2001, except that there are no photos on this digitized newspaper page from 1945, only as many names and pleas as the newspaper could jam into six narrow columns of text. With every page I imagined a chorus of voices, men and women of different ages, speaking German in anguish, the names of loved ones on their lips.

It was there on my computer monitor, among a cacophony of these imaginary voices, that several familiar names seemed to jump off the page. They were on page 26, the farthest column to the right, most of the way down the page. "*Suche meine Eltern*," the small classified ad began. "Find my parents." Next come names that are capitalized and bold-faced for emphasis. "***LEO und ROSE KATZ,***" it says, adding her maiden name, Lebenstein, in case that helped. "*Und Brüder* ***MANFRED und KARL-HEINZ KATZ.***" He provided their last known address, Sachsenstraße 13 in Essen. And he asked that messages be sent to "**Sgt. Rudy Katz**, Station Hospital Bks. No. 3, Camp Patrick Henry, Va."

It was as if my dad were shouting into the void. He never told me about this desperate attempt when I finally asked him about his experiences nearly forty years later. He had probably forgotten about it. Nothing ever came of it, and, as efforts go, buying a tiny classified ad paled in comparison with trying to return to Germany as a parachutist.

The last relatives he had been in touch with in Germany were his aunt Malli and uncle Franz, who were at that point seeking shelter in Duisburg and Düsseldorf.

The couple hid in different places during the war, helped by the fact that Franz wasn't Jewish. But as the years went by, even that didn't count for much. By 1944, Malli was ordered to be transported to a concentration camp. At one point, they avoided authorities by living in a monastery. Another time, they lived on a farm near Asperden, five miles from the Dutch border. She worked as a maid; he was the farm administrator.

Then, more trouble. They were detained by German authorities shortly before the war ended in Europe and held at an unspecified location. British troops arrived just in time to rescue them. My aunt and uncle pleaded with a British lieutenant to get in touch with my dad, handing him the Schulmans' address on 20th Street in Philadelphia. He complied.

"That was my first sign that they were alive," my dad told me about hearing from the lieutenant. "I was elated. I contacted them immediately." I asked, "And then they told you about your family?" He answered by repeating the question almost word-for-word as a flat statement, without further explanation: "Then they told me about the family." This was only the second time I remember asking my dad about that chilling conversation with Tante Malli and Uncle Franz. The first time, several years earlier, his response was also almost matter-of-fact. "They brought me up to date on what had been going on during the war," he told me then, "including the fact that my parents and my two brothers had been taken to an extermination camp in Litzmannstadt, Poland."

Perhaps the intervening years had dulled the pain so that my father could present the murder of his parents and brothers to me as simply a "fact." More likely the pain never receded, but he was determined as the sole survivor of the household to press on and restart his life in a new country and not burden his children with tales about the tragedies they had faced.

As to where his family members were taken, German officials created a ghetto in Łódź (they called it Litzmannstadt) in occupied Poland and forced Jews to live in overcrowded and unsanitary conditions. Such ghettos were initially created for Jews who already lived in the area. But in 1941, German officials began taking Jews from elsewhere in Europe there.

Karl-Heinz, who had lived for many years with his grandmother in Lembeck, had been sent home to Essen. Documents list him as having had an apprenticeship as a locksmith somewhere along the way. Manfred was also sent home to Essen after German troops overran Belgium and evicted him from the home where he was staying.

We've known that toward the end of 1941, Leo, Rosalie, Karl-Heinz, and Manfred were deported from their apartment at Sachsenstraße 13 in Essen. Cläre Mies, a friend of my tante Malli, saw them as they were about to be taken away. "Franz, Malli, and I were in Essen on their last day to say goodbye," she said. "A small suitcase with some shirts was being packed. Karl-Heinz and Manfred were very sad. The parents did not believe they would ever see each other again."

There's contradictory information about where they spent their final days. Not only did my aunt Malli and uncle Franz believe they had been sent to Litzmannstadt, but also word has been passed down through generations that a soldier from Lembeck later saw Karl-Heinz in Poland.

Why is it so important to me to know? I realize I'm getting further away from the mantra my parents adhered to when I was young, that their children "shouldn't know from it." I know now that the Holocaust enveloped my entire family. It's not enough to simply say someone *died in the Holocaust*, as if they had perished of a heart attack or from a house fire. They didn't succumb to a natural occurrence or a tragic accident. They were murdered.

Author Daniel Mendelsohn wrote that the refrain "killed by the Nazis" was used frequently to describe what happened to his grandfather's oldest brother as well as the brother's wife and four daughters. "It was hard to imagine just how they had been killed, to grasp the details, the specifics. When? Where? How? With guns? In the gas chambers?" To be lost in the Holocaust, he wrote, "referred not only to the fact that they'd been killed, but to their relation to the rest of history and memory; hopefully remote, irretrievable."

The German government—acting without objections from much of the populace in the country where my relatives had lived for centuries—systematically hunted down Jews, deported them, and murdered them. The world needs to know what these and other victims went through, for the sake of my family, the six million other Jews who perished in the Holocaust, and the millions of other victims of Nazi persecution and murder. The hope—which has been dashed several times since—is that humanity will be more likely to prevent other acts of genocide.

While we refer to the Nazi era as 1933–45, the mass murder of Jews occurred in a much more compressed period of time. About three-quarters of the six million victims were killed in the twenty months from June 1941 to February 1943. An astounding average of ten thousand Jews were murdered *every day* at its peak in 1942–43.

Hitler authorized the "Final Solution" to annihilate European Jews sometime in 1941. Heinrich Himmler, the *Reichsführer*, or leader of the SS, was the senior Nazi official responsible for conceiving the plan and carrying it out. The first wave of deporting Jews by trains to the east began on October 15. This phase included transports from Vienna, Prague, Luxembourg, and Berlin. The destination was the ghettos of Łódź and Ostland (generally the Baltics and parts of Poland and Belarus).

The second phase was from November 8 until mid-January 1942 and included twenty-two transports with some twenty-two thousand Jews. They were destined for recently conquered areas, including Riga, Kovno, and Minsk.

Documents now available make it clear that my father's immediate family members were deported about one thousand miles east to Minsk, then the capital of the Byelorussian Soviet Socialist Republic in the Soviet Union. German forces had been occupying Minsk soon after they invaded the Soviet Union in June 1941. A month later, they forced about eighty thousand people, including Jews from nearby towns, into a ghetto they created in the northwestern part of the city. In November, they began a year-long transport of nearly twenty-four thousand Jews, most of them from Germany and Austria, to the Minsk ghetto.

How do we know my grandparents and uncles were sent there? For one thing, Cläre Mies said after my family was deported, "Karl-Heinz later wrote a postcard: 'We are going to Minsk.'" Beyond that, the Germans kept good records. More of their documents have come to light in the decades since, and they've been increasingly digitized.

Matching the date of their deportation with train schedules, it now appears their ultimate destination was not Poland, as it first seemed. The train that carried deported Jews to Litzmannstadt left on October 27. While researching for this book, I found documents online that show they were on *Sonderzug* (Special Train) 52 to Minsk on Monday, November 10, 1941. Their names are on a typewritten list of deportees as numbers 55 to 58, with their birth dates and places, occupations, and home addresses. Black checkmarks, firm and precise, appear in the small space between their numbers and their names: Leo Katz, Rosalie Katz, Karl-Heinz Katz, and Manfred Katz. The list was carefully typed beforehand, the information neatly arranged into columns. The checkmarks may have occurred as they were about to board, standing before a Nazi guard dutifully taking inventory of the hundreds of people being sent to be slaughtered.

55✓Katz, Leo	18.1.91 Köln	Vertreter berufslos	Sachsenstr. 13
56✓Katz, Rosalie	7.2.89 Lembeck	Hausfrau "	Sachsenstr. 13
57✓Katz, Karlheinz	19.11.25 Essen	Schüler Schlosserlehrl.	Sachsenstr. 13
58✓Katz, Manfred	7.3.27 Essen	Schüler "	Sachsenstr. 13

This passenger list for the "Special Train" to Minsk identifies Leo Katz as unemployed, Rosalie as a housewife, and Karl-Heinz and Manfred as students and apprentice locksmiths.

They were first taken from their home in Essen to Düsseldorf, about twenty miles southwest, which served as a local administrative division for Nazi Germany. They were among 728 Jews herded into the cattle hall of the *Schlachthof*, or slaughterhouse, Sunday evening, where they were registered, strip-searched, and robbed of their belongings.

Most of the passengers were from Düsseldorf. The synagogue was ordered to notify members of the Jewish community beforehand that everyone chosen for deportation was to follow strict instructions. I assume my relatives were given a similar edict. Each person was limited to forty-four pounds of luggage and provisions for a two- or three-day journey. Only a backpack was permitted on board. Each person could take fifty *Reichsmarks* in currency (equivalent to about $2,500 in 2025), but it had to be handed over to authorities by 6:00 p.m. on November 5. They were also required to sign a form renouncing their assets, monetary as well as real property, so they could be used by the German government.

Forcing the Jews to gather at the slaughterhouse offered the Nazis several advantages. It was a large space, directly adjacent to the train station, and relatively well concealed from local residents. A survivor from Düsseldorf later compared spending that Sunday night in the *Schlachthof* to being "like cattle on bare earth." A deportee from a train that left a month later said, "The hall is naked, wet and dirty and contains an unbearable stench." Another survivor said the hall was flooded with water "up to the ankles" and that it was impossible to lie down and sleep.

Monday morning dawned cold and mostly cloudy as they were forced to march from the slaughterhouse to loading ramps at the Düsseldorf-Derendorf freight yard. Frail, old people who didn't move fast enough were punished with dog whips. The train pulled out of the station at 10:40 that morning, stopping at nearby Wuppertal-Steinbeck, so that wagons with another 264 Jews could be coupled to the train.

Among those on board that day was *Hauptmann der Schutzpolizei* (Captain of the Police) Wilhelm Meurin. The thirty-six-year-old SS member was in charge of the sixteen guards on the train. He took copious notes about the journey. A report marked "*Vertraulich!*" (Confidential!) that he filed for his superiors twelve days later now resides in the Wiener Holocaust Library in London, where it was discovered by German historian Bastian Fleermann in 2012.

Meurin's seven-page, typewritten report has well-worn holes punched on the side, signs that it was once kept in a ring binder. The pages have turned varying shades of brown, darker along the margins. But his descriptions of the journey are as legible, vivid, and horrifying as if they were written yesterday.

The 992 Jewish passengers were treated as cargo, crammed into wagons, and unable to find a place to sit. Meurin wrote in great detail about delays along the way. The locomotive had to be replaced because it was pushed beyond its limits trying to pull an especially long train over steep hills. The wagons themselves experienced mechanical problems. Detours were needed as word reached the authorities that partisans lay in wait in some areas, hoping to thwart the Nazis.

The train stopped for seven hours in the middle of the night in northeastern Poland, in order to change the locomotive. It was -18 degrees Celsius, or just below 0 degrees Fahrenheit. "The heating pipe was so frozen that the locomotive was later unable to push the steam through," Meurin wrote.

Today you can take a train from Düsseldorf to Minsk in some level of comfort in under twenty hours. Meurin wrote that their journey took exactly ninety-six hours, arriving in Minsk at 10:40 on the morning of November 14. "The Jews were quite soft at this time," he wrote, an apparent reference to them being weak and unable to resist.

What caused them to be "*weich*," or "soft"? Not only were they packed so close that they couldn't sit, but they also were riding in unheated wagons. Passengers weren't provided any water once the train crossed the Russian border on day two. At that point, Meurin said, there was no means to boil water for them, and he didn't want to run the risk of an outbreak of dysentery or typhoid fever while on board. Meurin wrote more compassionately about the needs of his fellow SS guards, including requests that subsequent journeys provide them with more food and alcohol, warm clothing, torches, and better weapons and protective gear.

Once the Jewish passengers arrived in Minsk, they were forced to march about forty minutes to the ghetto. Survivors from other transports recalled seeing a "city lying in ruins." The ghetto was even worse, betraying scenes of a mass murder. Meurin explained how they made room for those who arrived on *Sonderzug* 52: "8,000 Russian Jews were removed from the Jewish quarter and shot by the Latvian police."

Author Petra Rentrop examined records and reports from the Minsk ghetto that describe "appalling" living conditions. There were seven people living in a sixteen-by-sixteen-foot room. There was no water, electric lights, soap, or a latrine. Hunger was widespread. "Hunger, hunger, hunger! The food in the camp was atrocious," Berthold Rudner, a prisoner from Berlin, wrote in his diary. "Sometimes the camp inmates were given water soup at 9 o'clock and some bread in the evening. Sometimes there is such 'food' only late in the afternoon. It even stopped altogether."

SS and police authorities shot or gassed most of the prisoners in specially equipped vans, usually upon arrival in the nearby village of Maly

Trostinets. Those who were spared were forced to work on labor projects in factories inside the ghetto. Germans finally destroyed the Minsk ghetto in the fall of 1943.

It's possible that Karl-Heinz survived a little longer. A soldier from Lembeck apparently recognized him doing road construction work in Poland in 1943. That would have been quite a sight, seeing the Jewish kid who once starred in the local nativity play now in a prisoner's uniform, emaciated, ordered to perform forced labor. Did it prey on the soldier's conscience that as much as he was instructed to treat Jews as subhuman, he knew this young guy had been welcomed in the village where they both once lived? It may have. The story goes that as he began to speak with Karl-Heinz with some familiarity, my uncle responded: "*Bitte rede nicht mit mir, sonst bist du auch dran,*" In other words, "Please don't talk to me, or it's your turn, too."

Assuming that they were killed soon after arriving in Minsk, Rosalie Katz was fifty-two, Leopold was fifty, and Manfred was fourteen. Karl-Heinz turned sixteen a few days after stepping off the train in Minsk; perhaps he lived another year or two if the story of him being seen later in Poland is accurate.

Most everyone else in the Lebenstein family who was still in Germany met a similar fate. That included the family my father briefly stayed with in Südlohn—Moritz and Antonia (Toni) Lebenstein and their three children.

Moritz Lebenstein married the former Toni Wolff in 1928, the same year he took over his father-in-law's butcher shop. Meir Wolff enjoyed a good reputation in Südlohn, where he routinely supplied soup to village infirmaries. He also won renown as the first local merchant to sell toys and firecrackers. Son-in-law Moritz Lebenstein had many fans of his own. "Lebenstein not only supplied his religious brethren with kosher meat, but he was also appreciated by the Christian residents because of his honest nature," according to a history of Südlohn's Jewish community.

But the family's business and apartment at Kirchstraße 38 were attacked by a drunken mob during *Kristallnacht* in 1938. Led by the paramilitary SA members, more than one hundred people actively took part in the riots. Thugs first destroyed the local, one-room synagogue. Then they came after the Jews in their homes. Only the intervention of the Lebensteins' next-door neighbors, the Hinske family, temporarily kept them from harm and their home from being completely destroyed, though it was hardly left unscathed.

The Hinskes—the father and two brothers—said they rushed outside shortly before midnight, after being startled by loud noises:

> We could see several men, some of whom were carrying sledgehammers and crowbars. Other members of this group were trying to break down the door to the Wolff-Lebenstein house with a wagon drawbar. We approached the men, who were under the influence of alcohol, with the words: "What's going on here?" As we stood in front of the door, arms at our sides, the answer came back: "When we're done here, we'll come to you!"
>
> We saw some familiar faces. On the opposite side under a two-trunked tree stood Gendarme F., the local group leader and a well-known third person. Meanwhile, the door of the Wolff-Lebenstein house opened and Mrs. Toni Lebenstein appeared with her children. She asked reproachfully: "What have we done to you?"
>
> Then the local group leader broke away from the group, grabbed one of us by the shoulder and told us to leave, to close the doors and windows, that he had police powers. The rioters, who were aware of our physical strength, did not dare to continue their work of destruction. Then the order was given: "Enough here!"

The Hinskes' bravery saved the Lebensteins that night, but dangers remained. Toni Lebenstein and her children hid with neighbors in the days that followed, until the neighbors were given an "unmistakable warning" not to let them do so. Still, some local residents helped sustain the Lebensteins by slipping them food and money. At some point, Moritz and Toni reached the same conclusion that my grandparents had and sent their eldest child to safety out of Germany. Sonja fled to Holland, joining other refugee children at the Nooderhuis youth hostel in Hoogeveen, which could house ninety children. But that only lasted a few months, ending when a diphtheria epidemic ripped through the facility and forced surviving inhabitants to leave by April.

The timeline gets more frightening from there, as she bounced from one place in Amsterdam to another. Her father showed up in one minority census in Antwerp, then two months later, with his son Kurt in Duisburg.

Sonja returned to Südlohn on December 5, 1941. Three days later, she and the other Jews of Südlohn were ordered to be deported. On December 10 she was at an assembly camp in Münster; two days later she's listed as part of a transport at Bielefeld and a day after that taken with her mother and two brothers to Riga, Latvia. Documents show they arrived at the Šķirotava freight station near Riga at about 11:00 p.m. on December 15.

German forces had occupied Riga since July 1941. At least twenty-five thousand Jews who had been forced into a ghetto there were shot by Germans and Latvians in a nearby forest. That made more room for some twenty thousand more Jews who were deported from Germany and elsewhere in Europe. An eyewitness saw Sonja, her parents, and her grandfather being ordered to dig pits for a mass grave before being shot. (The witness survived by dropping into the pit unseen, then escaping after dark, remaining hidden until the Soviet Red Army arrived.)

The Hinskes' courage wasn't forgotten by the Jewish families whom they helped. When a military train stopped in the Auschwitz area in 1943, a concentration camp prisoner approached a corporal from the Rhine region. The prisoner, a young man named Erich Wolff, asked if there was a soldier from near his hometown of Südlohn. When the corporal wondered why he was asking, Wolff said he wanted to extend greetings and thanks to the Hinskes "*was sie getan haben*," or "for what they have done."

But individual Germans who tried to save their Jewish neighbors were no match for the Nazi's determination to murder as many as they could, including my relatives.

The youngest Lebenstein sibling—Rosalie's brother Hugo, who proudly wore a uniform in the family photo years earlier—fled from the family home to the Netherlands in 1939. He was captured and deported first to the Westerbork transit camp in the Dutch countryside and then to the killing center at Auschwitz-Birkenau, where he was murdered in 1942.

Back in Lembeck, Sophie Lebenstein and two of her daughters continued to live in the longtime family home until January 24, 1942. That's when they were loaded onto a truck and taken to a collection point at the freight station in Gelsenkirchen, northeast of Essen.

Many decades later, a witness recalled the day they were deported. "In the morning there was a truck outside the house; three women neighbors and two children witnessed it," he said. "Nobody said a word. There was a strange silence when it happened. I was only allowed to watch from our front door and was not able to say goodbye to the grandmother. One woman neighbor passed some food onto the truck."

My uncle Franz kept tabs on his mother-in-law and, as a non-Jew, had more sway with German authorities than did other family members. He successfully appealed to have her released from the Gelsenkirchen collection point at Buchenwald because of her advanced age and poor hearing, which made her unsuitable for labor. She was taken to her birthplace of Raesfeld, about eight miles east of Lembeck.

The proud matriarch of this once-large family of German farmers, traders, entrepreneurs, and patriots died there on May 5, 1942. She was five months shy of her eightieth birthday. Most of her offspring would die at a fraction of that age. The two daughters deported with her, Selma and Bertha, were taken to Riga and then the Stutthof concentration camp near Danzig, Poland. Both died there in December 1944. Selma was forty-seven; Bertha was forty-four.

Lembeck itself was the site of a pivotal battle in the Allies' attempt to take the Rhineland, accomplished thanks to a heroic act by Technical Sergeant Clinton M. Hedrick. Transported far from his home in rural West Virginia, he initially fought with the 550th Infantry Airborne Division. But his unit was disbanded after suffering many casualties during the Battle of the Bulge in December 1944–January 1945.

Hedrick was then assigned to Company I, 194th Glider Infantry, 17th Airborne Division. He took part in the largest airborne operation in history conducted on one day and in one location, to establish an Allied presence east of the Rhine River. Hedrick's glider endured a severe antiaircraft barrage before landing north of the city of Wesel. The unit then headed east until facing heavy combat in Lembeck on March 27 and 28. Hedrick knocked out multiple German machine-gun positions, prompting one of his soldiers to describe him as "fearless through two days of heavy fighting." His Medal of Honor citation describes what happened in Lembeck on March 28:

> Three times the landing elements were pinned down by intense automatic-weapon fire from strongly defended positions. Each time, T/Sgt. Hedrick fearlessly charged through heavy fire, shooting his automatic rifle from his hip. His courageous action so inspired his men that they reduced the enemy positions in rapid succession. When six of the enemy attempted a surprise, flanking movement, he quickly turned and killed the entire party with a burst of fire. Later, the enemy withdrew across a moat into Lembeck Castle. T/Sgt. Hedrick, with utter disregard for his own safety, plunged across the drawbridge alone in pursuit. When a German soldier, with hands upraised, declared the garrison wished to surrender, he entered the castle yard with four of his men to accept the capitulation. The group moved through a sally port [secure entryway], and was met by fire from a German self-propelled gun. Although mortally wounded, T/Sgt. Hedrick fired at the enemy gun and covered the withdrawal of his comrades. He died while being evacuated after the castle was taken. His great personal courage and heroic leadership contributed in large measure to the speedy capture of Lembeck and provided an inspiring example to his comrades.

Of the nearly 15 million Americans who served in the military during World War II, only 473 received the Medal of Honor, the nation's highest honor for valor. Hedrick's medal was the war's last of its kind awarded for action in Europe. For decades, his actions received scant attention in Lembeck. Finally, in November 2021, a memorial plaque was attached to a sandstone archway inside the castle as a result of conversations between the Count von Merveldt family, which owns the castle, and descendants of the 17th Airborne Division. About thirty guests from the U.S. attended the dedication ceremony, including two ninety-seven-year-old veterans.

Some residents of Lembeck displayed their own acts of courage. After the war, Tante Malli wrote a letter vouching that the headmaster of a school in Lembeck helped her sister obtain school certification papers she needed to emigrate. “Mr. Storck did this even though he knew that my sister was Jewish,” Malli wrote. “He did so at great personal risk to himself.” She said this proved “that he had nothing to do with the Party’s criminal policy towards the Jews. We already knew this attitude from before and we also knew that Mr. Storck was not addressed as a proper Nazi.”

As laudatory as these and other acts of bravery were, they were no match for the Nazis’ extermination efforts. Once there were thirteen direct descendants of Isaac and Sara Sophie Lebenstein. Now there were three—Tante Paula and my dad in the U.S. and Tante Malli in Germany.

Malli and Franz tried to put their lives together after the war and reconnect with old friends. One of them, Cläre Mies, was, like Tante Malli, a Jew married to a Christian. She survived the war hiding with a family in Duisburg. “Despite all the dangers that threatened the Steinfals family,” she said, “the kind-hearted people told me that as long as they had a roof over their heads and something to eat, I could stay with them.” She stayed out of sight, disguised as “Aunt Else from Magdeburg,” and spent the last several months of the war hiding in their cellar.

Soon after Malli and Franz arrived home, they dug up a suitcase they had buried in the garden for safekeeping. The documents and clothes inside were ruined. A spice box survived and is now on display at the Jewish Museum of Westphalia in Dorsten. A Sabbath candelabra was rescued, too.

In June 1946, Malli sought reparations, on behalf of the survivors, for property stolen by the Nazis when they deported Sophie, Selma, and Bertha Lebenstein, as well as any assets or property that still existed. The real estate in Lembeck was finally returned to them in 1950. The heirs immediately sold the property. It must have been too painful to consider keeping, given the memories. And from a practical standpoint no one in the family lived in Lembeck anymore. And no one wanted to.

But some of their belongings—including crockery, a seven-branched candelabra, and books—were not returned and there was compensation.

My father's family received very modest assistance from Germany and, like many survivors, went through an arduous legal process to get it. Archival records show that the heirs of my great-grandmother Sophie Lebenstein received compensation for her having to wear a Star of David, signifying she was a Jew. The 1,050 Deutsche Marks they received in 1954 was equivalent to about $3,000 in 2025. They soon received additional compensation because the family's cattle trading business was boycotted and, consequently, abandoned. That was worth another $15,000 in 2025 dollars.

It wasn't until many years later that I asked my father to tell me about his journey to America. The first time was in 1981, when I was writing about the Cuban refugee crisis. We sat in the living room of his home in suburban Memphis. He told me about his escape in a gentle, level voice, betraying relatively little evident emotion. But his eyes had a thin mist by the time he reached the end.

On his bookshelf that day was a copy of the book *While Six Million Died: A Chronicle of American Apathy* by Arthur D. Morse. I have it in front of me as I write this. Published in 1968, it was the first book to grasp this country's completely inadequate response to the Holocaust. I'm not sure, as a youngster, whether I ever did anything more than quickly thumb through its pages. But I've been aware of those four words, "While Six Million Died," as shown on the book's spine, for as long as I can remember, an emblem of American inaction when there was knowledge of—and plans that could have minimized—genocide. When I finally knew enough to ask my dad questions about his journey, it was clear this sentiment weighed heavily on his mind.

Looking back, he said, "I feel very bitter because when it really would have meant something, this country took a very narrow view and a lot of lives could have been saved." While the affidavits of support were justifiable when seeking to help people escape the Holocaust, he said, the quotas on the number of refugees who could be accepted were much too low.

"I also feel that when I came over, I provided my own start completely," he added. "A lot of interfaith organizations are now providing a lot of services to get people acclimated to their new home and country and get them accepted into American society." Although some relief agencies in later years were reimbursed for some of their costs by the federal government, organizations like HIAS operated in those days solely on private contributions, he said.

"I feel a lot more could have been done in that respect," he said of providing Jewish refugees with a better start in the United States. "I was just fortunate that I could find my own way and get my own start myself."

Despite his disappointment with America's reaction to the tragic events in Germany, he left little doubt about his appreciation for being here: "I still think that with the kind of life we're living here—there really is only one country. This thought was reinforced after the war and I went to Germany and I didn't feel any bitterness, surprisingly. I also felt good coming back to the United States, and I wouldn't want to live anywhere else."

Still mourning his losses after the war, my dad was ready for a new start in America.

Chapter 9

NEW COUNTRIES, NEW LIVES

"I came to this country at age eighteen not speaking any English."

My mom and the other six Landauers who left Augsburg in 1938 were bound for Colombia, South America, looking for safety some six thousand miles away in one of the few places that would take them.

Any hopes they could relocate to the U.S. were dashed because they couldn't find a sponsor. Latin America was relatively more open to immigrants at the time, though the situation was changing rapidly there, too. Countries that previously accepted European Jews—including Argentina, Brazil, Chile, and Uruguay—became much less welcoming around 1938. So refugees turned to countries previously considered unattractive because of their climate, poverty, and economic and political instability. That put Colombia, Ecuador, Bolivia, and Paraguay more in play.

Colombia had a liberal policy toward immigrants through the 1920s. The ruling class, with its Spanish roots, especially valued white, Christian Europeans. But as economic conditions worsened after the Great Depression and other countries began to tighten their immigration policies, so, too, did Colombia. First it banned immigration from a large number of nationalities, which inhibited Jews trying to flee Poland. Then, sometime in 1938, German Jews were turned away, followed by a ban on all Jewish immigration from 1939 to 1947. Which means my mother's family was fortunate in their timing not only when leaving Germany but also when entering Colombia.

They traveled first to Frankfurt, then to Holland, and from there to England, where they boarded the SS *Orbita.* The ship was built in 1914 as an armed merchant cruiser, became a troop transport during World War I, then was retrofitted to serve as a passenger liner until being requisitioned as a troop ship again during World War II.

We get a glimpse of what my family's experience onboard might have been like from the memoirs of Michel (Mikhl) Radzinski, who had emigrated from Poland to Panama as a passenger on the *Orbita* a few years earlier. "It is a life in a narrow, restricted little world," Radzinski wrote, with many monotonous days. "Nonetheless, there were hours when I was full of an inwardly illuminated hope of establishing myself. In the light of this hope, I saw how happy the worried passengers would be with a similar feeling—that they were leaving their old homes on cursed soil, where Jew-hatred raged and Jews feared for the present and future."

My mom retained no memories of the long ship ride besides being seasick. "I was deathly ill," she said, "my father and I both."

From Augsburg to Cali: Hedwig Landauer (my grandfather's mother); Gerd Landauer (my uncle); Flora and Ludwig Morganthau (my grandmother's parents); my mom, Margot; and my grandparents Else and Julius Landauer, in 1945

At last, after three weeks at sea, they arrived at their new home in Cali, Colombia. Perhaps they could live in peace in the Valle del Cauca, a valley nestled by hills about sixty miles southeast of a Pacific Ocean port. My mother recalls other Jewish émigrés settling in Cali from Germany, Poland, and Turkey. The three groups formed separate enclaves, attended three different synagogues, and rarely socialized with their Jewish neighbors from other countries.

Her parents sent her to an all-girls Catholic school because the public schools were poorly regarded. She wasn't coerced to follow the religious customs, becoming one of about ten non-Catholic girls who didn't cross themselves at morning prayer.

She wasn't much interested in family conversations about their days in Germany, a place she hardly remembered. But they spoke German at home because her grandparents never learned Spanish. The family also retained their German sensibilities about a proper upbringing, my mother said. "There was a very strict adherence as to how a child is to behave." That was particularly true of her mother. "My brother and I would take turns at the table, who sat next to her, because you got a pinch, every once in a while, underneath. They were very, very strict."

Aside from the occasional pinches, my mom quickly adapted to life in Cali: "I was very happy, had wonderful friends, enjoyed my school, enjoyed my surroundings."

There wasn't much of a middle class in Colombia; you were either wealthy or poor. She fell in with a group of girls from well-to-do backgrounds and enjoyed being invited to their family's country homes and country clubs. Anti-Semitism was not a problem for her. In fact, all of her best friends were Catholic, and she rarely socialized with other Jews.

Her parents owned a factory in Cali, Industrias Metal Gloria, that manufactured stainless-steel flatware. It only made forks and spoons because Colombians at that time were unaccustomed to using knives. The company bought any knives it sold from another supplier. My grandmother worked in the company office every day. Household chores were largely taken care of by three maids—one who cooked, one who cleaned, and one who worked three days a week doing laundry.

My grandparents stayed in touch with the global German Jewish diaspora with help from the *Aufbau*, the same newspaper my dad turned to after the war for the desperate classified ad looking for news of his family. My mom remembers each weekly edition of the newspaper being passed from household to household in Cali, as German expatriates tried to learn about the fate of others.

They were also connected to Augsburg's now far-flung Jewish community, thanks to Ernst Jacob, the city's last rabbi before the war. Jacob was arrested in November 1938 during *Kristallnacht*, imprisoned in the Dachau concentration camp, and released a few months later. He emigrated to England in 1939, then to the U.S. the following year.

Jacob typed a series of eighteen newsletters from his new post between 1941 and 1949, circulating them to erstwhile members of his former congregation, now living in more than forty countries. There's a reference to "a whole colony of Augsburgers" in Cali in March 1942, including my family and their friends the Walutas. It takes note of my grandfather's silverware company as well as Alfred Waluta's comb factory.

My grandmother described their twelve-room home in the September 1946 newsletter. "Our house is particularly large and airy," she wrote, "and, what is most pleasant here, exceptionally cool . . . There are also three patios with lawns and flowers, in short, a veranda with walkways and a sunbathing area. The house is very busy and you can't be here without staff."

My mom's life took another dramatic turn when she finished high school at age eighteen and her parents arranged to send her to the U.S., a decision which she attributed to her dating life. "I was going with a Catholic boy and they did not want me to marry out of my religion," she said. Her destination was Philadelphia, to live with a second cousin of her mother's, Hugo Rosenau, and his wife, Carol.

"That was a tough journey. I did not speak English," she recalled many years later. The gist of that message became a frequent refrain at home, whenever my brother or I would complain about something being too difficult to do. Whatever challenges we faced paled in comparison to what she endured. "I came to this country at age eighteen not speaking any English," she would say. The language barrier started soon after she landed in New York. "I went through customs; they asked me to open my suitcase. And of course, I didn't know what a key was. So, they pointed with a finger to the lock and that's how I knew they wanted a key."

My mother attended the Pierce business school in Philadelphia for a year, then met my father on a date arranged by neighbors of her relatives. They were married in 1952 in a civil ceremony, which she told me helped her return to the U.S. later as a Colombian resident, after a Jewish ceremony held in Cali. At nineteen, she was so young that I recently discovered a consent document her father signed and had notarized to permit the "Marriage of a Child or Ward."

My mom had two life-changing events in February 1956. First, she received the shocking news on a Friday that her beloved father had died suddenly of a heart attack. He was fifty-five. She was unable to travel in Cali in time for his funeral. Jewish tradition calls for the deceased to be buried as soon as possible but never on the Sabbath, which begins at sunset Friday.

On Monday she received news of a different sort—she was pregnant with me. My mom was struck by the timing and would later say, "God takes one life and delivers another." I was given the name Jeffrey Lee—the first letters inspired by my grandfathers, Julius Landauer and Leopold Katz. Two years later, my brother, Michael, was born, the first letter of his name inspired by my dad's brother Manfred.

My maternal grandmother, Else, was the only grandparent I ever knew, and she lived two thousand miles away. I called her Omi, a German word for grandmother. She was what would once be described as a career woman. My mom was a highly efficient homemaker when it came to nurturing, shopping, cooking, cleaning, and organizing. My grandmother was not.

I remember her German accent and seemingly utter fluency in three languages (though it would sometimes take her a moment to find the right word in English). She delighted in reminding me, "You know, you're my oldest grandchild!" long after I knew it to be true. She seemed precise; I could see how she could be strict. But she also had a hearty laugh that made her whole body shake.

She would visit us occasionally in Philadelphia, and we went to Cali sometimes. I celebrated my first birthday there, then went again at ages three, five, and fifteen. Several family members still lived there—Omi and her second husband, Joe Isner; my maternal great-grandparents, Flora and Ludwig Morgenthau; and my uncle's family—Gerd Landauer; his wife, Diva; and their children, Jaime, Jackie, and Freddy.

We stayed at the large house on Avenida 4 Norte. You entered via a covered patio, then walked on linoleum floors into the entrance hallway. The large room down the hall and to the right was Omi's office. That's where she conducted business for the German consulate, assisting with passports and visas for German and Colombian citizens. To the left of the entryway was the dining room. Behind there was the kitchen. There were several bedrooms upstairs as well as a balcony, which was a good place to try to stay cool at night. My cousin Jaime remembers the upper floor as being something of a time warp. "It was like being transported back in time," he said, with "the smell of the fine German wood furniture, the fancy German rugs and the original vacuum tubes wooden radio that came also from Germany."

As a teenage visitor to Cali, I delighted in eating rice practically every day and still jump at the chance to eat fried, sweet plantains known as *plátanos*. I remember feeling Cali's intense heat and humidity, hearing the sound of street vendors loudly hawking their wares with sing-song refrains, and marveling at the intensity of fans at a soccer game. Combining my limited Spanish proficiency with an early appetite for good newspapers meant I sometimes supplemented Omi's copy of the local newspaper *El Pais* by buying the more prestigious *El Tiempo*, published in the capital of Bogotá.

Culturally, I had a German influence, too. My parents routinely deployed German as a secret language, a way to talk about sensitive subjects in front of the kids without us knowing what they were saying. I learned a smattering of German—I asked what they were saying about us whenever I heard *kinder*—as well as some Yiddish. My upbringing also included a heaping of German foods such as knockwurst and sauerkraut, spätzle egg noodles, the barley-like grünkern soup, a wide selection of deli meats, and spiced cookies at Christmastime.

Thinking back to earlier days in Philadelphia, my dad continued to work in the dental laboratory business while my mom largely took care of my brother and me. First, we lived in the Oak Lane neighborhood, then in Mt. Airy. My parents became friendly with another family who lived a few doors away, the Nathans. They, too, were German Jews—John (from Cologne), Trudy (from Coburg in Bavaria), plus their Philadelphia-born children, Bob and Nancy.

My parents divorced, as did the Nathans, and then they remarried one another in April 1964. My brother and I lived with my mom and John, while

Bob and Nancy lived with their mother and my father. The children also spent time with their father and stepmother. Looking back, I don't think it was a coincidence that my parents fell in with another couple who also had the traumatic experience of fleeing Germany, an observation my mom agreed with years later.

Though my stepfather was certainly something of a disciplinarian initially, he and I became especially close. He grew up in an Orthodox Jewish family with his parents and younger sister, Margot. After his father died in 1929, he moved with his mother and sister to the small village of Eich, southeast of Frankfurt, along the Rhine River. He was kicked out of school in 1933 due to prohibitions against educating Jews, returning to Cologne to apprentice for a great-uncle. The growing anti-Semitism and presence of Nazis led him to describe the early part of life as "confused, with a lot of upheaval."

Other Germans didn't care that his family had deep roots in the country and that one of his uncles was killed outside of Paris fighting for Germany in World War I. Aunt Margot later recalled numerous incidents in Eich when she was pushed, shoved, spat upon, and called a "*schmutziger Jude,*" or "dirty Jew." "As a Jewish child," she said, "there was no way to defend myself against these actions in Nazi Germany." The local synagogue was looted on a Friday night, its contents taken to the town square and burned. Individual homes were attacked, too. Some of the men, including John and Margot's grandfather, were dragged to one of the early concentration camps in nearby Osthofen and tortured.

"I don't want you to think that my family was sitting back and not trying to better our situation," Aunt Margot wrote of her early years. "All the Jewish families knew they had to leave, but how and where to? The United States had a quota system (still do) and everyone needed a visa to leave. Going anywhere in the world was difficult, no one wanted Jews except Israel, at that time still Palestine. It was very difficult to go there as well, the British were still involved in that part of the world and controlled immigration to Palestine."

They finally obtained an affidavit of support from a cousin of their grandfather's. Once their quota number was called, they sailed to America in October 1936, spending six days at sea on the RMS *Aquitania*. They had few possessions when they came ashore. "We only had ten dollars between the three of us," John recalled. He also had a different name, after their American sponsor convinced him to change from Hans to John because the former sounded "too German."

He finished junior high school and started high school in Philadelphia, then began working in a department store from 1938 until being drafted into the Army in 1943 as a clerk typist. He was assigned to a portable Army hospital that started in Africa, then went to Italy while supporting the 82nd Airborne Division for three years. He didn't see combat, though he saw plenty of wounded. They were ordered to go to a staging area in Okinawa once the war in Europe was over and prepare for a possible U.S. invasion of Japan. The unit disbanded at war's end.

His modest education and limited work experience left him few options at home in Philadelphia. He became a costume jewelry salesman, calling on local retailers. What he lacked in formal training he more than made up for with grit and motivation. When potential clients commented on his accent and asked where he was from, he took advantage of the situation. "I played on people's sympathy," he later admitted. He eventually got into the import giftware business, where he was an executive for many decades.

He obtained his American citizenship while in the service and avoided being labeled as a German refugee. "There was a feeling that refugees really should be kept at a lower level," he said, "and I sensed frequently among my own relatives at the time that there was a desire to not have them achieve a great deal of success."

He never forgot his roots in Germany, nor his relatives who perished there. He thought often of the grandfather who had a major role in his upbringing: "I remember when I visited the concentration camp where he was killed, coming totally apart when I visited the specific area where crematoriums were."

But John, like my dad, never held a grudge against Germany after the war. He regularly attended giftware trade shows in Frankfurt and even started a spinoff company in Germany. My mom occasionally accompanied him there, unenthusiastically. "I was never happy going to Germany," she said, and vowed never to buy a German-made car (until she did). She never forgot her first trip back to Germany as an adult and hearing a man exclaim, "*Vaterland!*"*or* "Fatherland" once the plane landed and the cabin door opened. Nazis frequently used the word to invoke nationalism and unify Germany.

Those types of misgivings obviously weren't shared by my aunt Malli and uncle Franz, who remained in Germany throughout their lives. The much-diminished Jewish population in Germany immediately after the war consisted mainly of displaced persons who were liberated by Allied troops or had emigrated temporarily from elsewhere in Europe. Relatively few Jewish survivors lived there permanently, and a number of those who did, like Tante Malli, had a non-Jewish spouse.

I wish my memories were more vivid of my aunt and uncle, especially because they visited the U.S. Language was a barrier—he spoke some English, but she did not. I recall my aunt as an old woman with a wide face, who liked to hold me by the shoulders and kiss my cheeks. Lots of kisses, much more than I wanted, that came with the smell of an old-fashioned perfume. "*Meine liebchen!*" she would say, with great joy, heavily emphasizing the first syllable of that second word: "mine-ah LEEB-shen!" It meant "my sweetheart!" and was always accompanied by a smile as wide as it could be. It was overwhelming and off-putting to a young boy.

Oh, how little I knew! How sheltered I was from the world they had lived in and survived. I had no knowledge, no appreciation for my aunt and uncle having spent years hiding from the Nazis and their sympathizers, with more close calls than they might have wanted to talk about with me, had I bothered to ask. They also endured the aching tragedy of most of Tante Malli's huge family being murdered, the Jewish presence in Germany reduced to almost nothing. My dad's escape from Germany must have been an unbelievable miracle to them, especially after he had started life anew in America, of all places. And what could they possibly have made of my brother and me, representing the hope of a new generation in a new land?

I have a slightly clearer memory of Uncle Franz, who lived several years longer than Tante Malli and worked at learning English. His companion in the later years of life, Hildegard, handed me his two small, well-thumbed

German-English dictionaries. My dad described him as gregarious, personable, and humorous, putting a *very* in front of each of those adjectives. "Give him two drinks or so, on top of everything else," my father said, "the guy would be hilarious." I remember him as relatively tall with a solid bearing, occasionally smoking a pipe, happily puttering around a garden, interested in birds and getting fresh air each day, and committed to taking a daily walk.

Tante Malli died in 1974 and was buried in the Jewish cemetery in Düsseldorf. Uncle Franz then took up with Hildegard until he died in 1981.

There are so many questions I wish I could ask them all. To Uncle Franz and Tante Malli—tell me more about hiding in Germany during the Holocaust. Why did you stay in the country afterward? What was it like for Tante Malli to be there, the only survivor left in Germany from the Lebenstein family? And what was it like to return to Lembeck after the war and to the house she grew up in, before they sold it?

And for Omi—how could you reconcile working for Germany after the war? How were you treated then?

I didn't ask these questions and so many others because I wasn't focused on where my family had been. I was too busy thinking about where my own life was headed.

Chapter 10

BUILDING BLOCKS

"I am a Jew."

Three building blocks carried me forward in the late-blooming quest to know more about my family.

One was that no matter what we went through, I could always count on my parents' love and support. Both lived with the searing experiences of the Holocaust for the rest of their days. I can only speculate about the ways in which they quietly suffered through the trauma from those terrible years, the way it tore apart their extended families. Ladle onto that any scars from their divorce and it was a lot to handle. But of all the privileges I've benefited from in my life, the most important was knowing that I had my parents' unconditional love.

A second was that I was Jewish. This wasn't only something I was told at a young age. I believed it then and I believe it now. I trust in the words of the *Shema*, the Hebrew prayer that is the watchword of our faith: "*Sh'ma Yisrael, Adonai Eloheinu, Adonai Echad*. Hear O Israel, the Lord our God, the Lord is One."

I think sometimes of journalist Daniel Pearl's final words before he was murdered in Pakistan in 2002: "My mother is Jewish, my father is Jewish, I am a Jew."

The synagogues I have been a member of throughout my life have generally been associated with the Reform movement, Judaism's most liberal branch. I do not read or speak Hebrew, beyond the ability to recite the basic prayers and songs I have known for most of my life and that are repeated at services. Anything else, I stumble through with the help of an English transliteration.

I appreciate the humanistic nature of my religion. We are taught there should be no difference between what we say and think on the one hand and how we act on the other. We fast on the holiest day of the year—Yom Kippur, the Day of Atonement—and ask for forgiveness for our sins against God. But to atone for sins against others, we cannot ask for divine intervention; we must seek forgiveness from those we have sinned against.

We are supposed to carry this humanitarian focus throughout the year. It emphasizes the importance of acting ethically and taking part in social action, as expressed in the Hebrew phrase "*tikkun olam*" or "repair the world." (The latter was particularly challenging for a journalist at mainstream news organizations dedicated to impartiality.)

By no means would I suggest that I reliably uphold these ideals. They are guideposts and aspirational. I frequently fall short, leaving me with remorse, regret, and even guilt.

One of the vital decisions I made as a Jew was to marry someone Jewish. This was not a given. I decided as a youngster that if I were blessed with children, they would be brought up Jewish. What little I knew of my family's history at the time was enough to make me determined to impart my children with a Jewish upbringing. I didn't care what religion my wife was, until a couple of serious relationships with non-Jewish women ended largely because I insisted our kids be Jewish.

That was not going to be a problem with Mollie, the granddaughter of Rabbi Milton Grafman of Birmingham, Alabama, who was himself a descendant of a long line of cantors and rabbis. As we were dating, she told me that her family observed the beginning of Sabbath on Friday evenings, if not at the synagogue, then at home. Would it be okay after we were married to generally not go out on Friday evenings? I agreed, though as the years have gone by, we've made more exceptions. Also, her parents began every dinner at home with the Hebrew blessing over bread, known as the *Hamotzi,* added the blessings over wine (the *Kiddush*), and lit Shabbat candles on Friday night. Could we do the same? she asked. Yes, of course, I said. Even with my limited knowledge of Hebrew, these were blessings I knew well.

We have made ours a Jewish home, with Jewish art, books, sacred texts, and the ritual objects used to celebrate the Sabbath and religious holidays. We have always belonged to a synagogue. We enrolled our children in a Jewish preschool and put them on a path in their religious training where they had a bar/bat mitzvah, the coming-of-age ritual at age thirteen where they lead the Shabbat service, read from the Torah, and are recognized in Judaism as an adult. We have fulfilled our responsibility to introduce them to the faith of their ancestors. Where they go from there is up to them.

A third building block while growing up was having firmly decided in the third grade that I wanted to be a journalist. I don't remember seriously considering wanting to do anything else. Journalism captured my imagination. It wasn't so much that I wanted to be the first to deliver the news. What most interested me was analyzing a situation and the people who made it happen. Other reporters specialized in breaking news or investigative reporting or wrote riveting features. I guess I was most jazzed by explanatory journalism that took on complicated issues and introduced readers to people and places they would never understand on their own.

I wrote for and edited school newspapers, from elementary school in Philadelphia to junior high in suburban Cheltenham to high school in the Chicago suburb of Deerfield. I started my own high school newspaper, which we published by mimeograph and financed with bake sales. (My mom had the essential role of baking Bundt cakes that I sold by the slice at school.)

Over the years I came to understand that daily journalism fit my personality, balancing my desire for perfectionism by being accurate and fair and getting the story right with my pragmatic streak of getting it done in a timely fashion and hitting a deadline.

My first summer in Memphis as a reporter for the morning newspaper, *The Commercial Appeal*, was an eventful one for the city. I covered a series of municipal worker strikes in 1978—involving the police, firefighters, and public school teachers—as well as the selection of the first Black school superintendent in a city that had long-suffering racial divisions. Along the way I learned to ask tough questions, never mislead the reader, and provide my own motivation even when discouraged to do so by editors.

A big break was getting an opportunity to temporarily cover the education beat. I decided to find one of the best-performing schools located in one of the poorest neighborhoods and write about it. Lauderdale Elementary, located less than two miles from the newspaper's office, was built in 1902 and literally falling apart. Even so, many students equaled or beat achievement scores of their peers in some of the best neighborhoods. Principal Sara Lewis essentially willed the school to succeed with stern but fair discipline, a commitment to the basics, a passionate staff, and continual reinforcement and motivation for students.

Once the metro editor heard that I was reporting this story, he told me to stop. In words that still linger in my ears decades later, he told me in a voice loud enough that others around us in the newsroom could hear, "We don't want initiative on the education beat right now." I was shocked that anyone would say those words to a young, ambitious employee. I went downstairs to the press room, watching the presses roll as they printed the afternoon newspaper, and wondered if I had made the wrong career choice, one where initiative was discouraged. I decided to make this one of the few times I would act first and apologize later if necessary. I pushed forward on the story, quietly doing most of the reporting and writing on my own time, and won praise from the editor-in-chief when it was published.

Focusing on journalism trained me to immerse myself in events but to also keep an emotional distance. I learned to ask tough questions, analyze situations, profile people making news, and try to write in engaging, accessible ways to attract the largest natural audience. Curiously and unfortunately, it took a long time to use those skills on my own family.

At the beginning of 1980, I was given the opportunity to become the newspaper's correspondent in Little Rock. It turned out to be three years of covering major news in Arkansas, including the surprising reelection loss and subsequent comeback of Gov. Bill Clinton, the enactment of a state law requiring creationism to be taught in public schools whenever evolution was taught, and a Titan 2 missile explosion inside an Air Force silo. The latter two events were followed worldwide.

Another long-running story with global interest was reporting on thousands of Cuban refugees who were detained at the Fort Chaffee military installation in Northwest Arkansas. U.S. refugee policies were in crisis in 1980 when about 125,000 Cubans—some of them criminals and the mentally ill, many others simply fleeing Castro's communist regime—reached South Florida in what became known as the Mariel boat lift. About 19,000 of them were transported to Fort Chaffee that May.

I reported regularly from the military base. I spent time speaking directly with the Cubans, accompanied by an interpreter from the base. During my initial visit soon after they arrived, a refugee handed me a small, tattered slip of paper with his name and the name and phone number of a relative in Miami he wanted me to call. I tried to tell him I didn't know if I could be of help, but he waved his hand and nodded his head. A crowd soon gathered around me, motioning for my notebook and pen and leaving me with page after page of names and phone numbers with Miami and New York area codes, in hopes I would contact "*mi familia.*"

One of them was Luis Robledo, age thirty-one, who got my attention because he spoke English. He told me he was a mechanical designer who had been in a Havana prison because he had tried to escape Cuba. Now he was eager to send for the family he left behind and to be with his mother, who lived in Miami and owned dry cleaning stores he could work at. "In Cuba, there is nothing," he told me. "Only hunger." He said he'd had his passport and all the necessary papers ready to leave Cuba in what he described as a battle of "twenty years to fight in order to come here." I wished him *buena suerte* (good luck), the only appropriate words I knew in Spanish. He shook my hand warmly.

By the end of the afternoon, I had notes from sixteen refugees. I handed them to a military officer who said he would give them to the American Red Cross, unsure what would happen next. That night at my motel in nearby Fort Smith, I realized I inadvertently left one name and phone number in my notebook. It was from Robledo, who drew an arrow from his name to the name and phone number of his mother. I called her and told her I had spoken to her son.

"Oh my goodness!" she exclaimed, then began to cry softly. "I appreciate it all very much, because nobody tells me nothing." She said she had last seen him when visiting Cuba six months earlier and found her family—including a sister, brother, and uncle—had gone two days without eating. She brought them clothing and food. Of her seventy-eight-year-old mother, she said, "No clothes, no food, no nothing." She sobbed again.

She asked me several times when he would be home. "Soon," I told her, though of course I did not know. She thanked me. "*Buena suerte,*" I replied.

My story was published in *The Commercial Appeal* on May 16 under the headline, "A Son Looks for a Home That's Not the Same." I ended it with these words: "*Buena suerte* to all the names and phone numbers the refugees have handed out. Mostly, *buena suerte* to all the broken families and to Luis Robledo and his mother." Ten days later, frustrated by being detained, the Cubans began a series of riots, setting off a political firestorm that contributed to Clinton's reelection defeat when he couldn't get relief from President Jimmy Carter.

It was after telling my dad about my interactions with the refugees that we eventually spoke about his own experiences. I occasionally thought of Robledo in the years since, especially when researching for this book. I doubt that he saw the story I wrote. I wondered if the internet could help us reconnect, so I could tell him how much our brief interaction meant to me and to find out how he had fared.

I typed the key words in the search window, hit enter, then gasped at the results. A Luis Robledo had been shot and killed in February 1986 by a former cop turned serial killer during a drug deal in Robledo's West Miami-Dade County apartment. He was thirty-seven.

Our paths crossed fleetingly one day in 1980. I was a reporter naive about my own family's journey to America. Robledo was a refugee, fenced-in and uncertain about his future in this new country, while his mother anxiously waited for him in Miami. I cast no judgment on how Robledo came to his fate, only profound sorrow. I cannot say what combination of bad choices, limited opportunities, and bad luck may have contributed to it. Only that I wish he had found a better, longer life in America.

BEGINNING TO TAKE RESPONSIBILITY

Chapter 11

UNCOMFORTABLE HOMECOMINGS

"It only brings us sad memories again and again."

Visiting your family's hometown was a traumatic and complicated experience for Holocaust survivors, no matter how warm and welcoming the current residents might be. My mother and father returned to Germany many years after the war, though they weren't interested in seeing their hometowns.

My mother went to Germany reluctantly and only when accompanying my stepfather on business trips, refusing to speak German while there. She was always eager to leave again and wanted no part of revisiting her early childhood home of Augsburg, at least until I prepared for my first visit as she approached the age of ninety, when she felt too weak to join me.

My father had no qualms about visiting Germany and enjoyed being with his aunt and uncle in Düsseldorf. But I don't think he returned to Essen, and I know he never went back to Lembeck.

Somehow my tante Malli and uncle Franz reconciled with Germany after the war, spending the rest of their lives in the only country they really knew. Their apartment in Düsseldorf was less than an hour away by car from her ancestral home in Lembeck, but I don't know if she spent much time there. She quickly sold the old Lembeck homestead once it was finally returned to her in 1950, not having any desire to live there again.

My dad and John continued to be interested in Germany, especially the World War II era. They were both drawn to history from that time. They were also avid readers of espionage novels set in WWII, which undoubtedly contributed to my own interest in the genre. They read from the safety of their own homes. But I also remember my dad speaking in his later years of having occasional nightmares about Germany.

I recently learned about two distant relatives who visited their hometowns in the Dorsten area several decades after they survived the Holocaust, unspooling raw emotions that stayed with them for the rest of their lives. Their experiences show how complicated it is when survivors try to reconcile with the country they had to abandon.

The first such visitor, Ernst Metzger, quickly came to regret his return visit. He was born in 1912 to the same deep regional roots that I have; Mendel and Sara Lebenstein were his great-grandparents. That made him an enemy in the Nazi era; he was deported along with every other Jew they could find. His account of his family's abrupt departure begins in a chilling fashion, literally and figuratively. "On Saturday morning, January 23, 1942, it was bitterly cold," he wrote, "a car stopped near our house at Wiesenstraße 24 to pick us up unexpectedly for deportation to Riga." He was accompanied by his parents, two of his brothers, a sister-in-law, and his young niece.

What follows is a 1,500-word tale of horror, set mostly in the Riga ghetto. "People were shot and hanged every day, often for no reason or because they wanted to exchange a piece of bread," he wrote. "It was all at the commandant's whim. We slowly got used to having death before our eyes." Practically his entire family was murdered—his parents in Auschwitz, other relatives in the Jewish ghetto in Riga.

Metzger wrote about his wrenching experiences four decades later for the newly formed group of Dorsten memory activists led by Wolf Stegemann and Dirk Hartwich. Metzger's harrowing account appeared in 1983 in the first volume of the group's book *Dorsten unterm Hakenkreuz*. "Throughout my life," Metzger concluded, "I will never forget how we 135 Jews, out of 14,000 remaining from the Riga ghetto, were able to survive the hell of the

German concentration camps. And just as I cannot forget my experiences, people and young people must not forget what people are capable of."

After his liberation, he emigrated first to Sweden and then to the U.S., eventually retiring to Miami Beach. But Metzger never forgot about Dorsten. He accepted an invitation to return in 1983,accompanied by his wife, Cecilia, a Hungarian Jew and survivor of Auschwitz. "His wife had actually only seen Germany from the perspective of cattle wagons," Stegemann later wrote, "only saw Germans in boots and uniforms with dog whips in their hands and only knew the German language from commands such as 'out, out!' 'quick, quick' 'into the shower!' 'stand still!'"

Longtime Dorsten residents who remembered Metzger collected money to pay for his homecoming. The city provided a subsidy, too, though the administration worried that other deported Jews might expect the same courtesy.

Local officials needn't have worried that Metzger's trip would lead to a sudden influx of former residents, or that he would even make a return visit. After a few days, Cecilia Metzger stopped leaving her hotel, unwilling to be constantly confronted by her husband's difficult past, which was similar to her own. Ernst Metzger continued with his visit, which included meeting with the mayor, former friends and neighbors, and members of the budding research group studying the Jewish history there. He also reconnected with Rolf Abrahamsohn, the head of the local Jewish community, whom Metzger had befriended when they were both held in the Riga ghetto.

"Not everyone he met was a friend," Stegemann wrote. "At an information event with Ernst Metzger, it was said that it couldn't have been that bad in the camps because 'he (Metzger) survived!'" The couple also heard local residents remark, "You don't look like Jews at all!"

Metzger returned home to Miami Beach and decided he had more than enough of Dorsten for one lifetime. He wrote to Elisabeth, thanking her for sending one of the remembrance group's books about the Nazi era. He said he admired her commitment to educating others about what had happened in Dorsten. "These facts are historical and can and should never be forgotten," he said. "Many of our old friends who survived the concentration camp with us always talk about our sad past. None of us are healthy." He ended by pleading with Elisabeth not to send any more such books. "It only brings us sad memories again and again," he said. "The ones we have will last us until the end of our lives."

Another distant relative had a better—and life-changing—experience when returning to the region, a visit he had insisted he would never do. Alexander Lebenstein was the only survivor among the nineteen members of Jewish families in the town of Haltern am See, less than ten miles east of Lembeck. He was deported to Riga in 1942, then held in two concentration camps before being liberated.

He emerged after the war having lost his parents, his home and possessions, and nearly his life. "Germany was no longer my home," he wrote in his memoir. "Everything that I had known as a child had been ripped away from me and destroyed. I refused the German citizenship that had been re-offered to me. After the manner in which it had been stripped away from my parents and me, I could not imagine ever wanting to be a German citizen again."

He made his way to the U.S., eventually settling in Richmond, Virginia, sure that he would never again visit his native land. He was offended when Haltern am See invited him to return in 1988 as it prepared to celebrate the 750th anniversary of the town's founding. "It added insult to injury as my memory went back to the time when vile anti-Semitism was preached from the Roman Catholic churches," he wrote. "I hated the people, the children, and even the dogs."

A few years later, Lebenstein received two handwritten letters from students in Haltern am See inviting him back. He refused to go at first, though friends and family successfully pressured him to reconsider. Once there, he was touched by the affection shown to him, especially by the schoolchildren he spoke to. He related an exchange with two young women who approached him with tears in their eyes. One asked if she could hold his hand; the other asked for his forgiveness. "Forgive you for what?" he asked. "You have done nothing wrong to me." He asked the young woman when her mother was born. When she said it was 1949, he responded, "It is your grandfather who is guilty, Not you."

But not everything went smoothly. He was accosted by a former acquaintance who accused him of not helping to pay for a cake when they were in elementary school, then of angrily removing the man's Nazi uniform when Lebenstein briefly returned to Haltern am See right after the war. "Get the hell out of here," Lebenstein replied, "or I'll tear you apart again."

Still, Lebenstein's heart was softened by the young people in Haltern, where a school was named in his honor and a small Holocaust memorial began. "Since my return from Haltern in 1995, I have changed a lot," he wrote in one of his many letters to schoolchildren there, this one in 2003. "My values have taken on a different meaning. The visits with the students there gave me a new perspective on life. We shared our mutual pain and suffering which we all inherited from the Nazi era."

Lebenstein died in 2010, seemingly more at peace with the country he once called home that had brought him such overwhelming tragedy early in life. As a child of survivors, my first trip to Germany was less about exorcising old memories than creating new ones.

Chapter 12

STANDING WHERE MY RELATIVES DID

"We have to live with oppressive, collective shame."

The only family memories I carried with me on my first trip to Germany in 1986 were imparted from my dad and Elisabeth. They served as a counterweight to a young person's Hollywood, World War II–era familiarization of Germans as ruthless, evil, and hapless butchers, courtesy of *Stalag 17*, *The Dirty Dozen*, *Hogan's Heroes*, and their ilk. I was used to hearing German regularly spoken by family members. I didn't associate the language, in that context, with the harsh, guttural, and clipped commands frequently featured on TV and movie screens.

My first stop in Germany was Mainz, to visit a friend I made in D.C. the year before, when we both had a congressional fellowship with the American Political Science Association. Three days later, I took the train to Düsseldorf, where I had to convince myself that a journey to my family's past was appropriate. Elisabeth met me at the station in a city I had long identified with Tante Malli and Uncle Franz. We toured Düsseldorf with Hildegard, then enjoyed eating a mild salt herring for lunch called *matjes*. Herring had long been a staple of our many Jewish holiday gatherings, so eating *matjes* from the North Sea seemed to further blend my Jewish and German cultural heritage. We rode an elevator to the top of the 789-foot-tall *Rheinturm*, or Rhine Tower, a telecommunications center that provides spectacular views of the city.

And we went to the *Nordfriedhof*, or Northern Cemetery, to see a most unusual gravesite. By then, Hildegard had put the graves of my aunt and uncle next to her late husband's, marking the spot with one combined tombstone. It had all four of their names, including Hildegard's. She proudly posed next to it for me. All they needed to do to the tombstone whenever her fateful day came (which it did in 2005) was to add the year of her death.

The next day, Elisabeth and I toured Dorsten, accompanied by an acquaintance of hers who served as an interpreter. The day was cold, damp, and gloomy, but it hardly mattered to me. I had a sense of continuity walking about the market square, watching vendors sell their produce and meats. I became conscious of my footsteps on the cobblestones, walking where my ancestors did and where they once traded their wares. I started to imagine what the sights and sounds might have been like to them then. But I could never allow myself to fully conjure anything resembling an idyllic image. The notion that they had been persecuted was never far away.

Next, Elisabeth said she wanted to go to the Dorsten City Hall so I could meet the *Bürgermeister*, or mayor. I didn't think much about it. I'd been around enough local politicians as a journalist to be cynical about these kinds of visits, where the elected official barely knows the person whose hand he or she is shaking.

That wasn't the case this time. Mayor Heinz Ritter greeted me warmly as we stepped into his office and invited us to have a seat. As I did so, I realized that this was going to be something more than a courtesy visit; it was a minor event being witnessed by reporters and photographers from two local newspapers. I learned later that the mayor was a supporter of Elisabeth's group. He told me I was only the second Jew from the Dorsten area to visit his ancestor's land. Presumably Ernst Metzger was the first.

Ritter was a spritely politician, a former miner, and an experienced chess player. During his successful mayoral campaign in 1984, he bought thousands of the square, iconic Ritter Sport chocolate bars and handed them to voters. He described his reasoning to a local newspaper: "So my name will melt on the tongue."

The mayor wanted to know during our conversation why I had come to Germany and what I thought of young people who weren't interested in learning about the Holocaust. This is a beautiful and historic country, I said. But it is also one that killed my relatives. I could not understand how that could have happened. Even so, I thought it was important to confront this personal history by seeing the country myself, walking where my family once did, and getting a better sense of the culture they identified with. I welcomed the chance to build bridges of friendship to a new generation.

I thought back to the sudden crisis of confidence I had experienced on the train to Düsseldorf and how I resolved it. It was better to directly confront the past and see my ancestors' country, I told him, than to ignore it. To ignore Germany, I decided, would not only condemn the innocent people living there now, but it would be, in a sense, turning my back on my family's heritage by neglecting the roots that existed before my parents fled.

My remarks seemed to be accepted and understood. The mayor said the German government had made mistakes and that many people were disconnected from that history. He said he was proud that I had visited my family's hometown and found my way to him in his official role, adding, "You're welcome here."

Ritter also said something that I thought was a step too far. He asked that when I returned to America, I should speak positively of this new Germany and urge others to visit, too. Now, suddenly, I felt that I had been used. Of course, I was eager to talk about my interactions in Germany. But I wasn't about to become a salesman for the country to those who were not prepared to reconcile. For the first time, I had the sense that I was being asked to play the role of a Jewish descendant giving his blessing to postwar Germany. It is one thing if I choose to advocate that people make a fair appraisal of modern-day Germany and quite another if I'm expected to do so. As we'll see later, others have also felt and resented this expectation, part of what's been called the "theater of memory."

I didn't say any of this to Ritter, keeping my thoughts to myself. Before we parted, he presented me with a commemorative plate illustrating the famous Lembeck Castle. "It's rare that people take an interest in history," he said, not knowing, of course, that I had been largely oblivious even to my own family's history until just recently, and at that point had only a tenuous hold on the facts. He said he would be glad if my father visited him as well.

Photographers snapped pictures of me as I received the commemorative plate, which accompanied stories by reporters in two local newspapers the next day. It seemed to symbolize both the heritage my family had been forced to flee as well as the goodwill offered by those who now lived there.

Elisabeth, her friend, and I went to Lembeck to see the castle, then to the place where my great-grandmother's house once stood. A beauty parlor had since been built on the plot. Elisabeth's grandmother's house was just a block away. Had the Holocaust not intervened, she and I might have been childhood friends. The church, so central to the early life of the village, was right nearby.

We then went to Elisabeth's parents' house for a lunch of German pancakes. Her father, Bernhard Cosanne, told me that the Lebensteins had traded clothes and cattle with their neighbors. They used a horse-driven cart, cultivated apples and other produce from their garden, and slaughtered cows for meat. He remembered my great-grandmother as a "fine, elegant woman." He recalled Sophie and Selma Lebenstein giving their porcelain to neighbors the day before they were deported. They also went to a shoemaker, asking him to fit their shoes. The shoemaker declined, saying he wasn't allowed such contact with Jews.

"There was only one way to think," Bernhard Cosanne said, trying to explain this kind of response. And that was, "Sorry, but I have to take care of my own problems." People had few options under the strong-armed Nazi regime, he said, and had to choose between protecting their own family or someone else's.

And yet, he said, the Lebensteins were very much a part of the community. He remembered being at their house for a Passover seder, the ritual springtime feast in which we retell the story of the Jewish Exodus from Egypt. He talked about the celebration of Corpus Christi Day, which commemorates Jesus' Last Supper, when the Lebensteins built an altar just as their neighbors did. He recalled my uncle Karl-Heinz who had dark, curly hair, playing baby Jesus in a Christmas play.

He then said the words that I've since heard elsewhere, in one form or another, that in January 1942, two days before being deported, my great-grandmother said, "I don't know what we have done that the Germans would do this to us." Anger and frustration welled inside me as I thought about her and my other relatives. They had worked hard both to keep their Jewish identity and to belong to their German community but were not considered worthy enough to live. More than ever, I believed that as a minority, Jews could never feel completely safe anywhere, no matter how accepted we might seem to be at any moment.

Before we left, Elisabeth's father gave me a present to deliver to my dad—a sturdy, handmade wooden walking stick. It seemed to symbolize so much, this gift between two people who might well have crossed paths in Lembeck some fifty years earlier but were now linked through their children's friendship, a friendship that spanned time, a generation, and history. Years later, I found that walking stick in my dad's Memphis home in the days after he died and made a point of bringing it home with me. It's a keepsake I would never part with, one that brought me particular comfort more recently when dealing with vertigo.

Once leaving the Cosanne household, we drove to the Jewish cemetery outside of town (Jews were not permitted to be buried in town), property that had once belonged to my family. Many of my Lebenstein ancestors who died in the 1800s and early 1900s are buried there, including my great-grandfather Isaak Lebenstein. State and local governments had seized it in 1939 and kept cattle there. The cemetery was the subject of reparations proceedings after the war, though it was largely neglected afterward. It hadn't even been marked as a cemetery until Elisabeth's research group installed a memorial plaque at the entrance a few years before I visited.

I stood in silence. At that point, there was nothing more I could say.

We also went to Essen, to visit some of the places that my father pointed out in his notes to me. Sachsenstraße, the street where his immediate family lived and where he was the only one to escape being deported, was much changed. The apartment buildings where the family once resided—first at 16 Sachsenstraße, then at 13—no longer existed.

We went to the old synagogue in Essen, where my father's family were members. The building stood in its broken state for many years after the interior was destroyed during *Kristallnacht*. The Allies had frequently attacked Essen, a target of heavy bombing because of Krupp's major role as an armament supplier. By war's end, much of Essen's center city was reduced to rubble. But the synagogue was still standing.

In 1949, the city displayed a clear sign of Germany's unwillingness to accept responsibility for Nazi-era crimes. It installed a stone edifice at the front of the synagogue, with an inane inscription that referred to the "more than 2,500 Jews of the city of Essen who had to lose their lives between 1933–1945."

The building was formally sold to the city in 1959. Soon thereafter it began to renovate the property, turning it into an exhibition house for industrial design, known as the Haus Industrieform. Pictures from that era show a soulless interior, devoid of traces that it was once a house of worship. "This shows that there was little awareness of the necessity to preserve the vestiges of Jewish history and life in Germany," says a book published by the synagogue in 2011. "German society had not distanced itself from the perpetrators, many of whom were still living, and had not yet mustered up the courage to realize that the present is at any given time the intersection between past and future."

In 1979, an accidental fire caused by a short circuit destroyed portions of the industrial design building, giving the city another chance to reconsider its use. This time, it came back as a memorial site and documentation center. The inscription outside was changed to say it was a memorial to Essen's Jews "murdered by the Nazi regime." "For the first time," wrote Edna Brocke, who later served as the synagogue's director, "the perpetrators of the genocide were named, yet no attempt was made to reflect upon the responsibility and role of society at large." She also observed that Jews were rarely given an independent voice in the exhibitions.

It still didn't look much like a synagogue when I visited in 1986. But then, it wasn't intended to. The building's permanent exhibit was now a memorial to all of Essen's citizens who were murdered by the Nazis, not just the Jews. The idea that it was once a sacred spot where people worshipped was beside the point. The exhibit, Brocke said, "was devoted primarily to proletarian resistance against the Nazi regime and documented the persecution of various groups from the perspective of the persecutors. The Jewish population was only one of many groups of victims, despite the fact that the former synagogue represented more a site of previous Jewish life than a site of destruction."

Slightly more than half of the building's visitors were young people, said a curator who met us at the synagogue that day in 1986. The site helped them better understand the Holocaust's toll on their own community. But only to a point. "They always feel a moral pull on their feelings," she said. "But they don't know why. They say, 'What do I have to do with that?'"

Religious services were still held then for the relatively few Jews of Essen in the mid-1980s, a group small enough that they could gather in a room in the basement. Their ranks were a tiny fraction of the five thousand worshippers in the synagogue's heyday. Most of the Jews who lived there in the 1980s had fled from what was then known as the Soviet Union. These newcomers had no roots in Germany.

The most moving aspect of the site to me was an object easily lost in the grandeur of the large building. It was a book in the old synagogue's library that contained the names of Essen's Jews murdered during the Holocaust. I stared at four of the names, one at a time—my grandparents Rosalie and Leopold, and my uncles Karl-Heinz and Manfred.

I had seen their names written elsewhere of course. But they took on an extra dimension here, in the very synagogue in which they had worshipped and where my dad had his bar mitzvah. More than ever, I wondered what they were like. I've thought about that book many times since and ache for having been denied the opportunity to know them.

At night we joined members of Elisabeth's group for a fondue dinner. They told me that even after studying the Holocaust, they still didn't understand why more people didn't defy the Nazis, especially in smaller towns like Lembeck and Dorsten where everybody knew one another. But they started to take a few steps—through their books, plaques erected near town halls, and gravestones—to ensure that others would be forced to confront this grim chapter of history.

Bottom row, seated, from left: Sister Johanna Eichmann, Elisabeth, and Christel Winkel (cofounder of the museum) Top row, standing, from left: Wolf Stegemann, Rolf Abrahamsohn, Brigitte Stegemann-Czurda, me, Bernd Winkel, and Meinholf Edelkamp (a friend of the Winkels)

They wanted to know when my father would return to Lembeck. I told them it would be an emotional trip for my dad, who was then sixty-six years old. I also told them I didn't think it was necessary. He knew where he was from and what was lost. It was more important for me, as a part of a new generation, to make such a trip, to rediscover my home.

All of us had made our own distinctive journeys toward wanting to know what had happened during the Nazi era, raised by families who weren't much inclined to talk about it. The silence was finally ending in many parts of Germany in the mid-1980s, in places large and small. Grassroots citizen groups formed as a new generation of Germans broached a difficult topic rarely spoken about at home or school.

I should say that I'm primarily interested in the area formerly known as the Federal Republic of Germany when the country was split after World War II, from 1949 to 1989. West Germany, as it was called then, was where both sides of my family lived for centuries and the only part of Germany I have visited, save for a day in East Berlin.

East Germany, despite its formal name as the German Democratic Republic, was communist during those forty years when it was separated from the West, part of the Soviet bloc. It had a somewhat different take on the war compared to Germans in the West.

East Germany characterized West Germany as a bastion of fascism that allowed former Nazis to influence national policies even after the war. East Germans liked to consider themselves members of a true democratic state and sought to emphasize the communist resistance to the Nazis. They turned major concentration camps into memorial sites well before the West did, though their focus was mainly on the evils of fascism, not the Holocaust. Jews were portrayed as but one of its many victims. East German communists also played up their own victimhood, having been targeted by the Nazi regime, too.

"The GDR emphasized the workers, the party, and the Soviet population as having suffered most from National Socialism," wrote Thomas Haury, a German scholar of anti-Semitism. "The genocide of the European Jews was only one crime among many, to which the GDR hardly paid attention." Haury wrote the East Germans "drew a clear line between the 'criminal Hitler regime' and the 'enticed German people,' declaring them innocent and indeed the first victims of Hitler's rule. In the eastern part of Germany there was no debate on the German people's participation in discrimination, confiscation, and mass murder until 1989."

West Germany during this time emphasized that the crimes of the 1930s and '40s were really just the responsibility of Hitler, the Nazi Party, and the SS. Even President Richard von Weizsäcker's groundbreaking speech on May 8, 1985, urging Germans to remember what had been done in order to achieve reconciliation, equivocated on the notion of responsibility. He referred to the formal end of the war forty years earlier not so much as Germany's surrender or defeat but "a day of liberation." He said, "It liberated all of us from the inhumanity and tyranny of the National-Socialist regime."

Weizsäcker made it sound as if the German populace were unwitting victims, much like every other group of people who were targeted by the Nazis, ignoring that the regime enjoyed public backing. The notion incensed contemporary German writer and poet Max Czollek, who wrote three decades later that Weizsäcker's characterization was obviously false. Most Germans weren't liberated on that day, Czollek wrote. "They were finally and definitively defeated after supporting the Nazi regime to the bitter end—and still further beyond. National Socialism was, after all, truly a popular movement."

Germany's confrontation with its past has thus been part of a slow-starting, slowly evolving process. For one thing, the generation old enough to be involved in or at least aware of what was happening during the Nazi era was fading from public and private life, one way or another. Some of their children, having taken part in 1960s peace movements, had been conditioned to question the establishment at a young age. Now they were in a position to take further action. Germany's violent history came to the fore again during the 1972 Olympic Games in Munich, the country's first since Hitler used the 1936 games as a propaganda vehicle. Palestinian terrorists broke into the Olympic Village, killing two members of the Israeli team and taking nine hostages. The hostages, five of the terrorists, and a policeman were later killed in a failed rescue attempt.

In 1976, West German teacher Dieter Boßmann collected two thousand compositions on "What I have heard about Adolf Hitler," written by students who were mostly fourteen to sixteen years old. Their widespread ignorance and confusion about Hitler made worldwide news. There was also a surge of violence by neo-Nazis, including a 1980 bombing at Munich's Oktoberfest that claimed thirteen lives, followed by the murder of a prominent Jewish leader in Bavaria a few months later.

The four-part American TV series *Holocaust*, first shown in the U.S in 1978 and in West Germany the following January, was a revelation, with its dramatic, Hollywood-style focus on crimes committed against the Jews. ABC News West German correspondent Kati Marton was struck by its impact. Reporting from what was then the capital of West Germany, Bonn, Marton said the show "has been nothing short of a thunderbolt . . . an American TV series, seen by twenty million Germans, provoked a long-overdue national debate on the past. Foreign observers, this reporter included, have been astonished at the overwhelming reaction to the broadcast."

More national self-reflection came from a rolling series of anniversaries of major events from the Nazi era, such as those marking fifty years since

Hitler's march to power in 1933 and forty years since Germany surrendered in 1945.

"The History Movement emerged as a varied collection of initiatives focused on researching, exhibiting, and commemorating history—especially of the Nazi period, of workers' lives, of the struggles of ordinary people," wrote Jenny Wüstenberg, a historian at Nottingham Trent University in England. "Though they were locally grounded, the activists were also well networked across the Federal Republic. They were united by a common commitment to an engaged and political—and clearly left-wing—perspective on history. Their motto was 'dig where you stand:' it was a call to scrutinize and publicize the meaning of the past in one's own social and geographic environment and to make the findings relevant to the current political decisions and struggles."

It wasn't always big issues that energized German baby boomers to confront their parents. Often the questions hit closer to home. Joel Obermayer is an American who runs the Widen the Circle awards program that honors Germans who fight racism and anti-Semitism and act to preserve Jewish history. Often, Obermayer told me, it began with a straightforward question. "Like, 'What happened to that house over there?' or, 'Were there Jews in this town?' or, 'You served in the Army, what did you see?'"

One of the people in Dorsten who started making inquiries was Dirk Hartwich. Hartwich was born in the nearby rural community of Gelsenkirchen-Resse, six months after the war ended in 1945. He told me he didn't ask the uncomfortable questions at home until he was twenty. When he did, he learned that his father's family included many active Nazi supporters, his seven aunts and uncles never disassociating themselves from their involvement in the regime. His paternal grandmother was a member of the *Bund Deutscher Mädel (BDM)*, or the League of German Girls, a wing of the Nazi youth movement. This devout woman, a regular churchgoer, said later in her life, "the Jews killed our Lord Jesus."

Hartwich's mother, in the last years before she died in 2010, began to speak more freely about the Jewish families she once knew in Berlin who were deported. Their apartments were immediately transferred to countrymen who, as Hartwich put it, "swam with the Nazi wave."

Hartwich's own political activism took a turn in 1966 when he participated in his first demonstration, against the far-right NPD, the neo-Nazi National Democratic Party of Germany. He was elected to the Dorsten City Council in 1975. He didn't know that there had been a local Jewish community until he was on the way to a committee hearing in 1982 and heard radio reports about nearby towns commemorating the Nazi pogroms against Jews that culminated in *Kristallnacht.*

It prompted the kind of straightforward curiosity that Obermayer mentioned to me. "My spontaneous question at the meeting as to whether there had been a Jewish community in Dorsten was strangely unanswered," Hartwich later recalled. "My next question as to who the leading Nazis in Dorsten were was rejected because it was not on the agenda."

He then read a newspaper article in the *Ruhr-Nachrichten* about how the local Jewish community was destroyed in 1938. The story by journalist Wolf Stegemann prompted him to ask more questions, some of which Hartwich repeated in a letter to the editor. Were the perpetrators of those who destroyed the local synagogue and vandalized the Jewish cemetery during Kristallnacht ever prosecuted? he wrote. "Who was responsible for the expulsion and deportation of the Dorsten Jews? What became of the houses and property of the murdered Jewish citizens?"

This was a particularly unwelcome topic in small-town Germany. Praise for Hartwich's inquiry was outweighed by condemnation, some of which was delivered through anonymous, abusive phone calls. "Acknowledging that one's grandparents were Nazis or that one's town was complicit with the regime," wrote historian Jacob S. Eder, "is a much harder process in a small, tight-knit community than building monuments that portray victims or talk about perpetrators in an abstract way."

Hartwich's determination stiffened. He and Stegemann formed a *Geschichtswerkstatt*, or "history workshop," to research such unpopular issues, meeting regularly and documenting their findings in brochures and books. They spoke first to school groups, then widened their reach to include parishes and trade unions. "When we started our research in November 1982, I suspected that Dorsten was no exception during the Nazi era," Hartwich said. "But I could never have imagined the extent of injustice in our city." The more questions they asked, he recalled, the more they learned, not from officialdom but more from the "'simple' residents of Dorsten who were willing to reveal the knowledge they had previously held back."

Their research and motivation were enhanced by testimony from local survivors like Ernst Metzger. As wrenching as Metzger's homecoming was, Hartwich said, "Meeting him affected us all deeply. His shocking report on the terrible atrocities that were committed against him, his family and other Jews in Dorsten is without doubt the most moving document" in the first book the remembrance group published.

Eventually non-Jewish Germans began to open up about what they had witnessed, too. Hartwich remembered an elderly woman calling him, saying she was eager now to talk about memories she had repressed. They met in a quiet corner of a Dorsten café. "I was very nervous and tense," Hartwich recalled. "She was initially composed and ready to tell me everything she had experienced with her Jewish neighbors, including friendships with their children. While I was making notes, she suddenly started shedding tears of emotion and sadness. A situation that really affected me emotionally and I will never forget it.

"These were moments that told me that I would always have to act correctly and speak frankly and honestly about the injustice carried out by my parents' generation. It was a terrible crime against humanity."

Helmut Kohl, chancellor of West Germany and then the reunited Germany for much of the 1980s and '90s, once spoke of "*die Gnade der späten Geburt*," or "the grace of late birth," of Germans who were too young to be involved in crimes committed in the Nazi era. Hartwich said he never thought that being born after Hitler's reign absolved him of responsibility in its aftermath. "I have always argued that we, who were born after the war, do not bear collective guilt, but we have to live with oppressive, collective shame."

As the research group continued, he said, "I learned that these crimes had only been possible because the overwhelming majority of the population supported the regime. Actively and passively. On the one hand, I was shocked by the continuing silence of the perpetrators and supporters of the Nazi regime. On the other hand, I was grateful for the willingness of some citizens to 'finally unburden themselves' and, in my opinion, appease their consciences."

One of the key early members of the research group was Sister Johanna Eichmann. Where Stegemann and Hartwich were lightning rods, bearing the brunt of criticism for asking questions many people didn't want answered, Eichmann was the popular, widely respected head of a grammar school. She also had a unique perspective as the daughter of a Jewish mother and Catholic father; both she and her mother converted to Catholicism in 1933.

"She was the face of the group and opened more doors," Hartwich said. "Our volunteer research team grew and was joined by many highly motivated people from all walks of life in Dorsten. The stone that we threw into the water created more and more ripple effects."

Sitting across the dinner table from me that night in November 1986 was the only other Jewish guest, Rolf Abrahamsohn, a remarkable survivor of seven concentration camps. Abrahamsohn was born in 1925 and raised in Marl, just east of Dorsten, where his father ran a clothing and shoe store. He attended a Protestant school until the mid-1930s, when anti-Semitism grew so prominent that he left. After *Kristallnacht*, his family was required to live at a *Judenhaus*, a ghetto house where Jews were forcibly taken.

That began a period of terrible suffering for Abrahamsohn, who was ordered to perform forced labor at a gas company by age fourteen. He was deported to Riga in January 1942, along with his mother and the other remaining Jews in the immediate area. He told me he remembered seeing my aunts Selma and Bertha Lebenstein in Riga that summer. He also recalled going several days without drinking or eating and spending eight days in unheated wagons when it was about 42 degrees Fahrenheit.

He survived the ghetto, the Kaiserwald concentration camp (where his mother died in the harsh conditions), the Stutthof concentration camp near Danzig, and months of forced labor in the Buchenwald concentration camp. He was transported to Theresienstadt during the last weeks of war before being liberated by the Russian army. He weighed sixty-eight pounds.

Abrahamsohn returned to Marl much weakened but hopeful of finding surviving family members. He discovered instead that his father and brother were both deported from Belgium and had been murdered, as had other relatives. He briefly considered emigrating to the U.S. But that wasn't realistic because he was ill, hardly had any education since he left school at an early age, and had spent so much time in concentration camps. So he stayed in Marl, rebuilt his parents' old business, and became a successful textile entrepreneur.

He also took on a role as the leader of whatever was left of the Jewish community across the rural area of Recklinghausen. When I met with him, he said there were sixty-one Jews living in a region where three thousand once lived. He was there to help them get together to pray and have some connection to one another.

His was an incredible life, one that required great fortitude, commitment, and faith. Why stay in Germany? I asked. How do you live in an area where so much harm befell the Jews and where we now exist as a tiny fraction of the community that was once there? He never flinched in his response. People depended on him to continue to make his rounds and to let them know "what was going on," he said, especially with other Jewish survivors scattered across the area.

He paused briefly then said with full conviction, "Therefore, I am in the right place in Germany."

Abrahamsohn didn't have a formal role with the research group or with the museum that was built later. He was instead a valued advisor as well as a popular spokesperson about the Holocaust to groups at schools and the museum. It was vitally important, he added, for people to know about the past. With that, he folded his arms at what I took to be a hint of frustration. "People don't learn about history," he said, with a certain weariness, "so they make all the mistakes again."

Elisabeth later told me that it took a special effort to work with some survivors of the *Shoah*, like Abrahamsohn. He was a good storyteller and even showed a sense of humor in his talks, as well as an ability to captivate the young people he spoke to. That was, Elisabeth said, what he considered his "mission." But the group had to listen carefully to Abrahamsohn. "In every encounter, it was important to take his point of view and his problems seriously, even if they were trivial to us. He noticed that we always gave him our full attention. After each presentation to groups, he always needed confirmation from us (mostly from Christel Winkel) about his work."

Shortly before midnight, Elisabeth and Paul drove me to the station to board a train to West Berlin, where I would visit friends. That's when I noticed the same train was continuing east to Warsaw and Moscow, stirring more anxiety.

Back then, whether you were in the East or West, Germany wasn't much into memorializing the lives that were either lost or diminished in the Nazi era. Only those of us who knew where to look, who had a guide like Elisabeth or one of her colleagues in the research group, could find traces of those who once lived there.

I later wrote about my visit—including my friendship with Elisabeth and my internal debate as to whether I truly belonged in Germany—for *The Milwaukee Journal*. Elisabeth wrote to me the following month, saying she was moved by my story. "I must confess I enjoy it to be praised by you, a friend, an American Jew," she said. "Your praise strengthens my engagement for all the Jews, for their history and, above all, for the better understanding between Christians and Jews. Especially I'm happy to see that you have found a new perspective with my help. Only—I think I'm talked about and praised too much. But most impressed I was about your deep thoughts you felt when you were here. The strong stress [on] 'a right to be here' is very good as well as the hint that you as a young Jew try to meet history personally when you follow the traces of your family."

I read that now, consider when she wrote it, and think about the missed opportunities. There was so much more I could have, and should have, asked my dad when I had the chance. And I recall barely any conversations with Omi about her life in Germany and Colombia. How could I have been so callous as to think that since she and the rest of her immediate family made it out safely, there wasn't much to say?

Still, I was lucky. While my curiosity about my German Jewish heritage was limited at the time, it was top of mind to quite a few Germans I hadn't even met yet.

Chapter 13

STUMBLING INTO HISTORY

"What actually happened here?"

You'd expect a group called *Frauen für den Frieden* (Women for Peace) to have lofty ambitions. The social activists in Dorsten who adopted that name didn't disappoint. They were part of a national movement opposed to war and nuclear weapons.

It was the early 1980s, a time of heightened tensions in the Cold War between the Soviet Union and the West. A series of regional conflicts, instability in Soviet leadership, and an arms race between the U.S. and U.S.S.R.—including weapons with nuclear capabilities—dramatically raised fears that nuclear war could soon be at hand. The two superpowers deployed more troops and weapons to Europe, seemingly ready for battle.

Germany stood in the continent's geographic middle, split east and west. Fear of nuclear war was a global concern with a particularly local twist in the village of Wulfen, home to a huge munitions depot that was built in 1937, fell into British hands after the war, and later returned to Germany. Exactly what's stored in that heavily guarded facility has long been a source of unease. Anxiety soared in the 1980s when rumors spread that it was nuclear weapons. So Women for Peace went to work organizing marches and demonstrations. They displayed a clock set to five minutes before midnight, a sign that doomsday was near. Its members wore black as a form of protest.

Their actions went for naught. There was no evidence their protests had any immediate effect on local sentiment or federal policy. In April 1998, the ammunition depot at Wulfen was still described as "the biggest ammunition site in Europe." Looking back, Birget Lapke, one of the organizers, told me recently, "It seemed like the right thing to do. But now it seems a little pathetic."

The group foundered, unable to find another cause to rally around. Until 2003, when another member, Ulrike Matthäus-Robbert, read an article in *Stern* magazine about Gunter Demnig's nascent effort to memorialize Holocaust victims. He was honoring one victim at a time by installing small bricks in front of places where they once lived. He called these bricks *Stolpersteine,* or stumbling stones.

Matthäus-Robbert was intrigued, suggesting that her friends join her in sponsoring some stumbling stones. But it wasn't clear how seriously the group should take the project, especially since Demnig was primarily thought of as a German artist at the time. "At first, they were all, '*Ja, ja,*'" she recalled recently, pronouncing it "Yah, yah," with a tone of weariness.

But the Women for Peace soon warmed to it. "I think that remembering our past—although we are all born after the war, it is still *our* past—I thought it was a wonderful idea to show the threat was so universal, so widespread," Matthäus-Robbert said. "By this project you could see that. It's small, little thing, but it's like a net all over the country, all over Europe."

Stolpersteine may seem underwhelming when you first notice them. We're used to memorials that make grand statements by being, well, grand. Some of the most famous require us to look up and be overwhelmed by their sheer scale. They're almost always in just one place, a location that may or may not be relevant to the person or event being memorialized.

The most well-known memorials to victims of the Holocaust turns all of that on its head. You can find 100,000 *Stolpersteine* in 1,200 locations, in Germany as well as more than twenty European countries. Demnig installed his milestone 100,000th block in Nuremberg in May 2023. Each one is a simple design of about ten-by-ten centimeters (or just under four-by-four inches) of concrete, covered in brass.

These cobblestone-sized stones are typically installed in front of the victim's last known residence of choice. The bricks are easily missed. You could stand next to them and not realize it unless you're looking at your feet. You could step on them and not notice—one of the reasons *Stolpersteine* have their critics.

Demnig has personally installed nearly every brick. It began with an early-1990s commemoration of Roma and Sinti Holocaust victims, intended as a one-off exhibition. Praise for the work prompted him to keep going. Demnig no longer remembers how he settled on the name. He instead cites a schoolchild's response to a journalist who asked whether people could actually stumble on one of the bricks. "You don't trip on a *Stolpersteine*," the student answered, "you stumble with your head and your heart."

They contain the briefest of information. Only the victim's name, birth date and place, and where and when they were deported are displayed. Guidelines of who qualifies for a stone have broadened since he began, so that they now memorialize anyone persecuted by the Nazi regime, regardless of whether they were murdered. That includes those persecuted for their political views, religion, sexual orientation, or the color of their skin, as well as those considered deserters, prostitutes, or people without a home.

The *Stolpersteine* are distinctive in that once you pay attention to them, they become part of everyday life. You don't go to the *Stolpersteine*, by and large. They come to you. Collectively, these small, decentralized memorials are reminders that Jews and other victims of the Nazi regime didn't live in far-off places. They walked where you're now walking. They lived in your neighborhood. Their persecution, deportation, and murder were not secrets. They were done in plain sight, a history that should not be erased.

Demnig, helped by a small crew, is not a researcher or historian and doesn't pretend to be one. Every block laid into the ground must be researched and sponsored by a local sponsor, a literal manifestation of the slogan, "Dig where you stand."

In the Dorsten area that sponsor was *Frauen für den Frieden*, or Women for Peace. Three of the members—Lapke, Matthäus-Robbert, and Gyburg Sonnemann—reminisced about their activism with Mollie and me many years later over a light, healthy dinner in Lapke's home in the Wulfen countryside.

Three members of Women for Peace—Gyburg Sonnemann, Ulrike Matthäus-Robbert, and Birget Lapke—meeting again in 2022

Women for Peace were united behind certain beliefs, including that their ranks include only women. When a man asked to join the group, they responded with a polite but firm no, convinced that men were inherently conditioned to take over any group they joined. Matthäus-Robbert quickly added that they had nothing against men; all three were married. And in a bit of gender irony, they each had two sons, nary a daughter among them.

None of the three women present for our dinnertime conversation in 2022 recalled hearing much about the Nazi era when they were growing up in the 1950s and '60s. Matthäus-Robbert, who was born in 1949, heard nothing about it in school and little from her parents. She did recall hearing her grandfather saying he helped hide a Jewish boy during the Holocaust, a youngster who eventually escaped to Argentina.

Lapke remembered seeing a film about the Holocaust when she was a teenager, though the topic was barely talked about at home or at school. She once confronted her mother, who said she had a Jewish friend at school who suddenly moved out of the country, but otherwise knew nothing about the persecutions. Lapke pressed her mother on how she could be so unaware: "She couldn't answer me. You know how it is, you love your mother and at some point, you realize you were not going to get any more out of her."

Lapke believes her parents were not members of the National Socialist Party and said that her father generally questioned authority figures. She said he was a soldier during the war who got separated from his unit and eventually found his way home, unwilling to talk much about his experiences. So, like most of those involved in the nation's remembrance movement, the Women for Peace weren't necessarily motivated to action by their upbringing.

The campaign to bring *Stolpersteine* to the Dorsten area gathered momentum around 2005 when the group lobbied the mayor and city council. Members met twice a week for a couple of years, researching everything they could about the local victims, raising money to have the bricks made, and organizing public support. That meant cajoling at schools, at churches, and with political parties. When residents in Lembeck expressed skepticism about the project in September 2007 and claimed not to know about it despite the media coverage it had received, the women met with them to win them over.

"I told the attendees about the 200-year-old history of the Lebensteins in Lembeck," Elisabeth wrote to me soon after that meeting. "How they were involved and integrated in the community. They were active firemen, were part of the choir and so forth. They took part in all activities in the village. One attendee saw the Lebensteins being transported away when he was a child. He was very touched when he told me that scene. He mourned for years about the loss of Sara Sophie Lebenstein, because he used to visit her every day. The attendees were very affected by the Lebensteins, so that no more arguments were held against the laying of the stones."

"*Wir erinnern uns,*" began the invitation to mark the unveiling of the bricks on October 11, 2007. "We remember. Among us lived and worked people who were first humiliated and ostracized. Then they were transported away to be murdered. The memory of our Jewish citizens was to be erased. Today, 65 years later, we are still at a loss in the face of our history. How could so much injustice happen in our midst?"

How to make amends, it asked: "We not only denied people the right to life, we took it away from them. That cannot be made good. But we can try to give back the dignity of our former citizens and their descendants by remembering them personally and their fate."

It was signed by the Women for Peace: Nelly Beckers, Christa Bubner, Birgit Lapke, Ulrike Matthäus-Robbert, Gabi Schöneweiß, Gy Sonnemann.

Among the *Stolpersteine* Demnig installed in Dorsten that day were the first three honoring my family. Stones for siblings Bertha, Selma, and Hugo Lebenstein were laid into the ground just outside the property line where the family house once stood for a century. The owner of the beauty parlor that now resides where my family's house once did wanted no part of them.

"We don't really like stumbling blocks," Dorsten Mayor Lambert Lütkenhorst acknowledged to the crowd gathered for the *Stolpersteine's* unveiling. They are uncomfortable but necessary, he said. "They make us think about it: What actually happened here?"

Years later, I was eager to hear about the *Stolpersteine* from the artist himself. After months of trying, I finally caught up with Gunter Demnig by phone during the final days of 2022. He said the original idea of memorializing millions of Holocaust victims was conceptual and not meant to be literal. A friend told him, "Well, Gunter, you will never reach a million. But you can start."

He placed that milestone 100,000th *Stolpersteine* in Nuremberg, the German city associated with Nazi fanaticism, 1935 race laws that stripped Jews of their rights, and the 1945–46 trial of major war criminals. This quest has left him little time for anything else. He said he was on the road for 270 days one year. He was seventy-five when we spoke, acknowledging, "I have to slow down." And with that, he rattled off more than a half dozen cities in Italy where he planned to lay *Stolpersteine* the following month.

Like others in Germany's postwar generation, Demnig didn't learn much about the Nazi era in school and learned even less at home. He knew that his father was a German soldier, stationed in France, battling Allied airplanes. That's it. "He refused to talk about what happened," Demnig said of his father. "There was no answer, nothing at all."

Like others of his generation, young Demnig first bucked the established order as a student. To protest the Vietnam War in 1968, he painted a U.S. flag on the window of his studio, replacing the stars with skulls. That earned him a brief stay in jail.

Many decades later, he continued to have students in mind as a primary audience for the *Stolpersteine*, hoping it would entice them to learn more about the Holocaust. "They really wanted to know how could this happen," Demnig said. "When they open a book, they're reading about six million Jewish victims. The idea was that there was a family just around the corner. And they were youngsters, 'The ages of us now.' And maybe sometimes there are some stones in front of the schools."

He's gratified that some schools in Berlin will have pupils polish the stones twice a year as part of understanding the dates' significance—January 27, when the Auschwitz-Birkenau concentration camp was liberated, and November 9, in remembrance of *Kristallnacht*.

Assessments of *Stolpersteine* invariably focus on their highly decentralized locations. Miriam Volmert, a postdoctoral researcher at the Institute of Art History at the University of Zurich, wrote of the "tension between the stones' singularity and their multitude, a tension which at the same time reminds people of the sheer impossibility of ever representing the full extent of the Holocaust. A single *Stolperstein* can raise awareness of an individual victim's fate and the related fact of perpetration within the local space; and at the same time, it also calls to mind the incomprehensible number of individual Holocaust victims."

Critics say the inscriptions are too brief to be meaningful. They object to Demnig being the sole arbiter of who is memorialized by a stone and what the inscription says. And they cannot accept that people will walk on them, intentionally or not, and possibly defile them.

That last point is especially galling to Charlotte Knobloch, a Holocaust survivor and leader of Munich's Jewish community. "It is my firm belief that we need to do everything we can in order to make sure that remembrance preserves the dignity of the victims," she has said. "For me, stumbling over a piece of metal in the ground is anything but dignified." Knobloch persuaded the Munich city council to ban *Stolpersteine*, despite there being some support for the memorials. The city has opted instead to remember local victims with plaques on columns.

I got an earful from a critic of *Stolpersteine* during an international conference of Holocaust survivors and descendants in Washington, D.C., in 2023. The first four speakers on a panel presenting international perspectives on Holocaust commemoration spoke warmly of memorials that they were personally connected to in the Netherlands, U.K., and France. Their words of support and praise for the memorials were completely at odds with the fifth speaker, Gabriella Meros, an Israeli-born, Munich-based photographer. She launched into a long, personal attack against Demnig, whom she referred to as a "so-called artist" interested only in enriching himself. "The daily life of a *Stolperstein* is really in the dirt," she said, while deriding left-wing anti-Semites and displaying pictures of stumbling stones that had been defaced and neglected.

I practically jumped out of my chair in my zeal to ask the first question. It wasn't so much a question as bewilderment that a conference would book such a one-sided critic on a panel that otherwise heaped praise on Holocaust memorials. Other audience members, including several I spoke to afterward, talked with pride about their family's connection to *Stolpersteine*.

Demnig has scoffed at such criticism, saying it represented a small, minority view. He mentioned having visited St. Peter's Basilica in Vatican City and walking on gravestones laid into the ground.

A bigger concern than opposition to his work from those who find it disrespectful is opposition from Holocaust deniers and anti-Semites. *Stolpersteine* are occasionally stolen, then replaced as quickly as possible. Demnig, who's not Jewish, has not been exempt from acts of anti-Semitism. He said he had received three death threats, delivered anonymously. When I expressed alarm, he played down their significance, emphasizing that they occurred over a period of twenty years.

He'd rather talk about how the *Stolpersteine* have brought people together. Like the descendant of a Holocaust victim who traveled halfway around the world, from Tasmania to Cologne, to witness the installation of a *Stolperstein* and met a relative they'd never seen before. "So many handkerchiefs," Demnig recalled.

Or the time he installed a series of stones in front of a house near Bremen, Germany, including two for a couple killed in Auschwitz and two for their daughters who left on a *Kindertransport*—one to Scotland and one to Colombia. The sisters saw one another for the first time in sixty years when the *Stolpersteine* were installed, Demnig told me. "Now we are together with our parents," they said. "You can imagine," he told me, before pausing briefly. "That's a reason to continue. That's a reason to make this foundation," referring to efforts to make installing *Stolpersteine* a long-term project that extends beyond his lifetime.

I'm quite sure my dad would have been touched by these memorials to those persecuted during the Holocaust. But he didn't live long enough to see them. His health became more of a concern as he aged, and my brother and I tried to convince him to leave Memphis and move closer to family in Chicago or Washington, D.C. We had a particularly unpleasant hour-long phone call on July 22, 2002, when I pushed hard for him to move. Too hard. We didn't talk to one another for several days.

He had previously let me speak directly to his longtime doctor, so I could better understand his underlying medical conditions. That privilege didn't last beyond one conversation. I mistakenly repeated his doctor's advice that he stop driving. Not only did my father refuse to do so, he told me not to speak with his doctor anymore.

I should have realized that giving up his car would have destroyed his independence and forced him to move, something he refused to do. He had lived on his own terms. He wanted to spend his last days, however many there were, that way. I had trouble accepting his wishes to live independently and alone, but he made it perfectly clear that's exactly what he wanted. He'd had two coronary artery bypasses—in 1976, when that surgery was still relatively new, and again some twenty years later. He told me he wasn't going to put himself through more heart surgery of any kind no matter what the circumstances. By that point he also had been living with late-onset diabetes for several years.

Looking back now, I wonder if having been forced to leave his home as a teenager and under such traumatic circumstances made him unwilling to budge. He told me he still had occasional nightmares about Germany. Perhaps, even subconsciously, he was fiercely devoted to the notion of staying in his home because that privilege was denied to him as a youngster. I never thought to ask. But I did ask my mom years later, when she resisted similar appeals to leave her home in her late eighties and move into an assisted living facility, whether her reluctance had anything to do with being forced first from Augsburg, then from Cali at her parents' insistence. She told me it probably did.

Regardless, my father's visits to family in Chicago or D.C., or when some of us traveled to be with him in Memphis, always raised his spirits, though I wish they had been more frequent. My children, thirty-one and twenty-nine as I write this, still recall Grandpa Rudy fondly and with much love. There was something about his kind, patient manner that connected him to them, and he seemed charmed by almost anything they did. Emily and Ben frequently ordered him to "make mistakes!" when he read familiar children's books to them when they were young. They had memorized the books and were delighted when he replaced the author's words with something silly.

There was something magical about the first time my dad saw Ben as a toddler. I remember eating dinner in our snug dining room, Ben in his high chair, frequently interrupting conversations by shouting with great exuberance, "Hey, Wudy!"—the *R* came out as a *W*—"Look at me!" At first, I thought it was disrespectful to call your grandfather only by his first name. I couldn't have been more wrong. My dad was tickled by it. "I see you, Benjamin!" he responded. "I see you!" In that moment it felt like one generation connecting to another, betraying some distant, hidden, unspoken recognition from them that our family's existence was itself a miracle.

My dad had had plenty of sadness by then that hardly ended when he had to leave his family behind in Germany. Divorcing my mom in 1964 was followed by two marriages that ended in slow, agonizing deaths of his wives—Trudy in 1979 from cancer and Pat in 2001 after she'd been in a coma for five years following her own heart bypass surgery.

Yet he wasn't one to complain about what life had dealt him. He didn't want to talk much about his health or his outlook. I've often thought my parents both possessed a sort of German stoicism, made of a hardy stock that you don't always find in an era that seems long on widely displaying your emotions. I seem to remember my dad once describing his life as "charmed," an extraordinary claim for someone who experienced such trauma.

Displaying my own stubbornness, I didn't call my dad for several days after our difficult conversation that Monday in July 2002. I finally called him on Friday. I'm grateful that I did. It was a wonderful talk with no hint of unpleasantness. "You should write a book about my life," he said at one point. Dad, I said, you never told me that. I'd be delighted to. He said he had told me.

It was our last conversation. He died at his home in Memphis on Sunday, July 28, 2002, alone. It appeared he'd had a heart attack.

Later I conjured a mental image of what those last moments might have been like—his heart pounding, a fall, and what came after. Perhaps a swirl of memories and images going back to his early days in Essen, his once-large family, his parents and younger brothers, a daring escape from Germany and lonely entry into America, a new life in Philadelphia and a long career in the dental industry, three wives, two children, two stepchildren, grandchildren . . .

I imagined these images somehow playing as his consciousness ebbed, simultaneously depicted in visual form in his house, a concise rendering of eighty-one years, a holograph of sorts wafting from his bedroom to the living room with its high, pitched ceilings. Once there, music started playing from the huge speakers of the stereo system that brought him so much joy over the years. The tune I imagine playing from his vast classical music collection is Samuel Barber's impossibly beautiful and sad "Adagio for Strings, Op. 11," performed by the St. Louis Symphony Orchestra, conducted by Leonard Slatkin. It has to be that version because days later, as we went through his belongings and I brought home as many of his CDs as I could, that's what I found and that's what now plays, as I type this, that particular album ripped into my computer and now playing through its speakers, summoning memories of his life and his death, and my need to carry on, as best I can, my parents' legacy.

My dad was laid to rest in the Temple Israel Cemetery, just off of Interstate 69 in the South Memphis neighborhood. The cemetery first opened in 1846, four years before the Lebensteins built the house in Lembeck that they owned for almost a century. Grave markers bear the names of some of the city's famous families—including Goldsmith (of department store fame), Seessel (grocery stores), Lichterman (nature center), and Plough (Schering-Plough pharmaceutical drugs).

The gravesite service ended with the Mourner's K*addish*, the Hebrew prayer we recite in memory of the deceased. It brings special poignancy when a loved one dies and on the Sabbath that's close to the anniversary of their death. It's the practice in Reform Judaism to have the congregation stand as one and say the prayer together. I had always refrained from saying the words, determined to wait until one of my parents had died, even though my mother had urged me as a youngster to say it "for the six million."

Now was the time. Unable to read Hebrew, I held a laminated card with a transliteration of the prayer. "*Yitgadal v'yitkadash sh'mei raba,*" it begins. The prayer that follows never mentions death; it glorifies God: "Exalted and hallowed be God's great name in the world which God created, according to plan."

Afterward, we took turns shoveling dirt onto my dad's casket, following a Jewish tradition that mourners begin the process of burying a loved one. I was the first to do so. I then turned away, my suit soaked through from Memphis' oppressive summer heat and humidity. That's when the finality of it all hit me. His life was over. I was overwhelmed by sadness. My shoulders shook. Although my mother and Mollie quickly took turns hugging me, I felt totally alone in that moment. As we all must be at the end. Not long after, the intense heat and humidity combined for a drenching thunderstorm.

We went through the sad task of going through his belongings the next day. I was determined to find the letters he had exchanged with his parents in 1940–41, letters that my dad said had been lost years earlier when he moved from one house in Memphis to another. I never found them.

Most of my dad's belongings were soon donated or sold, though I packed some in his car as I drove back to D.C. I couldn't part with most of his audio CDs, a selection of his books, anything that looked like a valuable paper or document, some jewelry, a watch. And two Mont Blanc pens that I continue to use with great reverence.

"He was a wonderful friend with a good heart," Elisabeth wrote to me in a condolence note from Germany. She took solace in remembering their conversations, letters, and get-togethers. "Rudy always encouraged me to go on when we had difficulties with the Jewish history, the research and the Jewish museum. But I think hope and reconciliation has always been the main lead role in his life."

She concluded, "I'm sure we will stay good friends with your whole family."

A year later, on the Friday night closest to the anniversary of his death, Mollie, Emily, Ben, and I went to our synagogue on Sabbath to say *Kaddish* for my dad. But where would I go on the actual anniversary of his death, which was a Monday? I was drawn to the U.S. Holocaust Memorial Museum. The Holocaust was but one chapter in my dad's life, but it was the most impactful, affecting everything that came after.

I didn't tour the museum that day. I had already done that a few times. What beckoned me was the museum's Hall of Remembrance, a hushed hexagonal room that invites reflection after visitors have absorbed the horrors of the Holocaust. It also provides an opportunity to light a candle in memory of a loved one. The room has an eternal flame and an inscription from Deuteronomy 4:9: "Only guard yourself and guard your soul carefully, lest you forget the things your eyes saw, and lest these things depart your heart all the days of your life. And you shall make them known to your children, and to your children's children."

Our children—we had a responsibility to teach them what we knew. In a way, Elisabeth highlighted that responsibility when she and Paul were guests at Emily's bat mitzvah in 2007. Elisabeth spoke at the reception afterward and invited Emily to visit Germany. It took a while for us to make the journey, in part because we were then focused on Ben's bar mitzvah two years later. Afterward, we decided the time was right to plan for all four of us to visit Germany.

Chapter 14

RETURNING WITH MY FAMILY

"We made it."

The most remarkable, life-affirming meal I've had wasn't any sort of gourmet extravaganza. It was a simple Italian dinner in Germany. The pizza at Trattoria Sardegna in Dorsten wasn't what made the evening so special. It was dining in a restaurant exactly one block from where my family had lived for a century.

No words do justice to what it felt like that evening, surrounded by Germans, enjoying an ordinary-sounding meal under such extraordinary circumstances. My wife and our children were calmly and safely eating dinner a few doors down from where my relatives once lived and gathered for rousing family dinners and from where some of them were deported.

My emotions were conflicted then, just as they were when I prepared to step off the train on my first trip to Germany years earlier. Once again, I thought for a moment that perhaps we were doing something horribly wrong by sitting down for a meal in the very neighborhood where my relatives had lived for a century before they were persecuted, dispossessed of everything they owned, and then sent off to be murdered. As if none of that mattered.

And yet . . . our German hosts had painstakingly researched, documented, and memorialized the lives and deaths of Jewish families, including mine, who once lived peaceably amongst their own relatives. They then shared that knowledge with me and the rest of the world. Their actions don't make up for anything that was done during the Nazi regime, not one bit. Nothing could. But I wasn't going to honor the past by turning my back on it. A new generation was extending a hand to help us better understand the tragedies that occurred there and forge a new path together. We embraced the opportunity.

Our children were teenagers in June 2011—Emily was a few days away from turning seventeen; Ben was fifteen. They would periodically ask us why so many Germans were making such a big deal over our visit. We told them, in ways they couldn't quite understand, that it was a miracle just to be able to freely walk about the village where our relatives were outcasts. We had survived as a family and as a people. And now we were connecting to a home we never knew in a country where our ancestors had long lived—thanks to the open hearts of an extraordinary group of people, almost none of them Jewish.

Our time in Germany began in Cologne, where Elisabeth and Paul met us at the train station. We enjoyed our German lunch (some of us had sauerbraten, others sausages, and the smooth Kölsch beer was a treat), the view from atop the Cathedral (509 narrow and winding steps in both directions), and a tour of the nearby Lindt Chocolate Museum. Mostly we enjoyed being with Elisabeth and Paul, who, regardless of the time and miles that keep us apart, always make us feel like dear friends.

Saturday dawned cold and rainy, dreary weather better suited for late autumn than the onset of summer. We began the morning in Lembeck paying homage to the *Stolpersteine* adjacent to where the old family homestead once stood, kitty-corner from the Catholic church. A hair salon now stood on the property my great-great-grandfather, Nathan Lebenstein, purchased in 1850. We started at the three stones marking the last voluntary place of residence for three of the Lebenstein siblings—Selma and Bertha, who were deported to Stutthof, and Hugo, who was deported to Auschwitz after he had fled for the Netherlands and was captured. Ever prepared and eager to help us meet the moment, Elisabeth brought several stems of roses for us to lay at the site.

My first impression of these unusual memorials was they were too easy to miss and too easy to step on. The text was exceedingly brief, bereft of any context or any sense of their lives. It was hard to see how someone would learn much from it. (Years later, there would be a handy booklet, website, and app for those wanting to further explore the Dorsten area *Stolpersteine.*) But even then, I was grateful that the spot where my family once lived now bore their names. They had no gravesite, no other place that marked their lives.

Elisabeth had arranged for a small group to greet us when we arrived—two local newspaper reporters, Dorsten's deputy mayor, and a former neighbor of the Lebensteins. Josef Langenhorst, age eighty, was a descendant of one of Lembeck's oldest families, with a verifiable lineage that goes back to 1715. His ancestral house on what's now known as Wulfener Straße used to be called Village No. 22; my family's house stood on No. 15.

Langenhorst told us he frequently visited the Lebenstein home and had vivid memories of the building and some my relatives, especially my great-grandmother, Sara Sophie Lebenstein. He's freely shared his memories with the local history workshop and was eager to meet me and my family. A friendly man with an easy smile, Langenhorst handed us a bottle of locally made schnapps and a photograph, taken around 1930, of a marching band wending its way through the street in front of my relatives' house.

Heinz Denninger, Dorsten's deputy mayor, asked us to tell other Americans that Germany takes responsibility for the evils of the Nazi era and is much different than it once was. Once again, that desire to turn descendants of victims into cheerleaders for a new Germany. I said I understood the importance of creating new ties between our countries and successive generations, that I thought turning my back on Germany and my heritage there would give the Nazis another victory.

A reporter asked if being a Jew in the U.S. still posed difficulties. I said we're watchful, aware of being a minority, and cognizant of the past. As a Jew, I said, you can never fully relax, and that is true of ethnic groups the world over. Mine was a deeply rooted German family—Jewish, yes, but also very much a part of the broader German culture. And yet when the Nazis ascended to power and my relatives were persecuted, why did no one stand up for them? Emily talked about protecting the rights of other ethnic groups around the world, including the tragic events then happening in the Darfur region of Sudan. "We have to be active for minorities, that is our responsibility," she said.

Next stop was a street in a new housing development that Elisabeth and the Jewish museum had pushed to be named after my family. This was a moment Elisabeth had long envisioned, at least since 2005, when she and her allies first sought formal approval from Dorsten.

Her frustration with the slow process boiled over in a letter to then-Mayor Lambert Lütkenhorst in July 2007, a few weeks after talking with us about the street while attending Emily's bat mitzvah. The city's building committee had been slow-walking the proposal for two years, the latest objection being that streets in the vicinity of the new development ought to be named after bushes.

"Just what reminds you of the murdered family members, of the Jewish family in Lembeck, what traces can they follow?" Elisabeth asked in her letter. "A first sign is the laying of the stumbling blocks in October of this year in Lembeck and Wulfen. How should we argue with the Katz/Lebenstein family when they come to Dorsten. Maybe like this: The new streets were named after bushes because you couldn't deviate from the 'principle.'" She pleaded with the mayor and the building committee, urging them "to reconsider our application, whether a street after the Jewish family Lebenstein would not be just as well placed as the name of a shrub."

Elisabeth's persistence eventually won out. We drove to a development of new houses on a street named Lebensteinring. There it was, my family name, known for centuries in this community of Germany, then exterminated, now back. Not as small stones laid into the ground, but as clear as day on a street sign, and as an address to be used by a dozen or so homes. Before we left, Mollie suggested we say the *Shehecheyanu*, the Hebrew prayer for thanks. We said it first in Hebrew, then in English, though the lump in my throat made me the quietest participant. "*Baruch ata Adonai, Elohenu Melekh haolam, shehecheyanu, v'kiy'manu, v'higiyanu, laz'man hazeh.* Praised be You, our Lord our God, King of the Universe, who has kept us alive, who has sustained us, and who has enabled us to reach this day."

Then it was time to visit two Jewish cemeteries in the area. The first was in Lembeck, where records show the property was purchased by my ancestors in 1860 and where many of my relatives were among those buried there. You wouldn't have known that by looking at it. The grounds were seized by the state in 1939 on the pretext they were needed for farming. The gravestones were destroyed, and cattle began grazing there. The property was part of reparation hearings in 1948 and was fenced off soon thereafter. The working group installed a memorial plaque in 1983, commemorating it as a Jewish cemetery and honoring those who perished during the Holocaust. We laid roses there, too.

The other cemetery we saw that day was in a remote spot in nearby Raesfeld. It was not destroyed during the Nazi era, perhaps because it was so remote. Now the grounds are lovingly maintained by Bernhard Brockmann, a tradesman who lives in the area. He tends to the cemetery each week, showing remarkable attention to detail. We marveled at how he had raked and smoothed the dirt behind him the day before in such a painstaking manner that not a single footprint was visible when we arrived. Brockmann and his wife stopped by the cemetery, in the rain, just to meet us and shake hands. We were honored.

The grave that drew most of our attention was the one for my great-grandmother. Befitting Jewish tradition, we wanted to leave a stone for her, a sign of memory and respect. Seeing no loose stones in the cemetery, Ben left the grounds briefly to find one just outside the fence. He returned and placed it on her grave.

I paused there before we left, thinking deeply about the notion of survival, not just for oneself, but for generations to come. I tried to think of what my great-grandmother went through, especially toward the end of her life, being reviled in the village where she had lived peaceably for decades. Forcibly removed from the house she had known her whole adult life and that the family had owned for a century. Her children and grandchildren being violently hurled this way and that, to parts unknown at the time, their fates in the hands of a regime sworn to their destruction. How dark and foreboding the future must have appeared to her after my uncle Franz was able to arrange to have her returned to her birthplace at Raesfeld, where she died three months later.

I reached toward her tombstone. I don't pretend to know if we can communicate, spiritually, to those who once walked where we now do. But as my fingers touched stone, my mind clearly fixed on three words that I wanted to say to her, as a broad message of our family's survival: "We made it."

That afternoon, we gathered with a few of Elisabeth and Paul's friends at the Raesfeld home of Elke and Gerd Gutschow. Our visit prompted a midday treat of *Kaffee und Kuchen*, featuring Elke's homemade strawberry and gooseberry cakes. Our companions, all of whom were involved one way or another with the memory culture, spoke of Germany's shame after the war, though they said they were motivated more by a desire or obligation to remember the past and promote healing.

Elke Gutschow handed me a wrapped package as we prepared to leave. I opened it later and saw that it was a book of photography. I leafed through the pages, looking at a collection of black-and-white pictures from the first half of the century, a chronicle of small-town Raesfeld by a lifelong resident. What struck me most was a heartfelt note from the Gutschows, written by Elke in English, on a card stuck inside the flyleaf. "Dear Katz family," it begins.

> Ignaz Böckenhoff was a photographer from Raesfeld, died in Raesfeld. Lots of pictures in his book were taken when Sarah Sophie Lebenstein (born Elkan), your ancestor, was alive. Several pictures show persons from the village as they were known, even as Nazis. We are very sad about what was done to Jewish neighbors. I know some elderly people who cried when they told me how helpless they felt in Nazi times. Let us work together, that everyone gets his human rights. The members of the "Stolpersteine group in Raesfeld" try not to forget what was done by our people to your family.

Her words impressed me, especially how they were phrased. She made it personal, using possessive pronouns—"what was done by *our* people to *your* family." Elke Gutschow was born in 1944. She wasn't to blame for my relatives' fate. And I wasn't personally harmed. But she had clearly internalized it as a personal responsibility, from her to me and other Jewish descendants.

Our German friends seemed to be saying and doing everything they could to make us feel wanted and welcomed, including at the Italian restaurant that night in Lembeck. Still, a Jew retracing German roots is constantly surrounded by ghosts of sorts and a mix of emotions. Later that night, while trying to fall asleep at Paul and Elisabeth's house, I heard sounds of young people partying at a nearby park, loudly whooping it up. I couldn't understand what they were saying, and it didn't sound threatening. Still, the rough, guttural pronunciation and mocking laughter made me think about what my relatives had heard decades ago.

The following day we were off to Essen, first to stand in front of what used to be the Blum department store where my dad and his aunt once worked, then to climb the steps and enter the stately synagogue. The interior had been redone since I saw it last, with brighter colors and seating more befitting a place of worship.

And we filled it with some joy, once Emily discovered an interactive exhibit consisting of a video loop of Israeli folk music, a small dance floor, and mirrors. She was soon displaying some fancy footwork, accompanied by hand claps. Then Mollie gave it a try, and Elisabeth, ever the good sport, joined in. My memories of that impressive synagogue include not only its attempted destruction but also its rebirth, a sign of life renewed.

Mollie and I returned to Germany in October 2022 to do more research for this book. I wanted to retrace family roots in Bavaria but also return to North Rhine-Westphalia. I was eager to focus on some of the Germans who had documented the life and death of the Jewish communities that once lived where they now do. Now I was deeply invested in documenting some of the work of these contemporary Germans. What had motivated them to act?

Elke Gutschow at a Jewish memorial in Raesfeld in 2011; Gerd Gutschow in 2022

One of the people I would have liked to have met with was Elke Gutschow. But she died in 2013. Her death underscored that, just as there had been an eagerness to document the memories of those who had survived the

Holocaust, so, too, was there a need to hear from those at the forefront of the memory movement.

Elke's widower, Gerd, was able to meet with us the day we arrived. We joined him in touring some of the hallmarks of former Jewish life in Raesfeld, including a cemetery, the outlines of a *mikvah* (a ritual pool of water, which, by ancient custom, is used to achieve purity, especially by observant, married Jewish women), and the *Stolpersteine* for Sophie Lebenstein and her family. Mainly I was interested in hearing more about Gerd Gutschow's life and motivations in the memory culture.

We sat around a table at Raesfeld's charming Gaststätte Bonhoff, a family-run, simply furnished bakery and café with limited hours that described itself as "more of a hobby than a business." You got that impression from the well-worn wooden sign outside that said,"*Hier bacht die Hausfrau!*" ("Here the housewife bakes!") next to a depiction of a sliced Bundt cake. The generous portions of *Kaffee und Kuchen* were a good antidote to jet lag.

Gerd Gutschow had a white beard as well as a bald head that he covered with a flat cap when we were outside—except when we were in the cemetery, where he donned a *kippah*, the small skullcap religious Jews wear (especially at holy sites) as a sign of reverence to God. Gutschow isn't Jewish; he used the *kippah* out of respect. He wore socks and sandals and relied on a cane, walking with some effort. He dismissed Elisabeth's concerns about his health with dry humor. He said he knew what the problem was: "My doctor tells me I'm old." He spoke English effortlessly and with a British accent, which is how he learned it in Germany.

It turns out Gutschow was born in Essen in 1942, the year after my grandparents and uncles were deported. Befitting his generation, Gutschow said he learned "really nothing" about the Holocaust while growing up. He knew his father, a flight trainer, was sent to Prague when Gutschow's mother was pregnant with him. But he never asked his father for any details about his actions during the Nazi era. "The thing is in those days, you didn't ask your parents," he told me. "It's a shame."

Gutschow's interest in the Holocaust and Judaism was piqued during his college years when he visited Israel with a group of students. It was the first time he met anyone Jewish and the first time he began to understand the atrocities committed by Nazis. He remembered meeting Jewish survivors from Germany, including a former Berlin resident who was the only member of his family to escape. "I felt smaller and smaller when they told me what happened to their families," Gutschow recalled. "Astonished is not the right word," he said, before pausing for a bit. He ended up studying theology, then taught English, history, the Protestant religion, and music. I asked if he could reconcile how people who considered themselves devout could participate in Nazi-era violence. "I can't," he said. But that didn't mean he hadn't tried, saying he had filled a ten-foot-long bookshelf with works on Judaism and the Holocaust. It was an interest he shared with his late wife, a primary-school teacher who also provided instruction about the Holocaust.

"I can't say I feel guilty," Gutschow said. "But I feel ashamed about what the generation of my parents and grandparents did." He said a number of people he knew refused to attend the ceremonies marking the installation of *Stolpersteine* in Raesfeld, their sentiment being, "We've done enough." He led us to a collection of seven stumbling stones in front of an apartment building at Dorstener Straße 12. He said residents opposed installing the *Stolpersteine*, fearing it would foster unnecessary attention and perhaps violence. They closed their blinds during the unveiling ceremony in 2013.

Gutschow obviously had a different response, fulfilling a lifelong interest in the Holocaust that took him to memorial sites at many of the former killing centers. He began to name some of them, including Riga, Auschwitz, Stutthoff, Mauthausen, and Dachau. "The thing is," he said, "every new concentration camp I found, they did other cruelties I hadn't seen before."

He said the writings of Holocaust survivor and historian Saul Friedländer had a profound impact on his thinking, day and night: "The thing is, you can't sleep sometimes." He's not optimistic that humanity has learned from the atrocities because people continue to succumb to ignorance. "I think lots of people who are involved in anti-Jewish activities have never seen one. They hear something or they have a friend in the group." For Gutschow, contemporary threats of genocide and anti-Semitism hit close to home. He has three Jewish grandchildren through his eldest daughter, whose husband is Jewish. He's also been active in recent refugee efforts, including hosting a husband and wife seeking refuge from Iran in 2018.

Also active are two more of Elisabeth and Paul's friends, Gaby and Werner Springer. Gaby, who was also born in 1942, remembers one of her teachers talking about the Nazis and the Holocaust when she was a teenager, which was unusual at the time. That helped spur her own interest. "Since I was fourteen, I was always asking, 'Where were you in the Nazi times. I must know.'" She heard few useful responses. "My father was the only one who gave me an answer to, 'Why did this happen?'" His explanation for why Jews were persecuted was, "They're successful and we are not."

The Springers were also determined to help those in harm's way from current-day war and persecution. During breakfast at their home, we noticed the top of a large, white tent on an adjacent property, visible through their backyard. It was a nearby refugee center. The Springers are providing aid to the effort and let one of the youngsters borrow a bicycle that's kept on the Springer's property for safekeeping.

At another point, we returned to the synagogue in Essen. We talked with Martina Strehlen, the synagogue's deputy director, who said records no longer existed of my family's membership there. But she did say that *Stolpersteine* in their memory had been installed near where they were deported at Sachsenstraße 13, a little more than a mile away. That became our next stop.

The building they lived in is long gone. Bland, brick apartment buildings now reside on the narrow, two-lane street, along with a few offices and a parking garage. There are also a number of schools nearby. We scoured the street looking for the stumbling stones, eyes fixed on the pavement, until Mollie and Elisabeth found them, clustered together, close to the intersection with Geibelstraße.

One of my first thoughts when I saw these *Stolpersteine* was to wonder who did the research locally and arranged with Demnig to put them here. I know my family was not consulted, not that it would have been easy to make the connection to us. I discovered later that Essen's stumbling stones were sponsored by the Historical Association for the City and Foundation of Essen. The effort began in 2004 at the behest of former Mayor Peter Reuschenbach, who brought together donors and sponsors to finance the individual stones. The organization listed 423 *Stolpersteine* as of April 2024.

The ones for my family were installed on July 1, 2005. The person now responsible for overseeing the city's *Stolpersteine* said she couldn't tell me anything about how they came to be. Those who initiated the local effort had since died.

I was underwhelmed when I first approached the bricks, which obviously looked like dozens of others I had seen. They were everything critics complain about. You really have to look hard for them, even when you know they're nearby. They're well-worn and scuffed. The one bearing Manfred's name looked like it may have been intentionally scratched. The information on the bricks is scant. You can't glean anything about them except their names, the years they were born, that they were deported in 1941, and murdered in Minsk.

I wanted to interact somehow with these small memorials to my family but wasn't sure just what to do. I took pictures with my phone and my camera, then sat on the ground, stared at them, and touched all four simultaneously. Soon these stones began to make an emotional pull, just as when I saw their names in 1986 in a memorial book at the synagogue. Now I was seeing them embedded into the ground on the very street where they lived and were deported. The closest we could come to seeing an ancestral home there.

I kept staring at the *Stolpersteine*. Unlike a passersby, I could fill in some missing information about the victims. They lived right here, on this street, with my dad. This is where two SS officers looked for my father and grandfather on November 10, 1938, the day after *Kristallnacht* began. This is where my dad hugged his parents for the last time in January 1939, as he began his escape. And this is where authorities came to deport my relatives to their final destination in November 1941.

I thought of what it might have been like that day. Perhaps the Nazi thugs asked once more about my father. *Where is he?* I can almost hear them saying, their uniforms and guns making a fearsome sight. *What do you mean you don't know where your son is? You there, tell me, where is your brother? Okay, never mind, the four of you, come with us.*

They see the suitcases my family had packed the day or so before, the ones that Tante Malli, Uncle Franz, and their friend Cläre Mies had noticed. *Yes, bring them along.* Everyone saw this for what it was. My relatives may not have known for sure what their immediate fate would be. But they knew it was deeply ominous.

The more I stared at the *Stolpersteine,* the more transfixed I became. They *were* different than anything I'd seen before. They represented *my* grandparents. *My* uncles. Their lives were taken, as was any information about their murders. I don't know the day they died, so I can't accurately mark their *yahrzeit*, the anniversary of their death. That's when we would typically light a candle and chant the Mourner's *Kaddish* in their memory. Taking a cue from my father, I have instead marked their *yahrzeit* on the anniversary of their birth.

I continued to sit on the cold pavement, not wanting to leave, but not knowing what else to do. I rested my hands on the ground, on either side of the bricks. It was as if I was trying to protect them from outside influences—to save not the *Stolpersteine*, but my long-deceased relatives. There was something almost sacred about this space, these bricks, their names on the street, *their* street. My thoughts were jumbled. I regretted I couldn't have done something to save them before I was even born. At that moment, I couldn't have cared less what others thought about these particular bricks and whether their names sparked anyone's curiosity about who they were, what their lives were like, and whether anyone from that family survived. Their names were now where they once lived. Now, briefly, so was I.

I knew who they were, much more than before I first came to Germany. I also had a better sense of where they had come from and, as chilling as it was, where they were going. I sent photos from that spot to my brother in suburban Chicago. His thoughts quickly went to the implications that one member of that immediate family had survived and started a new life and new family in America.

"How lucky are we?" he texted back.

HOLY GROUND

Chapter 15

FOUR HUNDRED YEARS IN HÜRBEN

"May their death always be a warning."

Church bells pealed in the distance as we looked for the old Jewish cemetery in Krumbach where some of my relatives were buried. Mollie, Elisabeth, Paul, and I were flummoxed when trying to find it. We had parked nearby, then followed the directions of a local resident who said we should follow a path alongside a meadow. No such luck.

The "aha!" moment came only when I looked up from my phone and its surprising recommendation that we should now embark on a twenty-minute-long circular path. That's when I noticed the white walls directly behind us, a couple of tall tombstones peeking out from behind them.

We cut across fields, wet with rain from the day before. I led the way because my impatient, long strides propelled me, chagrined that we would be a few minutes late for our 10 a.m. meeting that Sunday in October 2022. So much for living up to the German quest for punctuality. Turning the corner to the entrance, I noticed our two guides' cars parked out front, beneath a sign identifying it as the Jewish cemetery: "*Friedhof Der Ehem Israel Kultusgemeinde Krumbach-Hürben 1628–1948.*"

Entrance to the old Jewish cemetery in Hürben (now Krumbach)

I walked through the open wrought-iron gate, greeted the two men who were waiting for us and then paused to take in the scene while the others caught up. We had driven south from Dorsten the day before, leaving behind western Germany, where my father's family had lived for generations. I was finally in Bavaria, where my mother's family had lived since at least 1700. We began our visit in Hürben, the once-independent village where the first five generations of Landauers were born, as well as a few of the sixth.

I stood where they once did and where some of them are buried. The rising sun cast a warm glow on the unshaded, northern part of the cemetery. There were no trees in that section, no obstacles keeping the sun's rays from shining on the old tombstones there, arrayed in close rows with the deceased and the markers identifying them facing east, down a gently sloping hill. This quiet, pastoral scene was enhanced by the view just outside the cemetery's six-foot-high white walls. Beyond adjacent fields that grew wheat, corn, and grass for cows was a hilly line of trees. They provided a green and gold outline in the unseasonably warm, mid-October air.

It didn't take long to notice the cemetery's tallest gravestone was a large, black obelisk that I had first noticed from outside. Etched on its base were the names Klara and Moses S. Landauer, my great-great-great-grandparents. Once again, I felt at home, in a sense, standing at this final resting place for my ancestors and their contemporaries.

It's also a special place for a small group of citizens interested in the long history of their town. They've researched, documented, and memorialized the Jewish community that once lived there and serve as guides for the curious. They are not Jewish, but they appreciate the cemetery's sanctity. "This is a place to remember what it was like before the war," one of our guides, Wilhelm Fischer, told us. "It's holy ground."

So, too, was the place where the deceased had worshipped back in the day, about a half mile west. It's identified now by an ironically named street sign, *Synagogengasse,* though there's been no synagogue on that street for eighty years. What you'll find instead is a rectangular outline of bricks laid into the ground, marking the former synagogue's floor plan. It was blanketed by wet, brown leaves on the morning of our visit. A memorial stood on one end of the property, topped by the Star of David. I thought it was a tombstone at first. A couple of vines partially obscured the fading words: "*Hier stand von 1675–1939 Die synagoge der Israelitischen kultusgemeinde zu Hürben.*" Or, "The synagogue of the Jewish religious community in Hürben stood here from 1675–1939."

On another corner was the fragment of a white stone wall, forming a right angle. One side depicted a lit menorah, evoking candles burning bright. The other side honored the presence of the local Jewish community, from 1504 to 1942. The years etched into the wall spoke volumes, a symbol that weighed heavily on Mollie's mind long after we saw it. More than four hundred years of a documented Jewish presence in this place—*more than four hundred*—totally obliterated by a year that evokes images of widespread torture, deportations, and murder.

There's also a plaque that's designed to appear broken with a jagged upper edge. "In memory of the Jews who were deported from Krumbach to Piaski, Poland, on April 1, 1942, and murdered there," it says. Their names and ages, which ranged from four to sixty, are listed, followed by a brief plea: "*Möge ihr Tod den Lebenden stets eine Mahnung sein.*" Or, "May their death always be a warning to the living."

Our guides that morning, Fischer and Herbert Auer, were active members of the town's history group, Heimatverein Krumbach. "The corner of the old synagogue and the grounds themselves were built by the local history society on its own initiative and at its own expense," Fischer said. It's consistent with their motto, "You have to do something, not just talk."

The inscription at the synagogue memorial, he continued, "is intended to admonish the living to always ensure that the events from 1933 to 1945 in Germany, and by the Germans in the war zones, are not repeated."

Herbert Auer and Wilhelm Fischer at the Jewish cemetery in Hürben/Krumbach

Fischer and Auer have done invaluable work researching the Jewish community that once lived there. Neither is Jewish. Neither is a trained historian. They are purveyors of a memory culture who have dug deeply into the local archives and sought to make it visible and relevant in a modern era.

In this, they were like the civic activists in and around the small towns of Dorsten. If Americans know about Germany's remembrance movement, it is likely to be about memorials and museums, because that's mostly what's been written about. But what distinguishes Germany's actions are not, primarily, bricks and stones that were assembled at the government's order. It's the thousands of individuals who worked to research and mark local history on their own initiative.

"The crucial point here is that the activists' primary goal was not dismantling the statues that symbolised a memorial culture that they saw as inadequate—though they did practice this kind of 'memory protest,'" wrote historian Jenny Wüstenberg. "Much more of these activists' time was consumed by the quiet and slow 'memory work' of archival research, conducting interviews, creating exhibits, planning alternative walking tours, and more.

In undertaking this work, those involved came to understand the intricate workings of Nazi rule and the local structures of power and resistance and carried this understanding into all branches of society. They demanded—usually against considerable resistance—that the sites of Nazi terror and of Jewish suffering be marked and the perpetrators be named."

Fischer had been interested in history, religion, and geography since he was young. "That may also have been the reason why I was elected museum director in Krumbach in 1992 and have been active in the local history association ever since, most recently as a member of the board," he said. He was first introduced to Jewish history in a religious education class and was struck that locally, at least, there was a "prosperous coexistence of Jews and Christians since about 1600, which was so different from that in the Nazi era from 1933."

Fischer said, "Exploring the past, understanding the present, shaping the future, will probably continue to be a guiding principle for me." Fischer was an amiable guide who wanted to leave us with a lasting, positive impression. Before departing the cemetery, he served us slices of a braided loaf of bread called *berches*, a local variation of challah that skips eggs as an ingredient but usually includes mashed potatoes. Like the street named for a synagogue that no longer exists, it's noteworthy that local bakeries still offer a local version of this traditional Jewish bread for a strictly non-Jewish clientele.

While researching the former synagogue, the local history association found a Hebrew inscription based on Isaiah 56:8 displayed on the building's east side, above the north window. "This house shall be called a house of prayer for all nations," it said. That the words were visible from the street, Fischer and Auer wrote, "testified to the self-confidence and self-image of the Jewish population, but also to the acceptance and tolerance of the Christian fellow citizens of Krumbach-Hürben."

The authors describe it as "a text of sobriety and clarity that leaves no room for doubt or uncertainty about its meaning; a text written 3,000 years ago, attached to the Hürben synagogue sometime in the 18th century and today more relevant than ever before, in the face of globalization and economics, but also of intolerance and xenophobia in our country."

Our guides were clearly moved by the Jewish history in their town. They were as enthusiastic in describing it to us as we were in hearing about it. Auer, then seventy-seven, literally took great pains to be with us that morning. He walked haltingly with the aid of crutches, the result of recent surgery gone bad, he explained. He was missing a few teeth. His clothes were loose and ill-fitting. And yet—his eyes were a vibrant, bright blue, fully alert and alive. When he spoke, he conveyed a gentle, learned, positive presence. He brought a black bag with him, from which he leafed through pages of the Landauer family tree, with its roots in 1700 Hürben. I pointed to my mother's name on the book's last pages. Doing so took on special meaning here, where our relatives once paid their last respects to our ancestors.

Auer's career had been in electronics and logistics. But his passion was for local history, especially of the former Jewish community. He spent twelve years researching, documenting, and writing a 634-page book that covers each of the Jewish cemetery's approximately three hundred gravestones. He titled it *Their Souls Are Bound in the Bundle of Life*, a phrase from the Bible's Book of Samuel. (Fischer also handed us a copy of Auer's book, along with a bottle of Israeli wine.)

Until the new cemetery opened in 1628, Hürben's Jews were buried twenty miles away in Burgau, a considerable trek in those days. They were granted rights to the new cemetery by Archduke Leopold of Austria, who took a somewhat kinder view of its Jewish residents than had other leaders. A *mikvah* was built in 1833, though it no longer exists. But a *tahara* built in 1898—where the deceased were cleansed, ritually washed, and dressed in a plain white shroud in preparation for burial in the Jewish tradition—still stands.

The cemetery's southern portion is shaded by birch, elm, oak, maple, and ash trees. A few tombstones reside there, though Auer and Fischer say there are many more unmarked graves. The less well-off were buried on that side, under wooden markers that didn't stand the test of time. Also, Nazis knocked down quite a few of the tombstones. U.S. Army troops who found the tombstones in disarray after the war placed them along the cemetery's western boundaries, uncertain just where they belonged. One grave sits isolated on the cemetery's eastern edge. It's for a man who committed suicide in 1882 and whose remains were separated from the others, in shame.

Having now walked in Lembeck and Hürben, the ancestral homes of both sides of my family, the time seemed right to see one of the many former camps where millions of Jewish lives came to an end. I could think of no better people to accompany us on this journey than Elisabeth and Paul, longtime friends invested in Germany's memory movement. Elisabeth has seen more than a dozen different camps, some multiple times, in seven European countries.

I asked Elisabeth why she saw so many. Quite a few were as part of a group from Dorsten's Jewish museum. Others were more or less on their own. "The first concentration camp I visited was Auschwitz-Birkenau," she said. "Paul worked nearby in Poland and we went there with a colleague. We didn't speak a word afterwards. Auschwitz is very authentic. There are mountains of suitcases, hair, glasses . . . There are still the former shelters. What impressed me so intensely? Not the barracks, the gas ovens, the photos. It was the real objects, the traces of people, for example—the suitcases, the children's clothes, hair, shoes."

Those are also the kind of objects that have left the deepest impression on my visits to the U.S. Holocaust Memorial Museum. Still, I'd never set foot on the site of a former camp. Elisabeth had asked if we wanted to go to Dachau later that day, some seventy miles east of Krumbach. After hearing and reading about concentration camps for much of my life, I thought it was important to see at least one of them in person, to witness the instruments of death and places of murder, to pay homage to the victims. I said yes, with some trepidation.

The Nazis opened their first and longest-lasting concentration camp at Dachau in March 1933. Visitors today walk through the iron gate with its chilling, Orwellian words—"*ARBEIT MACH FREI*," or "WORK MAKES YOU FREE"—and enter a world of almost unspeakable horror. The insidiously designed showers, the crematorium, places where human ashes were discarded or prisoners were shot, they're all still there, forcing you to reflect on the evil that people are capable of and the lies of Holocaust deniers.

The huge roll call area and immense grounds where barracks stood testify to the scale of the Germans' intentions. More than two hundred thousand people were imprisoned at Dachau between 1933 and 1945. Dachau alone would have been enough to recoil from the Nazis' actions. Then you remember that it was only one of more than forty-four thousand camps and other incarceration sites they established across parts of Europe. A huge map shows where they were located. It's part of a sprawling exhibit that adds context to this horrible, tragic site.

Visiting the memorial at Dachau is to be reminded of how Germans treated not only Jews but also political opponents, homosexuals, Roma, and Jehovah's Witnesses. Staring at the artifacts of torture and death, I tried and failed to grasp what went through the minds of the victims and their perpetrators, as well as the many neighbors of this mind-boggling, twenty-acre site in a well-populated town just outside of Munich.

Even after the war, Dachau's residents turned their collective backs on the former concentration camp and visitors who came to witness it. Historian Harold Marcuse wrote that the jurisdiction's representative in the Bavarian parliament tried to discourage visitors by having the crematorium torn down. Failing at that, he had the directional signs removed. Visitors in the 1950s and '60s, Marcuse wrote, "often reported receiving evasive answers to their requests for directions to the former Dachau camp."

A book officially published for the concentration memorial site now readily admits the widespread denial Germany adopted for decades. "Postwar society in Germany and Dachau generally sought to pass over the crimes committed in the Nazi years and repress the memory of what happened," it says. "Although the town had close economic, administrative, legal, and personal ties to the concentration camp, the population of Dachau asserted to the U.S. military government that they 'knew nothing' about the crimes committed in the camp. The residents claimed that they themselves had been victims of the Nazis and had tried to resist the regime. As everywhere in Germany, this refusal to face up to questions of guilt and responsibility went hand-in-hand with a relativizing construction of the 'other Dachau,' a town that had nothing to do with the atrocities perpetrated in its direct vicinity."

Whatever the shortcomings of the memory movement, Germany's eventual efforts to move past these decades of denial and reckon with its ugly past were signs of its success.

This was a lot of history for me to absorb, much of it upsetting, the kind of visit that would make any Jewish descendant think twice about returning to the scene of the crime. By day's end, we were ready to check into our hotel at Augsburg. Although my mother never had any interest in returning to her birthplace, it turns out I wasn't the first member of my immediate family to visit there after the war.

Chapter 16

VISITING AUGSBURG

"My heart laughed."

My grandmother could hardly contain her joy when visiting Augsburg for the first time since fleeing fifty years earlier. "My heart laughed when I saw the city again," she said in 1988, after she and my uncle Gerd had accepted an invitation from the city to return. Gerd was fifty-eight. Omi was described by a reporter for the *Augsburger Allgemeine* newspaper as a "lively 80-year-old," which certainly fits my memories of her.

"Ich bin mit Augsburg versöhnt," she told the reporter. "I'm reconciled with Augsburg." She added, *"Die Leute, die uns eingeladen haben, können nichts für unser Schicksal"*— "The people who invited us are not responsible for our fate."

My grandmother and uncle in Augsburg in 1988, fifty years after they fled (Photo credit: Fred Schoellhorn/Augsburger Allgemeine)

So much was packed into the words *"unser Schicksal,"* or "our fate." Generations of Landauers had contributed much to the city's industry, its small slice of religious diversity, and its civic life. And yet the survival of every Jewish family depended on having the means and foresight to flee Germany while they had the chance.

She was still haunted by years of persecution. "When she walks through the streets and encounters old Augsburgers who may have held 'office and dignity" during the Third Reich," reporter Alfred Schmidt wrote during her return visit, "it can trigger a feeling of unease in her. 'In a restaurant,' she says, 'two old Augsburgers were sitting at the next table the other day. I sensed immediately that they were two real Nazis.'"

Still, my grandmother cast no aspirations on the younger people in Augsburg—"It's not their fault," she said—as she and my uncle reacquainted themselves with the city. It took them a while to find the house at Beethovenstraße 16 where they had lived fifty years earlier. She recognized it immediately. "'Even the garden is still there,' she said happily," according to the newspaper account.

Omi died at home in Cali five years later. I wept at hearing the news of losing the only grandparent I knew. Mollie and I honored her nine months later by naming our daughter Emily, her first initial inspired by my grandmother Else. Even so, I knew little of her life at that time and nothing of my family's history in Augsburg beyond what I gleaned from that yellowing, complicated family tree.

I first visited Augsburg in 2022, coincidentally on my sixty-sixth birthday. I stood at Beethovenstraße 16 with Mollie, Elisabeth, and Paul at my side, staring at the apartment building and taking enough pictures that a resident asked what we were doing. Once Paul told her, she quickly left her balcony to avoid my camera.

But I wasn't in Augsburg only to retrace my family's steps and those of other members of the Jewish community. I wanted to better understand the motives and work of current-day Germans who already knew much more about my ancestors than I did. As in Hürben, Augsburg's main Jewish cemetery offered clues both about days gone by as well as insight into the present day. The lives of the people buried there have become a touchstone for a number of Germans, be they Jewish or not.

One of them, Michael Bernheim, straddles the lines in multiple ways. He's Catholic, his paternal grandfather having converted from Judaism when marrying his non-Jewish wife. Even so, the Nazis considered Bernheim's grandfather to be Jewish and his father half-Jewish. His grandfather escaped to France in 1938 and served as a French soldier in World War II, taking part in the Normandy invasion. His father was eventually deported to a labor camp in Thuringia in 1944, escaped, and hid until the war's end.

Michael Bernheim poses at the gravesite of family members buried at a Jewish cemetery in Augsburg.

Some of his other relatives were not so fortunate. Bernheim's paternal great-grandmother was murdered in the Theresienstadt concentration camp. His father's cousin, Wolfgang Bernheim, having been baptized at age seven, faced a life-or-death decision as a teenager. He was in the Benedictine Order in the Netherlands as a novice in 1942 when Germans began deporting Catholics who had Jewish ancestry. Wolfgang received his deportation notification in August of that year. But he had a convenient way out. A fellow novice who had contacts in the Dutch resistance arranged for Wolfgang to escape to Switzerland. But the monastery's leader, known as the abbot, objected, fearing the Germans would retaliate against the monastery if they discovered he was gone. Wolfgang had a terrible choice to make. If he escaped, as his fellow novice pleaded with him to do, he would defy the abbot and risk harm to those at the monastery he left behind. So Wolfgang stayed and was later killed at the Sakrau labor camp in Poland.

This was a lot of family history for Michael Bernheim to deal with when he was growing up in Augsburg. But it also meant that young Bernheim—unlike a lot of his classmates—didn't have to worry that his relatives were Nazis. "In these times, this is when teenage sons and daughters began to ask their fathers, 'What did you do in the war, what was your position, where you were working?'" he told me. "That was reassuring to me. I knew what my father was doing during those years, that he was not a perpetrator in the Nazi era and the Second World War."

Not that Bernheim got the full story as a youngster. "The victims didn't tell about what happened," he said. "My father had a tendency to talk about the good things, that some Nazis had helped him. He hardly mentioned the atrocities."

Bernheim, nearing seventy when we met, is a retired chemist, following in the footsteps of family members who used to run a chemistry business that served the local textile industry. As we spoke in person at the cemetery and during a previous Zoom call, Bernheim impressed me as earnest, well read, and proud of Augsburg. But when speaking broadly of the German history he had grown up with, he expressed shame about the Nazi era and the shadow it still cast over the country.

"There are some conflicts being both German and having Jewish descendants," he said. "I never found it attractive being German when I was younger. I would have preferred being Swiss, American, or British."

He remembered being a visiting student in Manchester, England, in 1974, and joining his host family at a restaurant that traditionally put the flag of the student's home country on their table. "I felt pretty uneasy," said Bernheim, who quietly asked that the German flag be removed. While working briefly at a chemical lab during that same visit, a local resident needled him by raising his arm in a Nazi salute. It was a gesture Bernheim pointedly told me he would not demonstrate himself as we stood in the midst of the Jewish cemetery.

Some of Bernheim's Jewish relatives are buried there, as are some of mine, including Heinrich and wife, Bettina Landauer. They are buried next to Hugo Landauer (whose tombstone notes that his wife, Hedwig, was buried in Colombia).

Bernheim and another member of the memory working group, Alfred Hausmann, pointed to other gravesites along the way, some of which prompted me to do further research later. Among them were four adjacent tombstones marking the remains of four couples who were forced to stay at a designated *Judenhaus* (Jewish house) before being deported to Auschwitz. The house was deeply meaningful to one of them, Hedwig Englaender, whose family used to live there. The pleasant memories she associated with it were obviously tainted by its also being the location of unspeakable horror. Her parents had committed suicide in the kitchen on November 6, 1941, just before they were to be deported.

A farewell note from her father, addressed to their children and grandchildren, is chilling, given what we now know. He wished them "a beautiful and sunny future which will not be darkened by the loss, though for you painful, but providing for us liberation from all the horrors of life." The note from Hedwig Englaender's mother struck a similar tone. "Perhaps you will still enjoy better times," she wrote, "you are still of an age where it is possible to have hope; that is the most fervent Wish of your loving Mama Linele."

Their last wishes were for naught. Sixteen months later, Hedwig and Paul Englaender gave up hope shortly before they were to be deported. On March 7, 1943, they joined three other couples attempting suicide in the same kitchen where her parents had taken their own lives. Seven were successful—the Englaenders, Ludwig and Selma Friedmann, Julius and Anna

Guggenheimer, and Louis Karl Kohn. The eighth, Erna Kohn, survived the attempt and was deported to Auschwitz, where she was murdered.

Perhaps the Englaenders had her parents' farewell notes in mind as they considered their own final words. They dictated a telegram to their children in America, via the Red Cross, dated March 5 but not received until that October. "Farewell," it concludes, "have a happy life and do not forget us."

We heard stories about others buried in the cemetery, including World War I veterans, quite a few children, and more recent Augsburg residents who had emigrated from Eastern Europe. We asked questions of Bernheim and Hausmann, took pictures, paused and reflected upon the tombstones, and observed the cultural differences between the simple gravestones of those from a Western European heritage and the more ornate memorials for those from the East.

As we prepared to leave and the rest of the group chatted near the exit, I turned once more to face the cemetery. I let my camera dangle at my side, shoved my notebook in my pocket, and purposely stood alone for several minutes, facing the tombstones. It was almost as though I was asking the deceased to address me. I bowed my head and tried to soak in the history and lives represented there, freely letting in whatever thoughts came to me. Nowhere but Germany have I felt such an urgent need to spend time alone in a cemetery, reflecting on what I had just heard and seen. But it seemed almost necessary in the country that my ancestors had long considered their home and where many were killed.

Every person buried there faced great challenges as Jews, no matter which era they lived in. They overcame obstacles to create and sustain a vibrant Jewish community filled with German patriots. Many of their offspring met an untimely, frightening end as Jews were targeted, threatened, and killed. The lucky ones who were alive as the Nazi era began left when they could. Some version of "we made it" crossed my mind, as it had when I stood in front of my great-grandmother's grave in Raesfeld eleven years earlier. The "we" represented not just my immediate family but something much broader. Some of us are still here despite unending waves of anti-Semitism, a genocide of historic proportions, and prejudice that still exists today.

I later thought of the many connections between those at rest in Augsburg's Jewish cemetery and those of us who are still upright and able to walk in and out of its gates. One connection in particular comes to mind. A tombstone had several stones on it, more than most, a sign of honor for the deceased. I looked at the name chiseled onto the granite: Mieczyslaw Pemper. Born in Kraków, Poland, in 1920, died in Augsburg in 2011. Bernheim pointed to it and asked if I knew who he was.

"No," I said, realizing I was about to be embarrassed by my lack of knowledge. Who was he?

"Mietek Pemper," Bernheim replied, using his informal name, was the man who typed Schindler's List.

Of course I was mortified. Why hadn't I known that? One reason is that in the movie adaption of Thomas Keneally's book, Itzhak Stern, played by Ben Kingsley, was actually a composite character based on Stern and Pemper. The real-life Pemper was forced to work as an assistant to Amon Göth, the sadistic commandant of the Kraków-Płaszow concentration camp in Poland. Entrusted by Göth with his correspondence, Pemper provided vital information to industrialist Oskar Schindler. It helped sustain a sham armaments facility Schindler operated that was actually designed to save some one thousand Jewish workers and two hundred other inmates. The ruse that they were essential to the German war effort worked; their lives were spared. Pemper, otherwise identified as camp prisoner 69514, was number 655 on Schindler's list. Schindler made sure Pemper's parents and brother were also included.

Schindler credited his two Jewish assistants when the company's workers were liberated in May 1945. "Don't thank me for your survival," he told his employees as they gathered around him. "Thank your own people who worked day and night to save you from destruction. Thank your valiant Stern and Pemper and the others who sacrificed themselves for you, especially in Kraków, staring death in the eye every moment as they thought of the good of all and looked out for you."

Pemper's real-life nightmares stayed with him, as they did for other Holocaust survivors. But he never tried to lock them away. He wanted to make sure the criminals were held accountable. Still only twenty-six, Pemper was the first witness called by prosecutors in the case against Göth, describing in great detail the atrocities he saw. Göth was subsequently found guilty and executed in Kraków in 1946.

Pemper continued to talk about what he had experienced during the Holocaust and what he learned about humanity long after those trials ended. After Pemper's mother died in 1958, he moved with his father to Augsburg, where his brother had settled immediately after the war. He became a German citizen and a management consultant. He actively tried to improve Jewish–Christian relations and pursue a postwar reconciliation. That quest led him to speak frequently with Augsburg's youngsters.

"I always find the new generation open-minded," he wrote. "They have no preconceptions and really want to know what it was like back then. For another, the future depends on these young people. It will be they who ensure that the darkest chapter in history is not repeated anywhere in the world."

One of those talks Pemper gave in Augsburg created a direct line to how Jewish history and culture are taught there today.

Chapter 17

SALVAGING A SYNAGOGUE

"Only actions count."

Eight youngsters from Augsburg introduced themselves to Mietek Pemper and settled in for what was supposed to be an hour-long conversation. Except that he had so much to say, and they had so many questions. A one-hour conversation stretched into five.

Meeting Pemper left a lasting impression on at least one of the students, Carmen Reichert, who still had vivid memories of him twenty-five years later. "He kept telling everybody that you can't judge people according to where they come from, what they look like, only about what they do," Reichert said. People may *say* a lot of nice things, Pemper told them. Only actions count.

Reichert took Pemper's words to heart. She was thirty-seven when we spoke, and the director of Augsburg's Jewish museum. A picture of Pemper sat on her desk, providing a continual source of inspiration. She remembered that he described "the hell that he saw in the concentration camp and ghetto. It didn't matter if it was a German SS or they came by circumstance. They acted the same. He said it's not a German problem, it's a human problem. And you never know how anyone would react if he was in a condition like this."

Reichert was talking with Mollie and me one afternoon at a coffee shop in central Augsburg, a few doors down from the museum. She knew the area about as well as anyone could, having been born two blocks away in 1985, just three months before the museum opened adjacent to the synagogue.

It's not as though Reichert had dreamt as a youngster of living and working in the very neighborhood where she grew up. Far from it. Her dream was to leave Augsburg. She considered the modest-sized city stifling in its uniformity of background and thought. "It was not a good idea to be different," she told us. "I felt that in school. I didn't feel comfortable with it." She was more at ease later when living in the larger, more cosmopolitan cities of Paris and Munich.

But she returned to Augsburg in 2021 to head up the Jewish museum. She left Munich, where she taught Yiddish at the Ludwig Maximilian University and worked at the European Janusz Korczak Academy, a Jewish organization that fights anti-Semitism through cultural education and dialogue.

There were a number of influences guiding Reichert, who is not Jewish, to a career in Jewish studies, none more so than hearing from one of those responsible for Schindler's List. "After the first meeting with Mietek Pemper," Reichert wrote in a letter introducing herself to the descendants of Augsburg's Jewish community, "I dealt intensively with the *Shoah* and particularly with the question of how loving family members could become murderers."

Ultimately, she concluded that she would probably never be able to answer that question, particularly in Augsburg, where she said Jews were more assimilated into German society before the Nazis' ascendance than in many other places. "There is definitely a German history of developments, a tradition of anti-Semitism, that helped this to happen," she told us over coffee. "But I do agree with Pemper and Levi," she continued, also referring to Primo Levi, an Italian chemist, writer, and Auschwitz survivor. "The fact that it happened, it can happen again. It can happen here again and it can happen in a different place."

One of the aspects of the post-Holocaust world that confounds Reichert is how relatively few bystanders talked afterward about what they had seen and heard. "Under a regime of terror, it's understandable," she said. "But once the war is ended, there's no reason not to talk. They felt guilty. They didn't talk at the moment." In memory culture, she added, "what's missing is the memories of the bystanders."

Reichert is heartened that the current generation of young Germans are learning about the Holocaust, which she consistently referred to by its Hebrew name, the *Shoah*. But she's wary about how it's presented. "It's the first time Jewish history is being taught at universities and schools. But it's still related today to the *Shoah*. That's a problem, in that we don't talk enough about all the other times. Jews are perceived as victims of the *Shoah* and not as agents of their own history."

I asked her why Germany was more willing than America to face up to its ugly past. "History's more recent here than in the U.S.," she said. "As long as you know the persons who were involved in this from either side, it's still there somehow. It's harder to relate to something that happened centuries ago and without knowing what part your family played in it."

Reichert has thought a lot about the role that a Jewish museum in Germany can play in educating the general public about Jewish history and religion. "Today, it is no longer about showing our visitors silver or gold *hannukkiot* or *besamin* cups and explaining what culture they once stood for," she wrote in her letter to the descendants' group, referring to Hanukkah menorahs and ritual spice boxes. "Today, I see our task more as being a place of encounter, exchange, and joint reflection on our past, present and future."

Augsburg's main synagogue and its Jewish museum are under the same roof. But the first aspects that struck me when we toured them the next day weren't related to religion. One was the extraordinarily tight security measures once we were permitted past the imposing front door. The other was a sign I saw as we stepped into the interior courtyard, inviting visitors to find something to drink or to read at the Lesecafé Landauer. I allowed myself a little family pride, that the Landauer name still meant something here, reinforced later when we saw an exhibit honoring Otto Landauer.

You can stand in that building today and imagine the world of Augsburg's Jewish community when the synagogue opened in 1917. Many of its members held important positions in industry and commerce. Their businesses—including banks and other financial institutions, as well as the textile trade—were among Augsburg's leading employers.

Worshippers were as proud of their city as they were of their Judaism and made sure you noticed that when you walked in. The congregation's symbol blends those two allegiances. It displays Augsburg's coat of arms, as shown by a pine cone, surrounded by the six-cornered Star of David. Their patriotism was also front and center. A plaque memorializes twenty-four worshippers who died defending Germany in World War I.

The synagogue's members were liberal and humanistic. A fountain in the lobby, suitable for ritual hand washing, is topped by a depiction of King David. This is unusual; most synagogues don't prominently display a human figure. The building also featured an organ, a musical instrument most often identified with churches. Their worship services inserted contemporary touches with more traditional practices.

The Jewish community of Augsburg was confident. How else to explain constructing a sanctuary with seating for nearly 800, representing a high percentage of the 1,200 Jews who lived there in 1917? That was more than they needed at the time, reflecting their optimism, said our guide, Frank Schillinger, the museum's education director. "You can see what the view of the future the community had."

The synagogue was a center of the Jewish community and a gathering place for the rituals of Jewish life. Prayer services were held at a daily *minyan,* a quorum of ten adults (traditionally, ten males) necessary to conduct a service. Congregants came to the synagogue to witness a *bris*, the ceremony of circumcision for an eight-day-old boy. They prayed at a bar mitzvah, the coming-of-age rite of a thirteen-year-old reading from Torah. They celebrated at weddings. They mourned at funerals. Beginning in the 1930s, the synagogue also hosted a kindergarten.

Schillinger, who's not Jewish, was forty-four when we met and had been working at the museum for a decade. He's from a small village in the Black Forest. He remembered visiting a nearby Jewish cemetery while growing up but not getting any context for it. Both of his grandfathers died before he was born. His parents couldn't tell him much about their family's involvement in the Holocaust, though they did share a few details. "My mother told me her mother supported the Hitler movement," he said. But he added, "I got the feeling that they didn't talk about the topic either."

Schillinger didn't learn about the Holocaust until studying history in his twenties: "I developed the feeling that I have to do something. Not that I'm responsible. But I'm responsible to make sure something like that doesn't happen again."

I practically gasped when he led us into the synagogue's sanctuary. It's a marvel that restoration efforts have remade it into a stunning, sacred space. Though the lighting was purposely dim, you could see that it combines elements of Art Nouveau, Byzantine, and Oriental architecture. The ninety-five-foot-high reinforced-concrete dome is covered with a green-gold mosaic and decorative imagery. Look closely and you'll find artistic depictions of the High Holidays, as well as the Twelve Tribes of Israel. Four stucco reliefs surrounding the dome portray the Torah as the tree of life, while biblical quotes are conveyed in Hebrew script.

The restored synagogue on Halderstraße in Augsburg
(Photo credit © JMAS/Franz Kimmel)

Staff are understandably uptight about public access. No photos are allowed. Visitors can only view the sanctuary from the second-floor Women's Gallery. They can't sit on the chairs. That hasn't been permitted since 2019, Schillinger said, when vandals drew swastikas on more than sixty seats, then drew twenty more just four months later. Police never found the perpetrators.

There was plenty of activity the morning we were there, from small groups of middle-aged and elderly friends to large groups of students. It was refreshing to see such interest in this sacred space, which had barely avoided total destruction by the Nazis and had only recently emerged from being shuttered during the coronavirus pandemic. Students typically visit the museum and synagogue in the sixth grade, when they learn about Judaism as part of a world religion course, and in the ninth grade, when they study the Holocaust as part of a course on the history of Nazism.

There's even more activity on the Sabbath, as the synagogue has once again become a focal point of Augsburg's Jewish community. The congregation now claims about 1,400 members, which exceeds the 1,200 it had in its prewar peak in 1925. That's right—more Jews live in Augsburg now than did so before the war. Some 90 percent of current-day members come from the former Soviet Union, the remainder from Israel, Poland, and Germany. They don't have the same familial history and ties to the country's Jewish heritage as do descendants of the prewar Jewish community now scattered across the globe.

The current leader is Alexander Mazo, born in 1955 in Tashkent, Uzbekistan, where his family with Belarusian and Ukrainian roots had fled. Mazo, an attorney, moved to Augsburg in 2003, three years after his parents did, as part of the wave of Jews leaving the former Soviet Union. The mix of background and languages is evident in its services, Mazo told me. The prayer books are in Hebrew and transliterated into German or Russian. When the rabbi speaks in either German or Russian, it is translated simultaneously into the other language.

There may be more Jews in Augsburg than ever, but they are not as prominent as they once were. There are not many captains of industry or leaders in civic life, like the Landauers, who could build on connections made over many decades. Many are still getting a foothold in society. "The Jewish community is not as integrated into the life of the city as it was before 1933," Mazo said. "To improve this is an important task. This must, however, not degenerate to assimilation. Religious rules are not negotiable. An example is an invitation to a public event on Shabbat."

But the Jewish community still has hopes and dreams, as evidenced by an ambitious project that began in 2022 to renovate the entire synagogue complex over several years, including the museum. It entails structural improvements as well as security upgrades that were estimated to cost about €26 million at the outset (about $29.4 million as of 2025). In a strong sign of public support, the German federal government is funding about half of the cost, the state of Bavaria nearly 20 percent, and the city of Augsburg 10 percent. "It's about preserving the traditions and the memory of all those who came before us," Mazo said, "so that the history of the congregation is not interrupted, so that there is a future."

There is also an ugly past, a hatred of Jews that persists to this day. "Anti-Semitism is no longer shameful anymore," Mazo told me in July 2023, three months before the Israel–Gaza war worsened the situation. "The number of cases of anti-Semitism unfortunately continues to grow. All of this cannot be left without attention and an appropriate response." Incidents are common enough that the synagogue designated someone specifically to handle such complaints, providing his contact information on its website. "This speaks about the seriousness of this problem," Mazo said.

A little less than three miles to the west, another historic synagogue stands in the Kriegshaber neighborhood, which has a history reminiscent of Hürben's. Once an independent village, Kriegshaber long served as a refuge for Jews who were expelled from medieval Augsburg in 1439. For the next four centuries, only a limited number of Jews were authorized to enter the city, and to do so through the Gögginger Gate. Even those privileged few were given access only during weekdays and only if they agreed to leave before nightfall. This became the traditional path for Jewish traders and tradesmen who commuted from their homes in the adjacent villages of Kriegshaber, Pfersee, and Steppach to Augsburg's commercial hub.

Kriegshaber had enough Jewish presence to have its own cemetery, *mikvah*, and synagogue, which opened in 1725. The Jewish presence began to dissipate after the Kingdom of Bavaria granted Jews freedom of settlement in 1861 and more moved to the city. The village of Kriegshaber was incorporated into Augsburg in 1916. The Kriegshaber congregation merged with the larger synagogue in the city center a year later. But members weren't enamored of the liberal, Reform services held downtown, so they continued to hold their own traditional services.

Until *Kristallnacht* changed everything. Services at the synagogue on Halderstraße ceased immediately, the interior of the venerable synagogue having been completely destroyed. But Kriegshaber avoided that fate. The building was ransacked, its ritual objects stolen and windows smashed. The congregation locked the doors afterward but not permanently. Within three months they opened again, and its remaining congregants returned to worship, at least for the next few years.

I was stunned when our guide at the synagogue, Ayleen Winkler, told us that. Its members knew they were in grave danger as hatred and persecution of Jews intensified. Yet they still gathered in that sacred building. It took courage to meet under such frightening conditions. Publicly expressing their faith put their lives and those of their loved ones at risk. They could have contented themselves by praying in their homes and in their hearts. But they would not be intimidated, even when that courted danger.

One of those worshippers was a young man named Sel Hubert, who fled to the neighborhood with his parents and older sister from the Bavarian village of Cronheim in December 1938. They made do in a room lent to them by relatives who lived a block from the shuttered synagogue, which they assumed would remain closed. The family was surprised when the building reopened a few days before Hubert was supposed to have his bar mitzvah on February 4, 1939.

"That was the first public Sabbath worship service since Kristallnacht," Hubert wrote in his memoir. "The small sanctuary was packed. Pain and worry were etched on people's faces." He felt not only his new *tallit* (prayer shawl) on his shoulders, "but also the hopes and prayers of my parents and all those present."

> After chanting the final blessing, a feeling of relief engulfed me and I silently thanked God for allowing me to fulfill my obligation. I will never forget the pride and love etched on the faces of my parents and my sister as I stepped down and the warm

> embrace and blessing I received from them later. It was a glorious and uplifting moment in a world bereft of hope.
>
> All Jewish parents dream of the day of their child's Bar or Bat Mitzvah as a joyous and proud celebration, to be shared with family and friends. My Bar Mitzvah, held in the midst of chaos and despair, was more a declaration of faith and hope and determination.

Hubert's family knew this was but a brief respite from the growing danger. Within a few months, Hubert's parents arranged for his sister and then Sel himself to travel to safety in London via the *Kindertransport.* It was the last they would see of their parents, who were later deported to the Jewish ghetto in Piaski, Poland.

Kriegshaber's worship services finally ceased at the end of 1941 as Augsburg's remaining Jews were systematically deported. The building was used as ghetto apartments the next year for evicted Jewish families, Winkler said. After the war, the city of Augsburg eventually took control of the building, and it was occupied for a while by the Russian Orthodox church. Local remembrance groups began to reclaim some of its heritage in the 1980s, and it became part of the Augsburg museum in the early 2000s.

The building was renovated for several years before opening to the public in 2014. It also serves as a temporary exhibit space. A small crew was actively and loudly preparing an exhibit on Ukrainian Jewish life while we were there. The sanctuary is much smaller than its more famous cousin in the city center. It looks solid, plain, unadorned, something more at home in the colonial era of America than the more ornate building three miles east.

Winkler, twenty-eight when we met, was younger than many of the Germans we talked to while in Augsburg. She grew up in northern Germany, wasn't Jewish, and described herself as not religious. It sounded like an unusual background for someone making a career as a curator at a Jewish museum. How did she end up there? I asked, as we paused in the Kriegshaber sanctuary. She said she started studying all religions before deciding to focus primarily on Judaism "because of German history." Winkler acknowledged that being immersed in Jewish history and the Holocaust isn't a popular choice. “As long as I can remember,” she told us, “people have been saying, ‘It’s been long enough, we can stop talking about it.’”

She won’t. (A year after we met, she became a curator at Dorsten’s Jewish museum.) She wants to also make sure that schools and museums go beyond the *Shoah* when describing German Jewish history. “It is more. It is alive,” she said of Judaism, “and it was alive before the *Shoah*.”

But it’s also important not to forget how fascism and anti-Semitism grew in the Nazi era “to show people what can happen if you’re not paying attention.” I asked why she thought there was still anti-Semitism in Germany, given the relatively low percentage of Jews there and low profile. Such hatred is transferred through the generations, Winkler said, as parents hand down their ideas to their children and grandchildren. “It’s always easy to hate people you don’t know.”

Which raises the question, Is it harder to hate people you at least *know about*? That is, in a way, why the postwar memory movement didn’t just restore synagogues where they could. It’s what led them to build dozens of Jewish museums throughout Europe, many more than had existed before the Holocaust, in hopes of educating the public.

AN UNEASY RECONCILIATION

Chapter 18

WHO TELLS YOUR STORY

"Running a Jewish museum can be complicated for non-Jews."

The end of World War II left a bleak landscape for Jewish survivors in Germany and elsewhere in Europe. Their synagogues, the central focus of Jewish spiritual life, were either totally destroyed or gutted. Their cemeteries, the sacred space for their loved ones, were vandalized, in some cases beyond recognition. Their homes, essential to celebrating Jewish festivals and the rituals of life, were seized and now had new owners.

Of course, the people themselves absorbed the most devastating losses of all. Two out of three European Jews who were alive when Hitler came to power in 1933 were killed. Most of the survivors fled and had no interest in returning; many displaced persons who had been ripped from their homes had no interest in staying. The continent's Jewish population of about 9.5 million dropped to 3.8 million in 1945 and kept diminishing, dropping by another two-thirds in the six decades after.

Into the void of the Jewish experience, eventually, came a concept that had a much lower profile before the Nazi era—the Jewish museum, a result of decades of spadework, figuratively and sometimes literally, of the memory movement. Almost everything about these new institutions differed from Jewish places that had come before, including prewar Jewish museums.

Before the Holocaust, German Jews faced outward as patriots who fought for their country, built businesses when they were permitted to, and supported public institutions where they lived. But when it came to practicing their religion, they tended to look inward. Some of their synagogues, like those in Augsburg, were built to blend into a neighborhood. Far from proselytizing others to believe as they do, Judaism traditionally makes conversion difficult.

By contrast, postwar Jewish museums are all about reaching a broader public. Generally speaking, they are of, by, and for non-Jews. Most began not as byproducts of the scant Jewish community that remained. There may be few Jews on the museum's staff or in the leadership because few live in the area.

The vast majority of Jews who live in Germany now have their roots in the former Soviet Union and Eastern Europe. They don't have the same connection to German Jewish history as, say, I do, as an American Jew whose family was an integral part of that history. And they don't have much interest in sharing it publicly. "Most likely this was because the history that was being retold in these places reflected the experience of only a small portion of the Jews living in the Federal Republic," wrote Inka Bertz, the head of collections and art curator at the Jewish Museum Berlin, "as the post-Holocaust Jewish community contained only a small minority of native-born Jews."

All of which leads to the phenomenon that many of these museums are places where non-Jews teach other non-Jews about the Jewish people and their history. That can be awkward for all concerned.

Take it from one who knows. Norbert Reichling was a political scientist and educator, a founding member of the supporting association for Dorsten's Jewish museum, a longtime board member, and its volunteer director for fourteen years—twelve of which he did while also holding a full-time job. "Running a Jewish museum can be complicated for non-Jews," he said. "It is necessary to keep a certain distance: we need and we want to reflect the diversity of Jewish life. It would be a serious mistake if we depicted Jewish life, Jewish identities and Jewish culture as something clear, something uniform, stable for centuries."

Circumstances dictate that the museums are largely disconnected from present-day Judaism. They typically feature religious artifacts and objects under glass that are no longer an integral part of a service or ritual; some objects may have been created and purchased specifically for display, without having ever been used. If a museum is part of a historic synagogue that's been restored from ruins, the sanctuary may be rarely if ever used for worship anymore. And though Jewish services don't by any means dwell on death—the Mourner's *Kaddish* we say to honor the deceased makes no reference to death; it glorifies God—the genocidal acts that virtually wiped out European Jewry cast a shadow over these museums.

Today you can find a Jewish museum of one sort or another throughout much of Europe. The most prominent are part of the Association of European Jewish Museums, which counts more than sixty institutions as members, from Norway in the north to Israel in the south, from Portugal in the west to Georgia in the east. No country has more than the dozen such museums that are in Germany. That includes the one in Dorsten, which has hardly had any Jewish residents in about eighty years, though Jews are scattered around the region that it serves.

Ruth Ellen Gruber wrote about the irony in 2002. "For decades after World War II," she said, "memory of Jewish history and heritage was often marginalized, repressed, or forgotten, not only in countries where the flames of the Holocaust had burned most fiercely, but also in countries less directly touched by the effects of the Shoah." As the memory culture movement got into full swing by the late 1990s, the nation's Jewish history was being increasingly recognized, including in official policy.

Gruber detected "an apparent longing for lost Jews—or for what Jews are seen to represent." Brocke said historians seeking to "objectively" examine the Holocaust rarely concerned themselves with Jewish people and "seemed to show more interest in dead Jews or 'victims.'" Dara Horn, author of the provocatively titled 2021 book *People Love Dead Jews*, was more blunt. "Jews were cast in the role of civilization's nagging mothers," she said, "loathed in life, and loved only once they are safely dead."

But not universally loved. Though these aren't spaces where Jews routinely gather, they—and the synagogues that remain—are still targets for anti-Semitic hatred and violence. A gunman shot and killed two Israeli tourists and two employees at the Jewish museum in Brussels in 2014. A Jewish man was killed and two police officers wounded near Copenhagen's main synagogue in 2015. Only a heavy, bolted door kept a gunman from firing at fifty-two worshippers during Yom Kippur services in a synagogue in Halle, Germany, in 2019. He shot and killed a passerby and a man at a kebab shop instead. A month after we visited Essen in October 2022, shots were fired at the rabbi's house adjacent to the synagogue there. The number of threats or security incidents at or near Jewish sites in Europe started increasing a year later, when the Israel–Gaza war began. That's led to stricter security measures, especially when entering a museum that's connected to a synagogue, as in Augsburg, and to fewer visitors.

It's difficult to generalize about the dozens of these diverse museums, most of which focus more on the centuries of Jewish history and culture in Europe than on the twelve years the Nazis reigned. Those who do spend considerable resources on the Holocaust must balance a series of seeming contradictions. They obviously have to reckon with how the Jewish presence in Germany was decimated by death and destruction while imparting that Judaism still exists. They're called upon to represent a local culture that may be barely present in the community or the museum staff. They have to explain that these acts of genocide were singular in their horror while trying to draw contemporary lessons from them. And they must do all of this representing a people who aren't eager to attract attention to their culture or beliefs, in a continent where their predecessors were persecuted for it.

"It's hard in European Jewish museums, getting the balance right between who is the museum for and who it should represent," Abigail Morris, the then-director of the Jewish Museum London, said in 2019. "In countries where the Jewish population has largely been murdered, it's particularly acute."

The heaviness that visitors carry from a Jewish museum, Holocaust memorial, or former concentration camp site is not the end game. It's how that experience changes you. "Guilt is not a forward-looking sentiment," said Irit Dekel, an Indiana University sociologist with a background in Germanic and Jewish studies. "Crying doesn't educate," said Volkhard Knigge, a German historian and former longtime head of the foundation for the Buchenwald concentration camp memorial site.

Whatever their precise focus, these places have a special responsibility to provide a broad context for the topic. "Jewish museums, more than any other kind of museum, are assigned a role in the politics of memory and identity, to 'educate' and—implicitly—to present a coherent 'big story,'" Bertz said.

One of the first tasks of a modern-day Jewish museum in Europe is choosing what should be remembered and which objects should be represented, Gruber wrote. But, she wondered, who decides? "What should Jewish museums in Europe show, teach, or represent? How? To whom? By whom? From what perspective? Where should they be located? Who should set them up? Should they be set up in the first place? Indeed, does Europe need so many Jewish museums?"

There were far fewer Jewish museums in Europe at a time when many more Jews lived there. Some sixteen Jewish museums of one sort or another existed on the continent in the decades before the Holocaust. Most of them grew out of private initiatives, usually with the support of the local Jewish community. The first was in Vienna, founded in 1895. The last prewar museum to open was in Berlin, on January 24, 1933, an improbable six days before Hitler assumed power.

An important function of this early Berlin museum was to provide contemporary Jewish artists opportunities to exhibit their work, in addition to honoring artists of the past. "Above all," Bertz wrote, "the museum bolstered its visitors' cultural self-awareness, as more and more Jews were turning to Jewish culture under the pressures of anti-Semitic policies. And yet, as with other Jewish institutions, the museum faced ever harsher constraints and harassment on the part of the German authorities."

Most of these museums had a relatively brief and troubled existence. Their buildings were closed after *Kristallnacht*, their collections confiscated by German authorities, their objects plundered and lost. The early museums primarily displayed Jewish arts and antiquities. Virtually all were associated with existing Jewish institutions. Gruber described the collections as something where modern Jews preserved treasures from a past that no longer seemed as relevant to them. "In a sense those museums were nonreligious

Jewish shrines to pious Jewish tradition," she wrote. "Today's museums, particularly those run by Jewish community organizations, still may fulfill this function in part, but often, too, they and their exhibits are enshrined as sacred relics of a destroyed civilization."

The Jewish sites in the places where my family once lived represent different aspects of the memory movement. The synagogue in Essen, which considers itself not a museum but a "House of Jewish Culture," reopened in its current incarnation in 1988, but only after the city zigged and zagged for years figuring out what to make of it. The Jewish Museum of Westphalia opened in Dorsten in 1992, a direct outgrowth of the region's history workshop.

The Augsburg museum was founded in 1985 as the first private, independent museum in the Federal Republic of Germany dedicated to the history and culture of Jews. The museum holds another distinction in that it was a rare such initiative started by the local Jewish community and not its non-Jewish neighbors. But the museum and remembrance movement in Augsburg has been sustained and led since then by Jews and non-Jews alike.

Many of the Jews who survived in Germany during the war—like Tante Malli and her friend, Cläre Mies—did so because they had been protected by non-Jewish spouses or parents. They weren't necessarily active in the Jewish community beforehand and weren't inclined to be active afterward. They were soon joined by a larger group of survivors from Eastern Europe, people the Allies considered displaced persons. Among them were Polish émigrés Cesia and David Blitzer, parents of longtime CNN anchor Wolf Blitzer, who met on a train while traveling between Poland and Germany looking for surviving relatives. Wolf Blitzer was born in 1948 in one of several places in Augsburg where displaced persons were being housed.

Many Jewish survivors from the east had no intention of returning to their hometowns to confront painful memories, destroyed property, and persistent anti-Semitism. With few immediate options, they migrated west to Germany and settled at least temporarily in areas liberated by Western Allies. Many were assigned to camps (sometimes former concentration camps), sheltered in barracks, or, if they were in a town, directed to houses or synagogues that were still standing in some fashion. Thus fate brought together Jews from Germany and Eastern Europe, though cultural differences remained. These tensions lingered for years in Augsburg, where the Jewish communities were split between German speakers and Yiddish speakers.

Into the breach stepped Julius Spokojny. Spokojny was born in 1923 near Kraków, Poland, deported to a labor camp at age sixteen, and liberated at Buchenwald in 1945. A year later he arrived at the displaced persons camp at Landsberg am Lech (where Hitler was imprisoned in 1923 and wrote *Mein Kampf*), then resettled in nearby Augsburg four years later. Most of Spokojny's peers eventually emigrated to the U.S. or to Israel when those paths opened. He stayed and became a leader accepted by all parties. He served as president of the Augsburg-Swabia Jewish community from 1965 until shortly before his death in 1996 and as a longtime representative of the Jewish Religious Community in the Bavarian Senate.

Spokojny was a prominent postwar bridge builder between the German and East European Jews who settled in Augsburg, as well as between Christians and Jews. One of his goals was to rebuild the large synagogue and worship there on the holidays. He wanted the synagogue opened to all residents of Augsburg the rest of the year, so they could learn about Judaism.

His dream came true on September 1, 1985, when the synagogue was rededicated along with the adjoining Jewish cultural museum. Spokojny acknowledged the synagogue was much too large for the relatively few Jews left in the city, except for special occasions. "But otherwise, we have placed it as the main exhibit in a museum which is to bring the culture of the Jewish religion closer to our fellow men," he said. "The museum and synagogue are open to the entire population of Germany and abroad, and we especially hope that the youth of all nations will take an interest in the culture and religion of the Jews with an open mind."

"Spokojny wanted to fill his museum as quickly as possible," wrote Sarah König, a former archive and research assistant at the Augsburg museum. He relied on the community's assorted Judaica, acquired ritual objects from rural communities or local municipalities and some items sent from Israel. The latter were purchased specifically for the exhibition. They had no connection to Augsburg or the Bavarian Swabia region and had never been used outside of the museum. A more historically accurate permanent exhibit opened in 2006.

An essential aspect of remembering the long Jewish history in and around Augsburg has been the research, documentation, and scholarship about it. No one accomplished more on that score than Augsburg journalist and author Gernot Römer. His work inspired superlatives. My grandmother's cousin Paul Rosenau referred to Römer fondly as "a good soul. He keeps our memory alive over there." A tribute by descendants of Augsburg's Jewish community began, "Gernot Römer may well have been the first person outside of our immediate family who ever inquired about our family's story."

Römer joined the local daily newspaper, *Augsburger Allgemeine,* in 1971 and became its editor-in-chief three years later. He earned a reputation as tough and demanding, retiring in 1994. "Römer was not an easy boss, not an easygoing boss," according to an appreciation in his own newspaper after his death in June 2022, at the age of ninety-three. "But he was all the more fair." That's also how Angela Bachmair, one of his former reporters, remembered him in a conversation with me the following year. "I admire him still," she said, adding quickly that "he was not easy as an editor-in-chief."

Römer's greatest legacy and lasting influence is less about his journalism than his devotion to the fate of the region's German Jews during the Nazi regime. He wrote or contributed to dozens of books, some written during his newspaper career, many others after he had "retired." Topics included the expulsion of Jews from Augsburg-Swabia, how Jews sought to defend themselves, Swabian concentration camps, and the fate of Jewish children émigrés. Of particular interest to me is his book, *Schwäbishe Juden*, ("The Jews of Swabia"), which has vital information on M. S. Landauer, his offspring, and the founding of the family's textile business in Hürben. I've also benefited from information about my family in a book he wrote that compiles the postwar newsletters written by Rabbi Ernst Jacob.

Bachmair remembered that Römer started his days at six or seven o'clock in the morning by doing research at the Bavarian archives, then left at ten o'clock to perform his day job as a newspaper editor. Nights were devoted to writing his books. He encouraged the newspaper staff to report on Augsburg's Jewish history, an initiative that drew mixed responses. "Some of my colleagues were not amused about this," said Bachmair, a member of the local remembrance workshop who, like Römer, is not Jewish.

I asked her why Römer was so devoted to learning about the Jewish community and sharing that knowledge with others. "I think it was the same motivation we all have," she said. "We are ashamed of what our parents and grandparents have done." She recalled asking him about his motives when they were together in Piaski, Poland, paying respects at the site of the old Jewish ghetto. He told her that as a boy he saw Nazis force Jews to march through the streets. "He was so shocked, that he never lost this image, this picture in his head. This was his motivation, not to forget, to remember."

George Sturm, among the last Jews to escape Augsburg in November 1939, offers a different explanation. Sturm said Römer told him about another incident from his youth. On November 10, 1938—the morning after *Kristallnacht*—Römer had an appointment with his pediatrician, who had a Jewish parent. "When he and his mother arrived, the doctor had disappeared, never to be seen again," Sturm wrote. Years later, when Römer came to Augsburg as a newspaper editor, he asked at the synagogue "what actually became of the Augsburg Jews since no trace of them was to be found. The Orthodox Russian rabbi there shrugged his shoulder and disclaimed both knowledge and interest, saying only that, 'We are here now.' Since Römer knew of the existence of the Jewish community going back to the 13th century, his curiosity was piqued and he decided to see how far his investigations might take him. Little did he know at that time he would be preoccupied with this effort for the rest of his life."

I can only speculate what I would have learned from talking directly with this dedicated soul. Alas, Römer died just as I was finally becoming aware of the depth of information available about Augsburg's Jewish history and the descendants' group.

Benigna Schönhagen, who led Augsburg's Jewish museum from 2001 until 2018, didn't know any Jews when she was coming of age in Koblenz in the 1950s and '60s. But she did know something of her family's activities during the war. Her father had been a prisoner of war in the U.S. before returning to Germany and becoming a soldier. "It took me much courage to ask him, 'Did you shoot somebody?'" she said, relieved to hear that he did not. Her maternal grandfather was a pastor whose skeptical views about Hitler, he told her, made the Gestapo wary.

Her interest in Jewish history began at the University of Stuttgart while writing her PhD thesis about the history of the nearby small city of Tübingen during the Nazi era. That brought her in touch with descendants of Tübingen's former Jewish community. It stoked Schönhagen's interest in local history, rather than national or global trends, which were a more common focus of German historians in the 1970s, she said. Other historians were more "occupied with the theories of fascism" than investigating what actually occurred in communities. Jewish history was relegated to laymen like Römer and memory activists, like the group that would form in the 1980s in Dorsten.

Historians who did write about the Nazi era tended to devote much more attention to the perpetrators than victims. German historian Nicolas Berg argued that many of the country's most distinguished historians in the early postwar decades purposely played down the Holocaust; some had shown a personal allegiance to the Third Reich.

I asked Schönhagen why she thought Germans had turned on their Jewish neighbors, even in modest-sized places where they surely would have known one another for many years, like Türbingen, Dorsten, or Lembeck. She paused at length, then said, "There are many reasons. There's a Christian tradition where Jews were the bad boys, they made Jesus Christ be put on the cross. I think a big reason is the economic situation after the First World War and the disappointment about not having victory and being the defeated. The bad economic situation where all the people were out of work. Not being used to use your brain. Not being used to being informed."

After the war, the most common refrain about the fate of their countrymen, she said, was "the Jews vanished. Eyewitnesses said, 'Yes, we had Jews in our classroom. But then one day, they were not there.' And nobody knew exactly where they were brought." And there wasn't much interest in talking about it years later.

Schönhagen's pursuits received a similar response from her friends as Elisabeth's did among hers. Common reactions, Schönhagen said, were, "Hmmm, maybe it's important but it's so depressing. Do you have to read all these cruel things? Won't you stop it?" After she obtained her doctorate in 1991 and created a public exhibition about Türbingen under National Socialism, one of her close colleagues told her, "Now stop. It's enough."

She was also admonished by those who were alive during the Nazis' reign and told her, "You can't see how it was because you didn't live at that time." She said, "That's typical. It took me much courage to overcome this." She said her response was firm: "No, I *want* to know it and I have a *right* to know it."

Schönhagen was self-conscious when starting her new job in Augsburg. She had a strong background in Jewish history, which she had studied extensively. But she was a non-Jew leading a Jewish museum. "For me it was helpful and encouraging that the Jewish colleagues which I met said, 'No, that's not important. What's important is that you want to know what happened.'" She also wanted to resist any temptation to over-correct from the country's long-standing neglect of the Holocaust and "to compress all Jewish history in Germany into the Nazi times."

Schönhagen said the museum had an impressive collection of Jewish ritual objects from Augsburg and nearby towns when she arrived. Many were made by renowned local silversmiths. They were supplemented by items on loan from private collectors and the Bavarian National Museum, one of the first national museums to set up a Judaica collection at the end of the nineteenth century.

What the museum didn't have, Schönhagen realized, was a way to tell the story of the local Jewish *people*. By 2006 the museum opened a permanent exhibit documenting the Jewish community in Augsburg and vicinity. A number of items were bequeathed or donated by Jewish descendants from the region.

The Jewish museum in Dorsten started more modestly than the one in Augsburg and without much Jewish input. The number of Jews in Dorsten proper began dwindling in the late nineteenth century and continued into the early twentieth century, until the last twelve Jews were deported to the Riga ghetto in January 1942. Hardly any Jews have lived there since, though some live in the wider region. The house that the Jewish community had purchased for worship services in 1869 was hit by a bomb on March 23, 1945, and destroyed.

So while Dorsten's remembrance workshop was enthusiastic about restoring some of the local Jewish history, there was no synagogue to build from and most of the nearby Jewish cemeteries had been destroyed. There were also few Jews to help with their tasks. In 1987, after memory activists began discovering historical documents, conducting interviews, and writing books, its members decided to build a documentation center. Eventually, they opted to build a full-fledged Jewish museum instead. Its doors opened to the public five years later. "We could hardly believe we'd really done it," recalled one of the founders, Anke Klapsing-Reich. "Before the museum was opened, we were standing by the display cabinets polishing trophies when Christel Winkel asked: 'Anke, can you pinch me, I think I'm having a dream, are we really opening a proper museum?'"

They really were. But many of them were self-conscious about their roles. As Gruber put it, the museum "baldly declared that its program of lectures, films, seminars, and other events on Jewish topics was 'conceived by non-Jews for non-Jews.'" I asked Reichling about that declaration from the museum's first years. "This was meant as an expression of modesty," he said, and was never meant to be read as one of exclusion. "We know that we aren't Jews. We know that we have a different perspective."

The museum has relied heavily on volunteers. It didn't have a paid, full-time director until Kathrin Pieren was hired in 2021. Pieren, originally from Switzerland, is also not Jewish. She remembers a washing machine repairman coming to her home shortly after she moved to Dorsten and asking about her occupation. When she told him she was the new director of the Jewish museum, "he was perplexed that you could do that sort of thing as a job." But he did know about the museum, having attended the grammar school headed by Sister Johanna Eichmann, the museum's first volunteer director.

Pieren emphasized that Dorsten's is not a Holocaust museum. "We're very much of the opinion it shouldn't be reduced to that," she told Mollie and me over coffee in the museum foyer, next to its bookshop. Visitors should know about regional Jewish history before 1933, she said, and that Jews have lived in Germany and elsewhere since the war ended. And while anti-Semitism is an important topic in Jewish museums across Germany, she added, the subject of hatred against Jews shouldn't be relegated to the museum or even thought of as "a Jewish problem." More broadly, the museum's goals include "how we live in a diverse society. We are diverse and we're becoming more diverse."

Still, she said, the museum has a unique role in educating people about the Holocaust. "It is important to remind people, of course, of the victims, but also of the deeds of perpetrators and bystanders on our own doorstep. And that there is a lot that German non-Jews can still do today to fill in the gaps in our knowledge as grandparents have died and left behind documents and memorabilia. Furthermore, I think we should remind people in the present about potential dangers in current thought and behavior. The conspiracy theories that have bubbled up recently are really a prime example of how much continuity there is in certain ways of antisemitic thinking."

But the museum can only work with those who are open to learning. "The people we would like to reach we cannot reach," she acknowledged. "They are not coming." One way the Augsburg museum tries to address this is with a mini exhibition on a cargo bike that goes to public places.

A statement of principles on the Dorsten museum's website may strike you, initially, as a boilerplate summary of pluralism. That's what I first thought. But consider the journey it took to get there. This kind of declaration by a German institution would have been unheard of even forty years after the country was defeated in World War II. The long history of Jews in the region had been suppressed for decades, as was the complicity of local townsfolk in persecuting and murdering Jews. The expression of personal responsibility that extends for generations may resonate with you, as it did to me, as may the call for human rights.

Here is what it says:

> Jews lived in Westphalia for centuries and took part in social life in a variety of professions and functions. They established Jewish communities and schools, built synagogues and were involved in everyday life. Their life among the large majority of Christians saw phases of tolerance, persecution and emancipation.
>
> The Nazi dictators persecuted and murdered German Jews and people of Jewish descent. The persecution and deportation of the Jews could be seen in the villages and towns. Only a very small number of non-Jewish people tried to help, provided hiding places or helped them to escape.

> Those of us who lived through that period or are the descendants of those whose actions or inaction helped to wipe out Jews and Jewish traditions feel a sense of responsibility to find and maintain traces of Jewish life in Westphalia. We want to contribute to understanding Judaism, its religion and culture.
>
> The history of the discrimination, persecution and murder but also the emancipation and positive life together as well as the development of new Jewish communities in Westphalia are an impulse for us to stand up for human rights and democratic participation of all people in the everyday life of our society irrespective or religion or ethnicity.

The museum is a generally accepted institution in Dorsten. It opened a greatly expanded building in 2001, with financial support from the state of North Rhine-Westphalia and town of Dorsten. But it is not universally popular. A manned police car stood guard just outside of the museum when we were there in 2022. Its regular presence serves as a reminder that hatred against Jews persists even when Jews are barely present. It doesn't seem to keep visitors from attending. Many of them come as part of a school group, usually in conjunction with studies about religion. Groups of adults visit, too.

A permanent exhibit on the upper floor is divided into several sections. One focuses on the Torah, synagogues, and Jewish community. Another shows Jewish life in relationship to the Torah and how it evolved over the years. A third is devoted to the *Shoah* and postwar German Jewish communities. There's also an exhibit on regional Jewish history and migration.

We observed colorful displays on Jewish holidays, how to braid challah, what it means to be kosher, and what a bar or bat mitzvah is like, with the companion expectation that the young person perform an action consistent with *tikkun olam*, a Hebrew expression meaning "repair the world." We did a double take when we saw the example they displayed of a bat mitzvah was Emily's, obviously Elisabeth's doing. Nearby, encased in glass, was a ritual spice box and porcelain place setting that Tante Malli and Uncle Franz had kept in the suitcase they buried just before they fled Düsseldorf.

Jeffrey Katz aus den USA erforscht Spuren seiner jüdischen Familie

DORSTEN, LEMBECK. Jeffrey Katz ist aus der Nähe von Washington nach Dorsten gekommen, um hier die Geschichte seiner jüdischen Vorfahren zu erforschen. Spuren führen vor allem nach Lembeck.

Von Petra Berkenbusch

Wenn seine Eltern vor ihren Kindern etwas verheimlichen wollten, sprachen sie Deutsch miteinander. Jeffrey Katz war lange nicht bewusst, dass er deutsche Wurzeln hat. Seine Eltern haben nicht darüber gesprochen. „Ich kannte die Geschichte meines Vaters nicht, bis ich etwa 20 Jahre alt war", berichtet Jeffrey Katz. Dass seine tiefen Wurzeln nicht in seinem amerikanischen Geburtsland lagen, habe er jedoch irgendwie gespürt. „Da war so eine Ambivalenz."

Jeffrey Katz ist Journalist geworden. Etwas anderes sei für ihn nie in Frage gekommen, erzählt er. Inzwischen ist er pensioniert und arbeitet ausschließlich an seinem Herzensprojekt: ein Buch über die Geschichte seiner Familie. „A home I never knew" ist der Arbeitstitel. Die Aufarbeitung des

Jeffrey und Mollie Katz vor dem Foto der Bat-Mizwa ihrer Tochter Emily im Jüdischen Museum. FOOTS BERKENBUSCH

Mollie and I posing in front of the bat mitzvah display at the Jewish museum in Dorsten. The story appeared in the Dorstener Zeitung newspaper. (Photo credit: Dorstener Zeitung/Petra Berkenbusch)

The photo of us aside, what you generally can't see in one of these Jewish museums are their connections to the families who once lived in the area.

An important aspect connecting the museum in Augsburg to its past is the *Lebenslinien* (Lifelines) program. This eyewitness project initiated by Schönhagen has invited a former Jewish resident (or, in recent years, a descendant) to Augsburg during annual commemorations of *Kristallnacht* since 2002. Visitors share their family histories in public gatherings and at discussions and workshops with high school students. The initial presentations were also collected into nine books. Schönhagen not only did much of the research, but she also obtained the funding for these events, too.

"They were very old," Schönhagen said of the survivors, "but they came, not for the first time, but for the first time told their story for a big audience." The guests stayed for a week, spoke before an audience of about two hundred people in a small theater and talked with students at three-to-four-hour gatherings. The visits made an impression not only on the people of Augsburg, she recalled, but "it was touching to see what it meant to the survivors."

One initiative led to another. The *Lebenslinien* program inspired Schönhagen to organize a reunion in 2017 to mark the centennial of the synagogue on Halderstraße. And that reunion spawned long-term efforts to connect the Jewish descendants from around the world with one another and with Germany today.

Chapter 19

DESCENDANTS DILEMMA

"My German citizenship represents a reckoning with injustice."

The most impressive sounds at an event celebrating the centennial of Augsburg's central synagogue probably weren't any of the words spoken from the pulpit. What resonated most in that stately, sacred sanctuary were the ancient Hebrew songs, resolutely sung, backed by a full orchestra. Music echoed throughout a building that had barely survived the devastating *Kristallnacht* fire, its interior a smoldering rubble.

And the most notable people in the audience that evening in 2017 weren't any of the dignitaries, though they included the president of the Federal Republic of Germany. They were the ninety-nine descendants of Augsburg's Jewish community. They came from around the globe for an emotional reunion in a city where their only surviving relatives were those who endured terrible hardships in camps, were aided by being married to a non-Jew, or escaped.

It was later left to Schönhagen, who, remember, is not Jewish, to remark on the poignancy of one of the biblical quotes tucked inside the dome. The words surely conveyed the congregation's optimism when the doors first opened in 1917 and reflected a tragic irony soon thereafter. The passage from Genesis 22:17 recalls God's promise to Abraham, Isaac, and Jacob to "make your descendants as numerous as the stars of heaven and the sands on the seashore."

That didn't age well, as Augsburg's Jewish population was decimated a little more than twenty years after the synagogue opened. Renewed optimism was still in short supply when the war ended, leaving only remnants of Augsburg's once proud Jewish community in its wake, the lucky ones having found safe harbor around the globe. The idea that their descendants would visit the land of their ancestors must have seemed far-fetched. Why set foot on soil that their loved ones felt blessed to leave?

And yet here they were, just short of one hundred strong, eager to embrace their ancestral roots—some for the first time, some with their own children in tow. They met with members of other families who had survived as well as those in the local remembrance movement who had worked to restore the Jewish history there. They visited places that were once important to their relatives and attended services in the glorious sanctuary of the synagogue, joined by members of the city's current Jewish congregation.

This chapter takes a closer look at the connections between descendants of Holocaust survivors and the places their family once called home. I believe Germany's remembrance movement is stronger when it works in conjunction with us, though there are plenty of challenges in trying to do so. Quite a few descendants want nothing to do with the country that persecuted their ancestors, carrying with them the understandable anger of preceding generations. Others simply aren't interested in their family history, content to confine themselves to the here and now, as I was for the first half of my life. Even those of us who do want to participate pose a challenge because we're scattered around the world.

I would have liked to have been there for the 2017 reunion in Augsburg. But I didn't know anything about it beforehand, nor did I know other descendants from the city's Jewish community. It was only while working on this book five years later and searching the web that I stumbled onto something called the Descendants of the Jewish Community of Augsburg. I've since spoken to or corresponded with several participants about it.

The historic nature of the gathering was noted by German President Frank-Walter Steinmeier. He recalled the words of Walter Jacob, the son of

Augsburg's last rabbi before the war, who connected Augsburg's Jewish diaspora in the 1940s with his newsletters. When the synagogue reopened in 1985, Steinmeier told them, Walter Jacob said that Jews had once felt "completely at home" in Germany before the Nazi era.

Steinmeier said he was heartened that Augsburg's Jewish community had been revitalized by an influx from the former Soviet Union. But he warned "antisemitism destroys home for all of us" and lamented that synagogues needed to be guarded by police. "The fight against antisemitism is not just a question of solidarity," he said. "It is a fight for everything that holds us together as a society. Or, in other words: Only when Jews are completely at home in Germany is this Federal Republic completely at home."

A few elderly survivors were also present at the reunion, underscoring the bittersweet nature of this particular homecoming. They brought reminders of Germany's hate as well as its kindness. A year after my mother left her family's Augsburg apartment in 1938, Henry Stern and his parents left theirs, one block away at 7 Mozartstraße. (His brother had already fled to London via the *Kindertransport.*) Stern remembered the day vividly, including when neighbors said they were sorry the family was leaving because, "You were the *good* Jews and we sincerely wish you could remain here." Stern then recalled, "I noticed my father's hand started to tremble as he asked them, 'Tell me who were the *bad* Jews in Augsburg?' There was no answer, except the words, 'You know what we mean!'"

A video taken during the 2017 reunion shows Stern, elderly now and a little stooped, staring at the apartment building and saying, "It was a hard time and a good time." He reminisced about another neighbor who said farewell to his family just before they left, a priest from the St. Ulrich parish, where Stern had attended elementary school. The priest was a friend with whom Stern had exchanged Passover *matzahs* and chocolate Easter bunnies in spring.

Stern said he was standing with his parents when he saw the priest for the last time. "And he came out, and at this spot," he said, pointing to where several potted plants now sat along the walkway, "all of a sudden he raised his hands." Stern raised his arms to mimic the gesture, then paused. His arms still outstretched, he began speaking again, this time choking on the words: "And he blessed us."

The priest was reciting the words of the ancient Hebrew benediction: "May the Lord bless you and keep you. May the Lord make His face shine upon you and be gracious to you. May the Lord lift up His countenance upon you, and grant you peace." And now Stern started to full-on cry, thinking back on that tender moment many decades earlier. Still, he was determined to finish the story and describe how he felt. He repeated the words, "He blessed us." There was another long pause as Stern collected his emotions, stared at the ground, and considered that they actually did leave Germany safely, first to Great Britain, then the U.S. "You know what? We were blessed." He later wrote that the priest's blessings "remained with us throughout many years in our new lands and during the difficult periods that all immigrants experience."

Memories came flooding back to Stern throughout the visit. On the final day of the reunion, an older woman called out to him, "Herr Stern, Herr Stern . . . I have all your toys." She was offering to return the toys his father gave to her as they were about to emigrate to London.

This was not the first time Augsburg's Jewish descendants bonded with local residents over a possession given to them decades ago for safekeeping. Diane Castiglione tells the story of traveling to Augsburg in 2001 with her parents, brother, and son for the dedication of a Holocaust memorial. One day a German woman named Helma Landherr came to their hotel lobby and introduced herself by saying her family had been neighbors of the Einsteins, Castiglione's mother's family. And she had something she wanted to return.

Landherr explained that her mother owned a delicatessen where Castiglione's grandmother shopped. Food was being rationed, and a line formed to get fresh herring. Castiglione's grandmother patiently waited in line, long enough to get the last fish. Other customers complained that a Jew didn't deserve such a precious commodity and reported Landherr's mother to authorities. But instead of refusing to serve Castiglione's grandmother, the delicatessen owner arranged to surreptitiously leave the rations at a side door, to be retrieved without drawing attention.

Diane Castiglione told me her grandmother deeply appreciated the gesture. When her grandmother was about to be deported to Auschwitz in 1943, she gave a porcelain plate to Helma Landherr's mother "as a token of gratitude for her help and kindness." Castiglione said, "Helma's mother never used the plate but took good care of it. Her mother told Helma that she should give it back if someone from the Einstein family ever returned to Augsburg. That's what brought Helma to our hotel. Somehow, she had figured out that my mother was in Augsburg for the memorial dedication and she kept her promise to her mother.

"Needless to say, we were all stunned. My mother had known nothing about this story as she had already fled Germany when those events happened. The plate became a treasured possession that she hung on her wall. It is a reminder not only of her mother but also of the impact that one decision can have—in this case, the decision one woman made to help another woman and her family."

Beyond individual actions to return toys or a plate to Jewish families who left because of persecution, the German government now offers to return an arguably more valuable possession to descendants—German citizenship. As of 2021, a new law made citizenship even easier to claim for descendants of German Jews, Roma and Sinti, and political opponents whom the Nazis had stripped of citizenship or prevented them from acquiring it. The law was supported in the federal parliament by all political parties except the far-right Alternative for Germany.

Also in 2021, the Augsburg descendants group surveyed its members to see who had obtained German citizenship or were interested in doing so. An overwhelming majority of respondents said they were at least interested. A number cited practical considerations as the overriding issue, saying a German passport simplified their travel or working arrangements in Europe. This was especially true for citizens of the United Kingdom after it withdrew from the European Union in 2020, complicating their interactions with European countries.

Some descendants said their interest in German citizenship was more symbolic, enabling them to reclaim a small part of what had been wrested from their family. "My German citizenship represents a reckoning with injustice, a sense of loss, hope and responsibility all bundled in one document," one person wrote in explaining her dual citizenship. "This was a meaningful way to help right a terrible wrong done to my ancestors," said another. "I believed it was important to 'undo' what the National Socialists attempted," added someone else.

Others said they were motivated more by the current political climate in the United States. They feared rising nationalism, as represented by the Trump presidency and his most extreme supporters. They welcomed having a hedge from Germany, of all places. "The irony did not escape me," said one.

"I never thought I would want to repatriate," wrote another, "but when things started to turn toward fascism in the United States after the 2016 election, I decided it was time to look into it. My ancestors were not able to leave Germany when Hitler was in power because they had no place to go. I wasn't going to let that happen again," this person said, expressing relief they now had a "back-up plan."

One of those who claimed her German citizenship years earlier was Bettina Kaplan, whose mother had a similar background as mine—a Landauer descendant, born in January 1933, who fled Augsburg with her family at age five. Betsy Kaplan, her twin sister, and their parents emigrated to England for a year, before a monthlong voyage took them to Los Angeles. Bettina Kaplan said her family never dwelled on their need to flee Germany and that some relatives were murdered there. But she did remember Betsy saying that her parents pleaded unsuccessfully for her grandparents to join them and that her mother later went into her bedroom crying after receiving a letter from the Red Cross in 1941 saying they had been murdered.

Even so, Bettina Kaplan said her parents didn't bear any grudges against Germany and didn't object when, after living in Europe for a time and visiting Augsburg occasionally, she and her brother applied for German citizenship. Which is not to say the family history was forgotten. When her brother was asked during the citizenship application process whether he spoke German, he replied, "Well if they hadn't kicked my parents out, I would have."

A member of another branch of the extended Landauer family who does speak German is Jonah Landor-Yamagata. Jonah lived in Germany from 2012 to 2018, when he completed a master's degree in urban ecosystem sciences in Berlin. One of the endearing images from the 2017 reunion is his then-two-year-old son, Ansel, playing in the courtyard of the synagogue designed by Jonah's great-grandfather, Fritz Landauer.

Jonah and I spoke by phone in 2023, when he was back in Berlin for a month while his wife was on a teaching assignment. I asked if it felt a little like being home again. "I wouldn't say immediately, because of our family history, that it feels like reclaiming a home," he said.

Then he thought about it a bit more as he looked outside a window to the apartment building where they had lived a decade earlier. He noted that their son was born in Germany, the country where many of his ancestors had also been born. "That kind of history does have weight and it kind of figures into, it complicates and deepens the experience of being here, it makes it more meaningful, more familiar," Landor-Yamagata said. "I've gone into buildings that my great-grandfather designed. There's a feeling I belong here, there's a reclaiming in a sense."

Like many others, he thought about getting German citizenship, acknowledging that the rise of American nationalism under Trump and the practical advantages of traveling with a German passport were incentives to do so. Still, he added, he wasn't ready to be considered a citizen of another country "that doesn't really reflect me or my experiences."

I've thought about pursuing German citizenship for myself and my children, mainly for symbolic reasons, to officially reclaim my family's connection to Germany. There are a few practical considerations, too, I suppose. It might help to have a German passport when traveling in Europe. But as I write this, I've done nothing except talk about it; the application remains in a folder in my computer hard drive. Being a German citizen seems like a big step and probably an unnecessary one. My lack of proficiency in foreign languages is but one of many reasons why it's hard to imagine actually living there. And as Landor-Yamagata said, the weight of history looms large.

To be sure, some descendants of Augsburg's Jewish community have no interest in pursuing German citizenship, and no one was less interested than my mom. Her affiliation with Germany ended when she felt lucky to flee the country with her family at age five, and she couldn't imagine turning back. She was appalled when I told her I would even consider becoming a German citizen. Several of those who responded to the Augsburg descendants group survey felt the same. "I don't want to be German," said one. "I am an Israeli citizen. I have no need to be a citizen elsewhere," said another.

A number of those who weren't interested made it clear that it was less about their animosity to present-day Germany than their allegiance to the U.S. Castiglione has known about her family's history—her parents' escape from Germany and that some relatives were either murdered there or committed suicide to avoid being transported to a concentration camp—for as long as she can remember. She appreciates her connections to contemporary Germans but draws the line at becoming a German citizen.

"Having lost their German citizenship, my parents became very proud American citizens and raised my brother and me to share that pride," she told me. "I am therefore loyal to the country that took in my family and gave them the opportunity to establish roots, raise a family and build good lives for themselves. I have nothing against Germany or its people today. I enjoy my visits there and I value the relationships I've developed. German culture and tradition have indelibly influenced me. However, I am first and foremost an American citizen. Germany lost its chance to get my loyalty when it stripped my family of its rights and citizenship."

Contemporary connections are delicate between Holocaust survivors and descendants and the country where our families once lived. They're often nuanced, more subtle than broad-brushed generalizations allow. Even those who, like me, have achieved some semblance of a reconciliation, retain a certain level of wariness that our goodwill not be exaggerated for broader purposes.

Lawrence Kahn felt this acutely after his cousin Eva Eckert died in 2022 at the age of ninety-five. Eckert was born in Augsburg to a Jewish mother and a Protestant father who died before her birth. Being only half-Jewish helped Eckert survive the Holocaust while remaining in Europe, though she was expelled from school and ordered to perform forced labor. Her mother was taken to the Theresienstadt concentration camp in Czechoslovakia, where she emerged after the war, broken but alive. Eva and her brother, Wolf, survived a series of travails, including the bombing of their Augsburg apartment, though Wolf succumbed to cancer in 1947.

Eva and her mother emigrated to New York in 1948, where they reunited with several members of their extended family and became U.S. citizens in 1954. Eva became a librarian, earning a master's degree and embracing life in her adopted country. "I am an American," she said. "For 55 years or longer I only think in English and hardly speak German. Augsburg was for me the city where I grew up. New York was my home."

Kahn and his wife, Beth Handler, were frequent companions of his cousin, who never married. Kahn said his own father, who fled his native Augsburg in 1938, never imparted an anger toward Germany. "There was no hiding what had happened" in Germany, Kahn told me. "But they had faith in the ability of people to change." As did Kahn, who was impressed that organizers of the 2017 reunion were not the descendants of Augsburg's Jewish community themselves but were part of the Jewish museum and local remembrance movement. "Clearly they have made a tremendous effort to remember what Germany had done to the Jews, to try to remedy it, recognizing that it could never be remedied in a complete sense."

What troubled Kahn several years later was how Eckert's wishes for her final resting place were reflected in a newspaper story in the *Augsburger Allgemeine* after she died in 2022. Eckert had asked that her remains be cremated and the urn containing her ashes be interred at the Jewish cemetery in Augsburg, near the graves of her parents and brother.

Her posthumous homecoming was an irresistible hook for the newspaper. "American Holocaust Survivor Finds Final Peace in Augsburg," was the headline over a story about her life, the day she was to be interred. "Only after her death did the daughter of an Augsburg factory owner return to her old home," it said. The story relegated to "assumption" and "conjecture" that she wanted to be reunited with her family, saying instead her primary motive was returning to the city of Augsburg. This explanation relied on a relative in Berlin, who said Eckert's fond childhood memories of Augsburg prompted her return.

Kahn and Handler say that notion is absurd. They said Eckert never visited Augsburg after she emigrated in 1948. The city isn't what drew her back at the end, they said; it was being at rest next to her parents and brother. It would have been, as Handler said, "so not Eva not to be buried with her family."

This might seem like a small quibble. But for Kahn, it's a disturbing sign of Germany's overeagerness to burnish its reputation by showing just how willing Jews are to applaud the country for its efforts at reconciliation. The same newspaper took it a step further the next day, reporting that a growing number of Jewish descendants were visiting Augsburg to trace their roots. It attributed this uptick in interest to the city's good work at memorializing its Jewish heritage. This was a self-congratulatory story. It relied solely on participants in the city's remembrance movement to explain the motives of Jewish descendants and praise Augsburg's efforts. The views of the Jewish descendants themselves were deemed not necessary to consider why they acted or what they thought.

This tendency of Germans to pride themselves for honoring the Jewish past has led critics to consider their actions performative, assigning roles in what's been termed the "theater of memory." It's an important topic to consider in any assessment of the memory movement.

Chapter 20

UNFINISHED BUSINESS

"Each generation has to find its own way through history."

It took Germany four decades to take responsibility for the evils of the Nazi era and another four decades to deal with the consequences of its actions. But the ripple effect from one terrible day in Israel made it clear Germany's attempts at reconciliation were unfinished.

It began with Hamas' barbaric murders of some 1,200 people in Israel on October 7, 2023, and their capture of about 240 hostages. Israel responded to this terrorist act by invading Gaza, hoping to eradicate Hamas. But that also inflicted further misery and death on Palestinians, stirring widespread condemnation of Israel, built upon its oppressive policies toward the more than two million Palestinians in Gaza. It didn't take long for that to seed latent anti-Zionist, anti-Israel, and anti-Semitic views worldwide.

Jews were widely seen by others as supportive and even responsible for Israeli actions, though many Jews increasingly objected to them. In 2025, as death and destruction mounted in Gaza, so, too, did Jewish criticism of Israel. By March 2025, fully half of all Jewish American adults said they lacked confidence in Israeli leadership. In July of that year, as starvation in Gaza became widespread, the largest Jewish movement in North America gave voice to many of us. "No one should spend the bulk of their time arguing technical definitions between starvation and pervasive hunger. The situation is dire, and it is deadly," said the Union for Reform Judaism. It dismissed arguments that "the Jewish State is not also culpable in this human disaster," adding: "denying basic humanitarian aid crosses a moral line. Blocking food, water, medicine, and power—especially for children—is indefensible."

But differences of opinion among Jews regarding Israel were largely lost in the global rise in anti-Semitism. Israel was increasingly seen as a pariah on the world stage and individual Jews were made to feel the blame, regardless of their personal views or connection to Israel.

Germany was no different. Perhaps it could have been if the remembrance movement had fully changed hearts and minds. Maybe then Germans could have separated their feelings about Israel from their thoughts about Jews. But that isn't what happened. Whatever goodwill the German public had built over the years with Jewish communities now seemed especially fragile.

Within weeks of Hamas' attacks, hatred of Jews was heard in chants at large pro-Palestinian and anti-Israeli rallies, felt as assailants hurled Molotov cocktails at a Berlin synagogue (causing only a small fire), and seen as the Star of David was painted on some buildings where Jews lived.

German officials responded by remaining steadfast in their support of Israel and condemned anti-Semitism. Large marches were held opposing anti-Semitism. But the chorus of voices condemning Israel was rising. Much of it, as in the U.S., was centered on college campuses and came now from the left, their anger toward Israel tending to blur into anger toward Jews. When protesters were banned from spray painting Stars of David on buildings and Jewish-owned homes, pro-Palestinian activists sprayed inverted red triangles, a symbol used by Hamas.

The speed with which hatred toward Jews accelerated in Germany forced those in the remembrance movement to reconsider what they had actually accomplished. "All this really deep and honest 'learning from the past' has been and still is an 'elite project' shaping many intellectuals, the media, the churches, the schools, the active citizenship—but not the majority," Norbert Reichling lamented in an email. Carmen Reichert disagreed with that interpretation. "Schools represent all parts of society, as well as media and church," she told me. "We have volunteers, especially in the countryside, with no academic background, that keep memory sites or cemeteries clean, give guided tours or keep keys of graveyards, etc. And we see universities at the top of anti-Israeli and anti-Jewish agitations."

But where hatred of Jews once focused primarily on the Nazi era, now attention turned to the present day. "Unfortunately, anti-Semitism has grown rapidly here," Alexander Mazo wrote to me in early 2024. "This can be seen from the fact that here in Augsburg there are many 'pro-Palestinian demonstrations' that loudly advocate for a 'free Palestine and the destruction of the state of Israel.' The two Israeli flags that hung on the town hall square in Augsburg were also torn down. Of course, this has increased the police presence in the city."

Mazo attributed the surge in hatred against Jews, in part, to the growth in Muslim immigration, as well as the lack of effective measures against racism and anti-Semitism and Germany's unwillingness to mobilize against it. "It is still the case that textbooks in schools still inadequately cover the Holocaust," he said. "Unfortunately, I have to say that the 'Nazi propaganda' of the time worked better than today's educational attempts."

Security is a major concern at Jewish-related sites. The 24/7 police presence outside the Dorsten museum can't prevent tensions inside. In January 2024, three months after the Israel–Gaza war began, words expressing hatred toward Jews were scrawled in pen on an inside staircase.

It's clear that absorbing German Jewish history has become a more complicated experience for students visiting the museum. As part of their visit, pupils are asked to write on paper what they most associate with Jews. Their responses are handled anonymously. Before the war, they typically mentioned a *kippah*, kosher food, Israel, and Hebrew, Pieren told me. Once the war began, there were more references to calling Israelis child killers and comparing Israeli Prime Minister Benjamin Netanyahu to Hitler.

It's a sign that students are processing a mix of conflicting messages and information that defies a tidy narrative. Emotions are running high, Pieren said. "People have a need to talk."

But conversations about sensitive matters lead to uncertain outcomes. Wüstenberg detected a new reluctance among German memory activists to engage those who have doubts about the Holocaust's relevance to their lives. She sounded troubled that a remembrance movement built on a democratic approach to the past had become overly rigid. "It became a doctrine, in a way, that is imposed on others who are trying to work through their other histories—the GDR past, the colonial past—and whatever you do, the Holocaust has to be the primary mover of German memory culture." She added, "You can't mandate when it's relevant, or to whom."

For years, a steady rise of German anti-Semitism had been fed by the growth of a far-right extremist party. This alarmed Max Czollek, a provocative Jewish writer who has long worried that Germany's remembrance movement had evolved into a kind of performance art, more theater than a sincere accounting of the country's continuing dalliance with its dark side.

Czollek identifies as being Jewish, tracing the heritage to his paternal grandfather. Born in Berlin in 1987, he is especially disenchanted with his parents' generation. He said they duped themselves and their children that Germany had successfully come to terms with its Nazi past. He tweeted that this was "gaslighting" and "the great lie of a generation that celebrated itself for something that is now proving to be false." Tellingly, he wrote that three weeks *before* Hamas' attack on Israel, prompted by the growth of the far-right.

I hadn't confronted much criticism of the remembrance movement when I first began taking stock of my German heritage. Most of the reporting and writing was laudatory, holding up Germany as a model for the world. And most of my interactions with contemporary Germans were with those at the forefront of the memory movement in the places where my family used to live.

They weren't interested in accolades. I asked many of the Germans I met whether their country ought to be held up as a role model for reckoning with an ugly past. None of them said it should. Benigna Schönhagen responded with a question of her own. She asked, "Did we, for this process, learn from another nation or did we have to do it ourselves? And that's the same for the Americans. Even because the problem is not the same."

My personal interactions and research have convinced me that these memory activists wanted primarily to set the record straight and, secondarily, to make amends. I will always be grateful for their commitment to addressing the horrors of the Nazi era against the Jewish people in general and my family, in particular. My goodwill toward them is unshakeable.

There's no doubt that locally based, citizen-led remembrance movements slowly forced many Germans to take responsibility for crimes committed in the Nazi era. The country boasts of new Jewish museums, Holocaust memorials, restored synagogues, and educational lessons designed to celebrate its Jewish heritage and teach tolerance. Germany has also been one of Israel's most steadfast allies and paid for the cost of resettling 500,000 Jews in Israel after the war. Its commitment to Israel's existence and security was described as its "*Staatsräson*," or "reason of state," by then-Chancellor Angela Merkel, in an address to the Israeli parliament in 2008.

German reparations in the form of payments to Israel and Jewish Holocaust victims is one of the most remarkable aspects of the postwar reconciliation, benefitting Germany as well as the recipients. Academic researchers have described it as "an unprecedented landmark." Previous negotiations over postwar reparations, when they occurred, centered on the losing side compensating its opponent for damages during a war. Reparations went well beyond that in this case, encompassing the Holocaust and other actions during the Nazi era. Also, the agreement was negotiated by representatives of two countries, West Germany and Israel, that didn't even exist when the atrocities occurred.

Reparations were strongly supported by Konrad Adenauer, the first chancellor of the newly formed Federal Republic of Germany. He faced opposition from German citizens who also considered themselves victims of war and thought they were more deserving of aid, as well as government officials who worried about West Germany's battered finances. Adenauer eventually prevailed. The enactment of the so-called Luxembourg Agreement in West Germany in 1952 was attributed not only to moral arguments—that it was the right thing do—but for pragmatic reasons. Reparations were considered important to rehabilitating the country on the world stage and rebuilding its economy, integrating it with the West.

My dad was reluctant for several decades to accept all the benefits he was eligible for. He initially declined Elisabeth's offer in 1986 to help obtain more assistance from Germany than he had already received. "I can only tell you that, as a total sum, my share for my family was not that significant!" he wrote to her. "I received a lump sum for the loss of my education and a smaller amount for the death of my family—no pension or significant sum. For me, the act itself (a form of reparation) was more important than the amount!" However, he later relented and received what appeared to be a very modest pension from Germany.

By now, Germany has paid more than $90 billion in restitution and compensation to Holocaust victims and their descendants, including money for pensions, home health care services, food and medicine. The country has also returned to the rightful heirs about sixteen thousand valuable artifacts that were looted by Nazis, though there's no reliable estimate of how much former Jewish land and property has not been compensated or returned. "Thousands more pieces of looted art are still missing worldwide," according to a 2024 report by the U.S. State Department.

Germany itself benefitted from these initiatives, viewed as a moral leader for reckoning with an ugly past. The writer Ta-Nehisi Coates prominently cited West Germany's experience as "instructive" for America in a 2014 essay for *The Atlantic* magazine. "Reparations could not make up for the murder perpetrated by the Nazis," he wrote. "But they did launch Germany's reckoning with itself, and perhaps provided a road map for how a great civilization might make itself worthy of the name."

Others have extolled Germany's postwar virtues in recent books called *Learning from the Germans* and prominent magazine stories with subtitles like "America still can't figure out how to memorialize the sins of our history. What can we learn from Germany?" We also got newspaper essays titled "Germany faced its horrible past. Can we do the same?" and web essays called "'Germans & Jews' and Americans: What can we learn from Germany's reckoning with history?"

All this calls for a close analysis of Germany's attempts at reconciliation, recognizing that those of us who try to do so are influenced by contemporary circumstances.

I've already tried to point out some of the limitations of the movement, such as Germany's overeagerness to take credit for its warm relationship with descendants of its Jewish communities; the awkwardness of non-Jews teaching Jewish history, culture, and religion to other non-Jews; and the recurring presence of anti-Semitism and violence against Jews and other minorities. These limitations led to an important corrective inside of Germany to its exalted standing on the world stage. Until recently, the criticisms received far less publicity outside of its borders compared to the cheers for its reconciliation efforts. But they're worth considering in any serious appraisal of the postwar memory movement.

The critiques have found expression in the word *Gedächtnistheater*, usually translated in English as the "theater of memory." The German word for theater in this sense does not mean a form of entertainment. It has instead "an ironic connotation that something is insincere, untrue, fake, and deceiving," wrote Chunjie Zhang, an associate professor of German at the University of California at Davis.

The term was coined in 1996 by German-Canadian sociologist Y. Michal Bodemann in a book whose title translates to "Memory Theater: The Jewish Community and Its German Invention." It asserts that Germany's recriminations have less to do with making amends to the victims of genocide (and their descendants) than with redeeming the perpetrators (and their descendants). The country is interested in the Jews of today mainly to help differentiate it from the Nazi era, the thinking goes, to confirm that the Germans are good again. "Jews are ascribed roles that help stabilize the new German self-image: the forgiving Jewish victims on one side and the reformed German perpetrators on the other," Czollek wrote.

Czollek has been described as many things, including poet, author, playwright, publicist, and comic. Doubtless, few political scientists with a doctorate have done anything like posing as the "Bear Jew," the character in the 2009 movie *Inglorious Basterds* who took a baseball bat to the heads of German soldiers in Nazi-occupied France.

Czollek described his precepts in the book *Desintegriert euch!* published in German in 2018 and in an English translation in 2023 as *De-Integrate! A Jewish Survival Guide for the 21st Century*, as well as in many subsequent writings. He writes that Jews have been assigned a specific role in the "theater of memory," that of victims who are as forgiving as possible of modern-day Germany. They are considered relevant only on three topics: anti-Semitism, the *Shoah*, and Israel.

Confining Jewish history to the Holocaust, Czollek wrote, means, "Germans primarily know one thing about the Jews: that they murdered them." It's a concept that evidently stayed in Czollek's head, too. He said his own "conception of Jewishness began with an enormous pile of corpses. And for a long time, I was unable to think or write beyond this macabre mountain."

But that is to be expected, Czollek wrote. The "theater of memory" colors the perception of everything he does. "Jews are ascribed roles that help stabilize the new German self-image: the forgiving Jewish victims on one side and the reformed German perpetrators on the other." Jews can be dispensed with "when they become uncomfortably conspicuous. Razed synagogues can be rebuilt without Jewish carpenters, Jewish museums can be staffed by German curators, and one can also pat oneself on the back and drink Prosecco at joint commemorative celebrations even when no Jewish people attend."

Czollek also took aim at Germany's generational divide, saying young Germans aren't as interested in the Holocaust as their parents were. "It must have been a charming thing for the first generation to be born after: confronting their Nazi parents with a truly moral transgression. And that worked well enough. It allowed them to stand rhetorically on the other, better side of the debate. Patricide can be fun. But that fun had an expiration date."

Czollek's notion that "patricide can be fun" hardly does justice to the challenges faced by Germany's postwar generation. Nor does it accurately reflect their dedication to setting the record straight, especially given the resistance they faced in small towns like Dorsten. Helmut Walser Smith, a historian of modern Germany at Vanderbilt University, wrote, "After reading literally hundreds of accounts of towns from Bavaria and Baden in the south to Lower Saxony and Schleswig-Holstein in the north, I am especially impressed by the patience of these local actors. For it is they who put in the many years of work that often went into convincing town councils to repair a cemetery, put up a plaque, restore a synagogue, rename a street for a famous Jewish son or daughter, or add a monument in the central square of a hometown that had once wronged its former citizens."

Even so, Czollek's contention that Germany essentially faced an "expiration date" in regard to the ongoing relevance of the Holocaust has gained credence. Resentment of the country's ongoing commitment to Holocaust remembrance has fueled anti-Semitism and the growth in popularity of the Alternative für Deutschland (AfD). The AfD is a right-wing populist party characterized as nationalist, anti-immigration, and Islamophobic. The party's leader was praised by Elon Musk in the run-up to the 2025 federal election for the party's hardline stance against immigration. It emerged as the second most popular party in the country, with nearly 21 percent of the vote, buoyed by a strong base in the east. A couple of months later, U.S. Vice President J. D. Vance and Secretary of State Marco Rubio criticized Germany's domestic intelligence agency for designating the AfD as a "right-wing extremist" group.

The title *De-Integrate!* refers to Czollek's wish that Jews and other minorities resist roles assigned to them and provide Germany with a more pluralistic society that recognizes its growing diversity. This notion of assigned roles includes criticism of Israel, to which Germany has been, to characterize it broadly, intolerant. The German government and cultural institutions are prone to reflexively brand criticism of Israel as anti-Semitic. The German parliament in 2019 passed a resolution condemning BDS—the movement that calls for boycotts, divestment, and sanctions against Israel—and called the tactics anti-Semitic.

The country's reflexive support for Israel drew more attention after the brutal war in Gaza provoked outrage and protests. Germany's official and institutional support of Israel remained steadfast, as did its intolerance for opposition to Israel's policies, even from Jews. A high-profile example was when the left-leaning, German-based Heinrich Böll Foundation withdrew cosponsorship for an award for "political thought" to Jewish journalist Masha Gessen in December 2023. Gessen had just published an essay in the *New Yorker* comparing Israel's treatment of Gaza to WWII-era ghettos the Nazis created to segregate and then murder Jews.

That brought Germany's fierce protection of Israel's policies into sharp relief. "It appears that something has gone terribly awry in Germany's famed 'culture of memory,'" wrote Manuel Schwab, a professor of anthropology at the American University in Cairo who lives and works part time in Berlin. He mentioned a series of incidents that occurred in Germany within two months of the Gaza war, in which Jewish and Arab protesters were detained, conferences and art exhibitions canceled.

"Consider what we are seeing in these events," Schwab said. "German police are arresting Jews for political expression criticizing the state of Israel, all in the name of combating antisemitism, while the German descendants of perpetrators (virtually all of us are) are declaring a proprietary expertise, accusing Jews and Arabs alike of not understanding the political purchase of antisemitism in our present."

Berlin-based artist Candice Breitz, who is South African and Jewish, was outraged when the Saarland Museum in western Germany canceled a planned exhibit of her works. The museum said she hadn't sufficiently condemned the October 7 attack by Hamas. "Need I point out the absurdity," Breitz responded, "of Germans dictating to Jewish people how they should articulate their reactions to the heinous massacre of Jewish people at the hands of terrorists?"

Critics had long objected to what they considered Germany's selective campaign against anti-Semitism, saying it was more heavily (and wrongfully) weighted against Muslims instead of the greater threat posed by the right wing. "This country is not coping properly with its Nazi past, and today perhaps less than it ever did," Israeli writer Ilana Hammerman wrote in 2019, assessing the memory culture in the Bavarian town of Landsberg am Lech and throughout the country. "If Germany were coping properly, what it would certainly place in the forefront of its struggle against anti-Semitism is not a campaign against the Palestinians, but against the extreme right at home, which is once more making deep inroads into German society. After all, the fomenters of most of the anti-Semitic incidents come from its camp."

This has also been Czollek's frequent refrain. He said many Jews delude themselves that they couldn't be systemically persecuted again by the German government. "Next time, the mosques might be the first to burn. But then the synagogues will burn, as well. I don't entertain any illusions about this." He added, "Those who dream of a Germany without Muslims, also dream of a Germany without Jews."

In retrospect, the ongoing relationship between Germany and the Jewish people was likely to be strained no matter what happened after the Nazi era.

"The problem was that in voiding itself of Jews, Germany had forever voided itself of the capacity for a normal, healthy response to Jews and their ideas," wrote James E. Young, a professor of English and Judaic studies at the University of Massachusetts-Amherst. "Instead, it was all a tortured bending over backwards, biting one's tongue, wondering what 'they' really thought of Germans. It is a terrible, yet unavoidable consequence of the Holocaust itself, this Jewish aphasia, a legacy of mass murder."

The contemporary emphasis on memorializing the Holocaust—some would say *overemphasis*—has prompted more misgivings and criticism from across an ideological spectrum, as well as introspection from memory activists. "Have lessons about the Holocaust essentially reached their expiration date?" Wüstenberg said to me. "In other words, is it now too far removed from memory, has the notion of Jews as victims been overplayed over the years, that most people simply aren't interested any more? I see more and more signs of Holocaust fatigue."

Until recently, the harshest denunciations in Germany came from the far-right. In 2018, Alexander Gauland, a member of the Bundestag and coleader of the AfD at the time, told the party's youth division, "Hitler and the Nazis are just bird shit in more than 1,000 years of successful German history." A year earlier, Björn Höcke, the party's leader in the state of Thuringia, called for "nothing other than a 180-degree reversal on the politics of remembrance," describing Berlin's Holocaust memorials as a "monument of shame."

Which raises the question—does shame weaken a country? Bryan Stevenson, a lawyer and social justice activist in Montgomery, Alabama, believes it can be essential to getting past historic tragedies. He's cited Germany's memory culture as an inspiration behind his National Memorial for Peace and Justice in Montgomery, which commemorates lynching victims. "Collective shame about mass atrocities is a healthy thing because it moves you to get to the point where you say 'never again,'" Stevenson said. "We don't say those words when it comes to the history of racial inequality."

Nevertheless, Musk has repeatedly complimented the AfD, telling a party gathering a month before the February 2025 federal election that Germany has "too much of a focus on past guilt." I don't know how many

Germans Musk had spoken to about this or how much he studied the memory movement. The activists I've talked to emphatically denied feeling guilty about Germany's actions during the Nazi regime, though they did feel shame.

Skepticism about the impact of Germany's intense focus on the Holocaust has also come from more mainstream public figures. In 1998, German writer and novelist Martin Walser voiced concerns about "the historical burden, the never-ending shame" presented daily to Germans. "Auschwitz is not suitable for becoming . . . an always-available intimidation or a moral bludgeon or also just an obligation. What is produced by ritualization has the quality of a lip service."

Some advocates of Germany's remembrance movement have responded to criticism by adjusting their approach. Pieren said Jewish museums have become more open to how students in particular respond to history. She said there's less of, "You shouldn't think that, I'll tell you how it is. Instead, she said, "We want the children to think for themselves."

Joel Obermayer's nonprofit group, Widen the Circle, honors Germans who find more effective ways to fight hatred than expecting everyone to respond the same way. "When something becomes doctrinaire in the equivalent of high school in most places in Germany," he said, "it has become performative. 'We do the things, we learn the facts,' as opposed to something that has actual emotional content to it. That is a recipe for something that's doctrinaire and doesn't allow for the difference of opinion."

Obermayer related the experience of one honoree, Sabeth Schmidthals, who teaches history and German in an ethnically diverse, predominantly working-class Berlin neighborhood. Many students are from Arab countries and Turkey. Schmidthals assigned her teenage pupils the autobiography of a German Jewish Holocaust survivor, Inge Deutschkron. She then started a project called "My History, Your History," in which ninth graders described where their families came from and shared their stories of migration. During the project's early days, a student with a Palestinian background began to cry when speaking of her family history. Asked if she had ever talked about these experiences before, the student said, "'No, no one ever asked.' And then I began to understand," Schmidthals said. "In my opinion, their negative attitude to the theme of Jews and persecution is the flipside of the feeling that no one is interested in their [own] suffering."

This is an important point, Obermayer said. "You can't ask students to empathize if you haven't empathized with them."

Some historians also point out that Germany's highly selective memory culture fell short of doing justice to the full weight of its national crimes. "It is important to recognize that these are not solely the product of twelve years of National Socialism," wrote Joseph Cronin, a historian of modern Europe and director of the Leo Baeck Institute in London, which studies German Jewish history and culture. "A memory culture which focuses only on this period is incapable of addressing racism and anti-Semitism in the present day. Germany's memory culture—just like the United States'—therefore must include the longer history of European colonialism, its belief in white superiority, and its attendant subjugation of other peoples deemed inferior."

Compared to other European countries, Germany's colonial history was not long, lasting from 1884 until 1918. "It was brief," observed writer Paul Scraton, "but it was bloody." It included the genocide of the Herero and Nama people in German South-West Africa, in what's now known as Namibia, regarded by the United Nations as the first genocide of the twentieth century. It entailed deliberate starvation, concentration camps, medical experiments, and the murder of 65,000 to 100,000 people. And up to 300,000 people were killed during the 1905–07 Maji-Maji Rebellion against German colonial rule in East Africa, which encompassed an area now known as Rwanda, Burundi, and Tanzania.

These large, targeted murders may sound long ago and far away. But in some ways, so does the Holocaust's role in history, as decades roll by and there are fewer survivors or those who witnessed it firsthand. Czech-born Holocaust survivor Saul Friedländer, a professor emeritus of history at UCLA and one of the most preeminent historians of the Holocaust, was quoted as saying, "At some point people will read books about the Third Reich and the Holocaust like we do about Caesar's Gallic War today. That's how it'll be, there is nothing we can do about it."

I got a glimpse of this fading interest after I found a pdf online about the impact of the Holocaust in Essen, published in February 2020. It was created by students at the Erich Brost vocational college, now on the same street where my family once lived. The paper includes a concise history of the Jewish elementary school that used to reside where Brost now stands, as well as descriptions of the Nazis' persecution of Jewish children. I was touched to see a section devoted to my grandparents and uncles that also mentioned my father (spelling his name as Rudi). I wondered if some of the students or faculty might want to hear from a descendant. I was certainly interested in hearing from them.

Turns out the interest was not reciprocated. Curiosity about the school's proximity to events that played out eighty years ago has apparently faded. I tried for two years to correspond with some of the school's current and former staff, all of whom professed little knowledge of the project. I ultimately got a response from a former pupil who said it helped further her long-standing interest in Judaism and anti-Semitism, especially as she studied to become a teacher. She said the students who participated in the project were enthusiastic, as were the teachers, though she added, cryptically, it caused "quite a stir" at school. (She didn't respond to my request for more details.)

The postwar rallying cry of "Never Again" about the Holocaust essentially faces pushback from those who say "Enough," when the topic arises.

What might be the impact if the Holocaust continues to slide from public awareness in Germany and beyond? Dara Horn wrote in *People Love Dead Jews* that we've already experienced it. "The last few generations of American non-Jews had been chagrined by the enormity of the Holocaust—which had been perpetrated by America's enemy, and which was grotesque enough to make it socially unacceptable, even shameful. Now that people who remembered the shock of these events were dying off, the public shame associated with expressing antisemitism was dying, too. In other words, hating Jews was normal."

Susan Neiman, in *Learning from the Germans,* worried that in America, and to some extent in Britain, over-emphasizing the Holocaust's place in history had also taken a toll. "The claim that rounding people up and sending them to gas chambers is evil is the only claim that commands nearly universal moral consensus today," she wrote. As a result, "The focus on

Auschwitz distorts our moral vision: like extremely nearsighted people, we can only recognize large, bold objects, while everything else remains vague and dim. Or, to put the matter in psychoanalytic terms, the focus on Auschwitz is a form of displacement for what we don't want to know about our own national crimes."

I detected an increasing sensitivity among many Germans involved in Jewish museums and cultural institutions to being perceived as overemphasizing the Holocaust. It calls to mind the question that writer Sanders Isaac Bernstein posed in a review of *De-Integrate!* "As Czollek notes, in Germany it might be impossible to exit the Theater of Memory altogether," Bernstein wrote. "But couldn't we instead attempt to stage stories of Jewish life not framed, first and foremost, by a relationship to suffering?"

Reichert agreed that confining the teaching of Jewish history in German schools to the Holocaust means "students get to know Jews only as victims and linked to a very bad feeling. Schools—with the best intentions—link Jews with feelings of horror and guilt at an age where they barely can cope with their own emotions. I think that could be one of the reasons people avoid contact with Jews or Judaism and more easily respond to 'opinions' or fake news about them."

There ought not be, as was once put to me, an Olympics of persecution, a competition to see which group of people suffered most throughout history. There have been other genocides since the Holocaust, other attempts to destroy populations based on their nationality, ethnicity, race, or religion. That includes more recent mass murders in Rwanda, Darfur, and Burma/Myanmar. There's no need to compare which was more harmful or remains more relevant to each person. Each genocide stands on its own, each horrifically tragic with its own circumstances and lessons for the future.

I understand the fatigue that comes from talking about a historical chapter that ended almost eighty years ago or by frequently using the Holocaust as a measuring stick to compare against more recent acts of persecution. Even so, it remains a valid cautionary tale about how quickly democracies can tumble. How demonizing people because of their race or religion can turn longtime friends and neighbors against one another. And how each of us bears personal responsibility to connect with others, striving for tolerance while recognizing that as humans, we're destined to fall short. "This isn't only about Germany and Jews," Pieren said, "this is about an incredible failure of humanity."

"Realistically, I don't think there is any way to not use the Holocaust as a standard of measurement for antisemitism," said Adam Eisendrath, an American whose Jewish ancestors lived in Dorsten for hundreds of years and whose family has also benefited from Elisabeth's research. "Trauma has helped define the Jewish people since the Torah was written, both on a personal level and generational level. From the binding of Isaac to slavery in Egypt, to the Pale of Settlement and the Dreyfus Affair, the Jewish community has always been known as 'the other.' That otherness helps define the community and frankly becomes a source of strength for it. But removing it or lessening the Holocaust's role in Jewish history is like leaving out Napoleon from French history or slavery from the founding of America."

Julia Rymer Brucker, a descendant of Augsburg's Jewish community, concurred, but only to a point. "For those Jews like myself who continue to identify with and practice Judaism, the Holocaust was and remains a seminal event in the history of the Jewish people, affecting our communities to this day, even as the survivors among us pass away. It is part of the stories told in synagogues, and it looms large in our memories." But, she added, "For those who no longer identify with their Jewish heritage, I don't see it as a big issue anymore, but more of an abstraction."

Meanwhile, the challenges of relying on the Holocaust as a historical reference point are becoming more apparent. Brucker worried that it's already "to the detriment of celebrating our culture and traditions . . . And we don't educate non-Jews about our traditions because we barely educate ourselves." It would be much better, she said, "that a celebrity who publicly spouts right-wing, antisemitic drivel is asked to attend a Shabbat dinner, visit a synagogue or attend a Purim carnival instead of visiting a Holocaust museum."

Whatever the flaws of Germany's memory activists and the limits of their impact, many of the Jewish descendants I've spoken to have been among their biggest defenders. They may have occasionally been asked, as I have, to vouch for the country postwar. But they don't feel obligated to do so, nor do they consider this the primary aim of the memory movement.

I recently spoke to Alberto Dorfzaun, who's connected to a particularly ugly chapter in Essen's history. His great-grandfather was the *gabbai*, or rabbi's assistant, whom the Nazis forced (with his son, Dorfzaun's grandfather) to open the synagogue on *Kristallnacht* and retrieve the Torah scrolls so they could set it ablaze. Alberto, who now lives in Ecuador, where he runs his family's Panama Hat business, was the founder of a bank dedicated to microlending and has been president of Quito's Jewish community.

It turns out he has a connection to my mother's side of the family, as well. His father's roots were in the village of Fischach, not far from Augsburg. They initially emigrated to Cali, Colombia, where his grandparents went into the flatware business with my grandparents, before resettling in Ecuador. Dorfzaun was more inquisitive as a youngster about his parents' origins than I was of mine, though his parents discouraged it. "Every time I spoke about this," he told me, "I heard, '*Nicht für die Kinder*'—'not for the children.'" He kept pushing the issue when he got older and connected with a new generation of Germans. "I asked my mom many times what is her position. She always said, 'Forget, never. Pardon yes.'" When Dorfzaun and his mother traveled to Germany together, she was haunted by memories and claimed she saw Nazis everywhere they went.

Dorfzaun has a charitable view of postwar Germany, where he's enjoyed a warm welcome. "It's another generation," he said. "I feel with this generation, very reconciled. I truly, wholly believe they're not responsible, it was their grandparents and they want to make up for what happened." Dorfzaun is a German citizen, but he made clear to me the limits of his allegiance: "At the beginning, I was hesitant until my father-in-law said, 'You're an idiot because an Ecuadorian passport will not take you far.'" So he claimed his German citizenship, as a descendant of the persecuted, though he quickly added, "I wouldn't fight a war for Germany. This is only practical, a convenience."

He's also been embraced by the current-day Jewish community in Essen, not a commonplace experience, given the historical cultural differences between German Jews with an Eastern European lineage and those from the West. Dorfzaun, his four siblings, and their families were invited to return to Essen's historic synagogue in June 2022 when it ceremoniously inaugurated a new Torah. Dorfzaun was given the honor of inscribing the last of the scroll's 304,805 handwritten Hebrew letters.

Those most active among the descendants of Augsburg's Jewish community have been particularly close to members of the city's remembrance movement.

"For me," Diane Castiglione said, "if the remembrance stuff was only happening in major cities where there's a significant Jewish population or Jews from other countries may be passing through, I might think more about this idea as a performance. The fact that so much of this happens in small areas where there are no Jews, there is no audience expectation for the local residents."

Her colleague who organizes Augsburg's Jewish descendants, Bettina Kaplan, also expressed admiration for the remembrance movement. "They're acknowledging something that they had nothing to do with, but they're bringing it to light so that it doesn't happen again," Kaplan said. "It's very normal for us to have gratitude for that. It's genuine. You can still say what you want about theater, that's what life is. When you recognize good work, that promotes more of it."

I recently connected with Mark Bendix, a Lebenstein relative who lives in Toronto, though he grew up in South Africa, where his father emigrated in 1936. He and his wife, Gail, retraced his family's roots in Lembeck, with Elisabeth's help, as well as in nearby towns. He appreciated being able to tour Jewish sites with a local archivist in Dülmen, including an old Jewish graveyard. But Bendix said he and his wife were taken aback when the archivist proudly showed off the train station. "Clueless," was the word that popped into Bendix's head at the time. "That's where you marched our family and sent them off to the gas chambers."

He still has the same unabashed enthusiasm for Elisabeth and her fellow memory activists as I have. "I actually find it quite touching. These people are keeping a memory alive. Whatever their motivation is, so be it. But I do believe it comes from a good place." Yes, Bendix told me, some of the motivation may come from a sense of guilt. But, he added, "They're not getting anything out of it. A lot of people I find will do things because there's a reward at the end of it. But they're not."

I hope I'm not being naive in thinking that some of what the memory activists accomplished endures, and their dedication still inspires. More than a million people protested in January 2024 against the AfD in demonstrations held in about one hundred locations across Germany, including Dorsten. A public opinion survey conducted a year later found just under half of Germans agreed that Holocaust remembrance was still important. That was a few percentage points higher than those who wanted to leave the past behind. Support for commemorating the *Shoah* had actually increased slightly since the last such survey in 2021, though Germans' impressions of Israel worsened considerably during that time. Which indicates some support of Holocaust remembrance has endured loud and occasionally violent expressions of anti-Semitism, as well as revulsion toward Israel's pummeling of Gaza.

Even so, Germany's dedication to the memory movement appeared unsettled. Two-thirds of Germans surveyed agreed with the statement that "It is wrong to continue holding Germans responsible today for the crimes committed by the Nazis against the Jews." Hartwich, who cofounded the history workshop in Dorsten four decades ago, was hearing more complaints about "the Jews" from his neighbors. "I object always and everywhere, and try, clearly and unambiguously, not only to counteract the opinion expressed, but to promote more tolerance," he told me. "I don't have any other solution."

It's tempting to think Germany could have largely ended anti-Semitism within its borders if its late embrace of responsibility for the Nazi era had truly been successful. That it could have ushered in a new age devoid of hatred not only against Jews, but also against immigrants, people of color, and any group of people considered "different."

But that feels like wishful thinking, an almost impossible outcome. How could well-intentioned members of a generation or two replace centuries of mistrust and unease with peace and love? That sounds like the naiveté of the 1960s.

We're left with a more complicated assessment of what Germany's memory movement has accomplished and a tempered view of what it can still achieve. "It's not like the remembrance culture failed," insisted Joel Obermayer. "It has failings." Hatred and prejudice among groups of people will never truly be solved, he said. He recalled Bryan Stevenson telling him, "Each generation has to find its own way through history. It's never done."

Chapter 21

IMAGINING A HOME

"Reconciliation is possible."

Having just considered the larger implications of Germany's memory culture, let's end where we began by looking at the effect on Elisabeth and me.

As I've mentioned, Elisabeth was embarrassed when I praised her in a newspaper story in April 1988 about my first trip to Germany. But she said it encouraged her to learn more about Jewish history and seek better relationships between Christians and Jews. "The Jews have a long tradition, for they have taught for centuries, even for thousands of years, only one truth," she wrote to me. "In spite of sorrow, in spite of humiliation and in spite of persecution, they have been faithful to the tradition of the fathers—even those who often didn't take in earnest the orders of faith or forgot them. But they never forgot they were Jews—Jews in their thinking, in their feelings, and Jews especially in their hope for the future. This is a great, everlasting lesson."

Many years later, I asked her to reflect on ways her decades of activism changed the community around her and herself. Despite her obvious modesty, she expressed pride that a small, local remembrance group created a regional Jewish museum and sustained it for more than thirty years. "It was not easy, we often lacked the financial means, but I have actively participated in it," she said. "Women's power!" she wrote, attaching to her email a photo of her with three other founding women members.

Other tangible results included providing the impetus for numerous local *Stolpersteine*, getting a street named after my family, and organizing a large reunion in Dorsten in 2010 for the Eisendrath family, which culminated in a book of research and essays. She also went to Stockholm to track down the sole survivor of another Dorsten family, Elise Hallin-Reifeisen, who fled to Sweden in a *Kindertransport*—and whose parents had been deported in 1938 and murdered. Elisabeth turned her research about the family into a book published in 2013.

"Certainly the experiences of the last thirty years around the museum have changed me. Without my work, I would not have experienced so much suffering," Elisabeth wrote. "Sometimes I still can't understand what people have done to others. Maybe that is an impetus for me to never let it start again. Germany has made an effort to build a democracy, has a good Basic Law," she said, referring to the country's constitution, which took effect in West Germany in 1949 and for the unified country in 1990. "The first charter says, 'All people are equal.' But in practice it often looks different."

Elisabeth's motivation to connect with and help others began with those of us in the German Jewish diaspora. It now stretches far beyond. Having devoted so much time honoring those who were unable to leave Germany for freedom in the 1930s, she turned to helping those who arrived in Germany seeking freedom in her lifetime.

I asked whether assisting immigrants stemmed from her work regarding the Holocaust. "Maybe a little bit," she said. "It's also a result of my upbringing, which gave me values" to help those less fortunate. "It is also important to me to contribute to mutual acceptance in society, so that living together becomes easier for everyone. We all want to live together peacefully."

Working with immigrants played to her strengths as an energetic doer and organizer with a large circle of friends and family willing to provide additional support. She's also persistent. "At first, I was shocked by the bureaucracy in Germany," she said. "Until then, I had never had contact with people who were dependent on the social welfare office (and their staff). I was always the mediator and advocate, so to speak. When I called, all the vouchers could be issued; when the immigrants tried to do it themselves, it usually didn't work out. And I had something to do all the time, almost like a full-time job. Looking for flats, looking for jobs, booking German courses, looking for schools, the simplest social contacts had to be made."

Elisabeth has worked with families from Afghanistan, Pakistan, and Syria, many of them with several children. Now, she said, Germany's capacity to deal with migrants has reached its limit. Dorsten, with its population of about 75,000, had two huge tent camps of 800–1,000 migrants each as 2023 came to a close. "The cities and municipalities no longer have the means to accommodate them or even to support them financially," she said. "This has given the AfD an enormous boost. We often discuss the issue with friends. In many areas of society, tolerance has become very fragile. As soon as one's own job or money or something criminal is reported, the waters run high."

Tolerance was also in short supply among Germany's newest arrivals. She spoke of having "heated discussions" with Syrian families she was working with. "They grow up with hatred of Jews, with anti-Semitism from birth through school in Arab countries. They don't know any Jews at all and find it difficult to deal with our remembrance work. Social media is constantly sending new messages, which they quickly accept and convey." The situation became more difficult, she said, with constant reminders of Palestinian suffering in Gaza when Israel deepened its war on Hamas.

"Our educators go into schools, we have organized events for teachers," she said. "We keep offering these events and they are very well received. But it doesn't seem to be enough."

Israel's aggressive response to Hamas' October 7 terrorist attacks made the situation more difficult. "One form of anti-Semitism that is widespread today is Israel-related anti-Semitism. Here, existing anti-Semitic attitudes and world views are transferred to the state of Israel, which in this context is seen as a representative of 'the Jews.' This is done, for example, by denying Israel's right to exist or equating the role of Israeli policy in the conflict between Israel and Palestine with the perpetrators of the Holocaust. At the same time, conspiracy ideological aspects of anti-Semitism can also be transferred to the state of Israel, for example when it is assumed that Israel is an all-powerful state that has a major influence on global political events."

I asked if she believed that more could have been done—or still be done—to promote diversity and tolerance. Her response betrayed some of the weariness I had also heard from Hartwich. "I can't say that for myself," she said. "I send my messages to my circle of friends and relatives and everywhere else. Over time, of course, you notice that there is less interest. Sometimes they don't want to hear it."

Elisabeth's disappointment lands with a thud, even to a lifelong journalist whose natural instincts tend toward skepticism. One of the characteristics of the generation that launched Germany's memory culture that most impressed me was their confidence. They seemed propelled by an earnest desire to make their country better than the generation or two that had preceded them. A key part of their efforts was to deal honestly with Germany's past and make amends. Now they had serious doubts about their impact and legacy.

Mollie and I flanked by Elisabeth and Paul, outside of their home in 2022

Working on this book also prompted me to look back on my relationship with Germans during the past four decades. I'm taken with how prescient Elisabeth was. I reconsider the narrative history of my father's family that she handed Mollie and me at our wedding in 1987. It cuts differently now when I read her conclusion that following the "multitude of traces" my family left behind, "they give a clear picture of the life and death of the Jews who used to live in Lembeck."

I'm much closer to that than when I first read her narrative years ago. I've stood where my ancestors once did, not only in Lembeck and Essen in the west but also in Hürben and Augsburg in the south. I've walked on the streets where they once lived, shopped, and prayed. Most of the buildings they frequented are gone; only a few have been restored. Even so, there's something transformative about standing where they once did, particularly at the restored synagogues in Augsburg and Essen. This was where they gathered to express their faith, a faith that led to their persecution. My visits encouraged me to try to carry forward the same faith that helped sustain my ancestors during their lifetime. Even the mere outline of the synagogue that once stood in Hürben provided an opportunity to reflect on how that spot once provided inspiration and solace to worshippers.

I also carry with me memories of seeing where those who died by the 1930s are buried. I feel, in a way, that they spoke to me and I to them at that holy ground, a kind of manifestation of the ancient concept in Judaic scripture of "*l'dor vador*," "from generation to generation."

Stolpersteine serve a somewhat similar function for those whose burial grounds lie far to the east, their presence unmarked. I appreciate these small memorials at their last known voluntary place of residence, most of them honoring murdered family members, their lives cut short by countrymen fulfilling a hideous ideology based on hate, with no interest in the lives of the people they killed, in numbers that stagger the imagination.

I acknowledge the many shortcomings of these stumbling stones. But they accomplish something no other memorial has. They remind you that a crime against humanity occurred *right here*, where you are now. If you take a moment, they also remind you that six million victims are made up of six million *individuals*.

More traces of my ancestors recently surfaced in my home, on my desktop monitor, while searching for digitized documents and artifacts. It's where I stumbled onto the wrenching story of the train that left Düsseldorf for Minsk on November 10, 1942, and the checklist confirming that my grandparents and uncles were on board. The internet is where I found new details about my father's aunt and uncle whom he briefly stayed with in Südlohn and how they were temporarily protected by their neighbors until resistance to the Nazis proved futile. It's where I found my dad's desperate classified ad in the *Aufbau*. It's where I read the newspaper article about my maternal grandmother and uncle (sent by my cousin Jaime), that provided new insights about their life in Germany and reconciliation with the country they fled fifty years earlier.

Finding these and other digitized documents was a mixed blessing. I spent an inordinate amount of time staring at them, willing myself back to the moment in time when they were created. Each one unleashed a flood of emotions. I was grateful to have found another puzzle piece about my family, to have followed the traces. I was also pained thinking about their suffering, regretful that I couldn't share my thoughts in a meaningful way with the principals and deeply self-critical that I blew the chance to get more information from those whose lifetimes overlapped mine. These feelings lingered with me during the day and sometimes resurfaced in the middle of the night.

Powerful moments also came from conversations and visits with the many people I've met or reconnected with in the years since I started this research. They have been among the most rewarding elements of my quest. Each one is connected to my family's story in some way.

No email brought more joy than the response I got when I first wrote to the Descendants of Augsburg's Jewish Community after I discovered its website. I claimed my affiliation as a Landauer without any expectation there were others out there. "Cousin Jeffrey," began Bettina Kaplan's reply, my first sign that descendants on my mother's side of the family extended well beyond my imagination. I also appreciated reconnecting with my cousins Jaime Landauer, fifty years after we parted at the Cali airport, and Mark Bendix.

I spoke with Richard Aronowitz, prominently working in art restitution, after discovering an essay he wrote about his maternal grandmother being deported from Germany on the same train that carried my grandparents and uncle.

Few discoveries were more stunning than when I followed the suggestion of Martina Strehlen at Essen's synagogue to contact Alberto Dorfzaun in Ecuador. He's the great-grandson of the rabbi's assistant who was forced by Nazi thugs to let them enter and burn the synagogue during *Kristallnacht*. I felt like I'd come full circle when Alberto and I realized we shared a family connection not only in Essen but also in Colombia. Our grandparents were in business together for a few years in Cali. Alberto shared photos of the

Metal Gloria manufacturing plant our families once co-owned, the silverware they made, and business documents signed by our grandparents—none of which I'd seen before.

My visits to ancient cemeteries where my relatives are buried were enhanced by the conversations I had there with local guides Michael Bernheim and Alfred Hausmann in Augsburg, Wilhelm Fischer and Herbert Auer in Hürben, and Elke and Gerd Gutschow in Raesfeld. They share a remarkable dedication to the history of the Jews who once lived in their communities.

All of these experiences make me feel more rooted as to who I am and where my family comes from, part of a continuum I never knew existed. They've left me with a greater responsibility to make a positive impact with my life. But they also provide reassurance that my family's legacy doesn't rest quite so heavily on my shoulders, that I'm connected to a part of history that goes well beyond my immediate family and friends and extends to people and places I didn't even know.

My interactions with Germans who invested so much in the country's remembrance movement make me see more clearly the virtue in practicing forgiveness. Pemper addressed this when concluding a memoir of his journey from Kraków to the Płaszów concentration camp and on to Augsburg. He acknowledged being overcome with sorrow about the Holocaust and mourned the many victims. But Pemper said he didn't hate Germans: "Hate gets us nowhere and doesn't contribute to reconciliation." The Nazi regime, he wrote, coerced many people to "commit crimes they would probably not have committed under different circumstances." They must be held responsible for those crimes as individuals, he said, but he rejected the idea of a "collective guilt" among a group of people, be they a nation or a religion.

Nevertheless, he added, "It fills me with apprehension that it was so easy to manipulate so many people and that so few helped us in our need. For the sake of our future, we must not forget what happened. We cannot escape history. Mankind will only progress when the principle of individual responsibility becomes the golden rule, when refusal to play along becomes a virtue, and blind obedience loses its currency."

Practicing forgiveness is much easier in the abstract than it is in practice. I'm not disappointed in my mother or other survivors for carrying a grudge against Germany, given what they experienced. But I also think that reconciliation is possible, that people can find ways to not carry forward hate and animosity from previous generations. My dad, Omi, and John all established new relationships with Germany after the war.

Immersing myself in this sad chapter of history underscores the importance of practicing tolerance and embracing diversity. By that I mean accepting that we're all human, with our own strengths and weaknesses. That no group of people is better or worse than any other. The Nazis succeeded in dehumanizing and persecuting several different groups of people in addition to Jews, including the disabled, homosexuals, Sinti and Roma, as well as political opponents and dissenters. Nazi Germany is hardly the only nation to have done something like that. I think we are stronger as people when we recognize that our differences can be a source of strength and not a basis for hate. To do otherwise not only threatens lives, but it also threatens democracy.

I've also come to appreciate the value of family memories. I waited much too long to ask questions of my relatives who have since passed on. Preserve yours, if you can. Ask questions of your relatives, about where they came from (no matter where they come from) and what they've experienced, while you still have the chance.

I'm now part of a group of children of Holocaust survivors who are periodically invited to speak at local schools. We talk with students in middle schools or high schools who are studying the Nazi era, either in history class or English class (the latter, often by reading Elie Wiesel's *Night)*. I look into the audience during my twenty-minute multimedia presentation and see an extraordinarily diverse array of faces. They ask good questions afterward. "How do we know what you're telling us is true?" one asked. "Why didn't your father's family leave earlier?" is a common one. "What would you most like to say to your father and your relatives if you had the chance?" And there are also questions of a more general nature. "How do you practice tolerance?" and "Have you ever felt threatened when talking about history?"

I've also spoken about my family's experiences and the German memory movement at our synagogue. At one of them, a panel of us asked the seventh graders in attendance whether they had experienced anti-Semitism recently. We heard about swastikas being scrawled at their schools, a student being shoved by a classmate while being called a slur against Jews, and a middle school teacher who told pupils the October 7 attacks against Israel were a hoax. We asked how they responded to these actions. One student said it made him more determined to hold fast to his beliefs and be proud of being a Jew. Another said it made him feel even less inclined to conform and more sure about being different. This, I believe, is some of what it means to be a Jew today. To know about our heritage and be proud of it. To be aware of the long history of anti-Semitism and be neither intimidated by it nor wear heavily the cloak of persecution. To never back down in the face of hatred or evil no matter where it occurs.

It's only now that I've begun to grasp the quiet trauma experienced by my family's survivors. I remember Tante Paula, an especially forlorn figure in her later years as a widow, hands folded in her lap, her hushed voice in a downward turn, often saying in a thick, German accent, "I feel so blue." It would have taken an extraordinary effort to have felt otherwise. Her family was persecuted for years. While she and her husband managed to make a safe passage to the U.S., as did her sister, Malli, and nephew Rudy, practically everyone else in her large family perished. You have to be made of especially strong stock to push past that.

My parents had that, as did Omi. And though they never talked about it, they obviously connected to their home as much more than a brick-and-mortar place to live. As they aged and became infirm, living in their own house became more tenuous and impractical. Yet each adamantly opposed moving to an elderly housing facility. My mom would say her mother would only leave the house in Colombia where she had lived since 1938 when she was carried out of there. She was right. The most raw and difficult conversation I had with my father was when my brother and I pleaded with him to leave his home in Memphis and move closer to family in Chicago or Washington, D.C. He wouldn't budge, taking his last breath at his home six days later. Years later, my mother similarly refused to consider alternatives while her struggles with health problems deepened, until finally relenting at age ninety-one.

I believe they all shortchanged themselves by not moving from their home when circumstances dictated it. None of them saw it that way. They were forced to flee their home once before. They weren't going to be uprooted against their will again. Their homes represented hopes and dreams, security and independence. No one, not even their grown children, was going to convince them otherwise. I made myself a promise that if I were ever in the same position, I would listen to my children. I don't see my home in quite the same way as my parents or grandmother did. But then, I didn't live through what they did.

Some of the homes that most connect to how I came to be and who I am are in Germany. I feel like I make a statement every time I set foot on German soil. No, I don't necessarily see myself living there. But I reclaimed an important part of my identity and family heritage by embracing it and the Germans who welcomed me.

ACKNOWLEDGMENTS

I've treasured books and bookstores for as long as I can remember. I dreamt of writing a book myself, but as the years went by, it became more unlikely. It's remarkable that you can now hold these words in your hands, especially for a project as meaningful to me as this. I'm deeply grateful to so many people who helped make this happen—family members, friends, authors, and especially those who've worked so hard to restore the memories and heritage of Jewish communities in Germany.

For information about Dorsten, Lembeck, and Raesfeld, I am of course in awe of the dedication and help from Elisabeth Schulte-Huxel. Elisabeth and Paul are among our most valued friends. I deeply regret that this book was not published before the untimely death of Norbert Reichling. But he read drafts and provided both encouragement and information, and I remain in his debt. I am also thankful to those who spoke with me about the North Rhine-Westphalia region, including Rolf Abrahamsohn, Bernhard Brockmann, Bernhard Cosanne, Elisabeth Cosanne, Heinz Denninger, Sister Johanna Eichmann, Elke Gutschow, Gerd Gutschow, Dirk Hartwich, Josef Langenhorst, Birgit Lapke, Ulrike Matthäus-Robbert, Kathrin Pieren, Heinz Ritter, Gyburg Sonnemann, Gabi

Springer, Werner Springer, Brigitte Stegemann-Czurda, Wolf Stegemann, Tobias Stockhoff, Pat van den Brink, Peter van den Brink, Bernd Winkel, Christel Winkel, Angelika Zenge, and Otto Zenge.

For information about Augsburg and Krumbach, I thank Herbert Auer, Angela Bachmair, Michael Bernheim, Mario Felkl, Georg Feuerer, Wilhelm Fischer, Alfred Hausmann, Alexander Mazo, Karl Borromäus Murr, Carmen Reichert, Frank Schillinger, Benigna Schönhagen, Thomas Weitzel, and Ayleen Winkler. Among the descendants of Augsburg's Jewish community, I am grateful to Steven Anson, Diane Castiglione, Beth Handler, Lawrence Kahn, Jonah Landauer, and Deborah Rausch. A special shout-out to my long-lost cousin, Bettina Kaplan, who has been a gracious and encouraging guide ever since I stumbled onto the Descendants of the Jewish Community of Augsburg group.

I'm also grateful to Mark Bendix, Gunter Demnig, Alberto Dorfzaun, Adam Eisendrath, Ruth Ellen Gruber, Jaime Landauer, Joel Obermayer, Alina Penzel, Martina Strehlen, and Jenny Wüstenberg.

Many friends and authors provided help and encouragement, including Richard Aronowitz, Sarah Birnbach, Barbara Bradley-Hagerty, Michelle Brafman, Steve Drummond, Jeffrey Dvorkin, Pam Fessler, Richelle Fredson, Alan Greenblatt, Michelle Hainbach, Aaron Hamburger, Mark Jacob, Susan Jerison, Joseph Shapiro, and Eric Weiner.

My ability to describe my father's escape from Germany, his family's fate, and thoughts about Germany postwar was enhanced by the speakers' training program for children of Holocaust survivors offered by the Jewish Community Relations Council of Greater Washington.

The Holocaust Encyclopedia provided by the United States Holocaust Memorial Museum is a wonderful resource. It was particularly invaluable for definitions and a chronology of events.

A big shoutout to Naren Aryal and the wonderful team put together by Amplify Publishing Group that enabled me to turn the idea of this book into reality. They include: Jess Cohn, Camma Duhamell, Sarah Herse, Jeff Miller, CW Patrick, and Ben Simpson. And a special thanks to David E. Chandler for creating the map.

I believe that bookstores—as well as books—have a soul and a personality. Good bookstores reward readers with a sense of discovery, serendipity, and personal guidance that no website can replace. My journalism career was bookended by jobs at bookstores that helped nurture my love for the printed word and those who cherish it. I thoroughly enjoyed the two summers during my college years that I worked at one of the legendary Kroch's and Brentano's stores in the Chicago suburbs. And I'm grateful to Amy Joyce and Gayle Weiswasser for letting me work part-time at their little jewel of a bookstore known as Wonderland Books in Bethesda, Maryland.

Siblings Michael Katz, Nancy Eisenberg, and Bob Nathan offered encouragement, as did my aunt Margot Marx, in-laws Ruth and Jim Fromstein, son-in-law Eitan Sayag, and Mollie's uncle, Stephen Grafman.

I hope this is more or less what my father, Rudy Katz, had in mind when he told me, in our last conversation, that I should write a book about his life. The subject matter ended up taking me well beyond what he might have envisioned. My stepfather, John Nathan, had also urged me to write a book. My mother, Margot Nathan, despite her uncharitable view of Germany, was thrilled when Mollie and I called her from Augsburg with daily updates on our visit, eagerly embraced my writing ("Why don't you finish it already?"), and *kvelled* when reading the first draft.

My eternal thanks to my wife, Mollie, and our children, Emily and Ben, whose love, patience, and support know no bounds. Mollie, you make all things in my life possible.

NOTES

An Introduction "When Our Paths Crossed"

4 A psychological theory: Gilad Hirschberger, "The Collective Memory of Trauma and Why It Still Matters," Verfassungsblog, July 24, 2024, https://verfassungsblog.de/the-collective-memory-of-trauma/.

4 An executive order: "Restoring Truth and Sanity to American History," The White House Executive Orders, March 27, 2025, https://www.whitehouse.gov/presidential-actions/2025/03/restoring-truth-and-sanity-to-american-history/.

5 "What brought change": Jenny Wüstenberg, "What Is Memory Culture: Look at the Process, Not the Outcome," Goethe-Institut USA, accessed July 23, 2024, https://www.goethe.de/ins/us/en/kul/art/stp/22106958.html.

Chapter 1 VIEW FROM THE RHINE

15 "There can be": Richard von Weizsäcker, "Speech by Federal President Richard von Weizsäcker," Der Bundespräsident, May 8, 1985, https://www.bundespraesident.de/SharedDocs/Downloads/DE/Reden/2015/02/150202-RvW-Rede-8-Mai-1985-englisch.pdf?__blob=publicationFile. Also https://www.bundespraesident.de/SharedDocs/Reden/DE/Richard-von-Weizsaecker/Reden/1985/05/19850508_Rede.html?nn=129626.

16 used similar language: Alfred Schmidt, "Eine Rückkehr ohne Groll im Herzen: Nach 50 Jahren sieht die Jüdin Else-Helene Isner erstmals ihre Heimatstadt wieder," *Augsburger Allgemeine*, September 21, 1988, 38.

Chapter 2 FLOWERS ON A GRAVE

18 "Elisabeth is back": Elisabeth Schulte-Huxel, email to author, April 30, 2022, the source for much of the information in this chapter.

18 Moises had been taken: "Juedischer Friedhof," Heimatverein Wulfen 1922 eV., accessed November 19, 2024, https://heimatverein-wulfen.de/wp01/juedischer-friedhof/.

18 soon emigrated: "Gedenktafel Familie Moises," Heimatverein Wulfen 1922 eV., accessed November 19, 2024, https://heimatverein-wulfen.de/wp01/gedenktafel-familie-moises/.

19 "Public anti-Semitism": Ruth Ellen Gruber, *Virtually Jewish: Reinventing Jewish Culture in Europe* (University of California Press, 2002), 52.

19 It was the first time: Damien McGuinness, "Holocaust: How a US TV Series Changed Germany," BBC News, January 29, 2019, https://www.bbc.com/news/world-europe-47042244.

20 "How could Germans": Wolf Stegemann, "Spurensuche zwischen Schuld und Scham," in *Dorsten unterm Hakenkreuz, Band 1, Die jüdische Gemeinde,* ed. Dirk Hartwich and Wolf Stegemann (privately published, 1983), 9.

20 The tide turned: Wüstenberg, *Civil Society and Memory in Postwar Germany* (Cambridge University Press, 2017), 63.

20 "*Grabe wo du stehst*": Wüstenberg, *Civil Society*, 130.

20 It said my dad: "Jüdische Bürger," in *Dorsten unterm Hakenkreuz, Band 1, Die jüdische Gemeinde,* ed. Dirk Hartwich and Wolf Stegemann (privately published, 1983), 67.

20 made her first appearance: Stegemann, ed., *Dorsten unterm Hakenkreuz: Band 3, Der gleichgeschaltete Alltag* (privately published, 1985).

20 One reader insisted: Schulte-Huxel, letter to author, October 1985.

21 So she asked: Schulte-Huxel, email to author, April 30, 2022.

24 "You and your colleagues": Rudy Katz, letter to Schulte-Huxel, June 27, 1985.

25 history of my father's family: Schulte-Huxel, *Chronik der Familie Lebenstein, Lembeck,* typed booklet in German with English translation, August 1987.

26 "We can only keep": Schulte-Huxel, email to author, December 7, 2023.

Chapter 3 A VILLAGE IN GERMANY

31 a popular saying: Hugo Hölker, Hans Hatkömper, and Bernard Stachauer, "Lembecker Stories" (Wietholt, 1984). Excerpted in "Alte Sitten und Bräuche," Lembeck A-Z, accessed June 6, 2024, https://www.lembeck.de/lembeck-von-a-bis-z/alte-sitten-und-braeuche/.

32 It was first mentioned: "Story," Schloss Lembeck, accessed June 6, 2024, https://schlosslembeck.de/index.php/schloss/historie.

32 Episcopal bishop: "Lembeck und die Herrlichkeit Lembeck—die Entstehung," Lembeck A-Z, accessed June 6, 2024, https://www.lembeck.de/lembeck-von-a-bis-z/lembeck-die-entstehung/.

32 The pastoral setting: "Wissenswertes über Lembeck," Lembeck von A bis Z.

32 officially dates to 1217: "Chronik der Kirche St. Laurentius Lembeck," accessed June 6, 2024, https://www.lembeck.de/st.laurentius/kirche/.

32 "sandstone Baroque splendor": John Dornberg, "Germany's Island Fortresses," *New York Times,* May 2, 1993, Section 5, 15, https://www.nytimes.com/1993/05/02/travel/germanys-island-fortresses.html.

32 Count and Countess: "Lembeck Castle," Musterland Das Gute Leben, accessed June 6, 2024, https://www.muensterland.com/en/tourism/topics/adventure-region/castles-and-palaces-in-the-munsterland/lembeck-castle/.

32 nine-year gap: Gerd Osterholt, "Lembeck, Schloß, Kirche und Dorf im Wandel der Zeit," in *1000 Jahre Lembeck in einem Buch* (A. Schrecklein, 2017), 16.

33 would never prosper: Elisabeth Schulte-Huxel, "Lebenstein/Katz Family," booklet printed by Schulte-Huxel, June 2011, 2.

33 "Their way of life": Mayor Frank Brunn in "Wissenswertes über Lembeck," Lembeck von A bis Z.

33 spinning flax: Schulte-Huxel, "Chronik de Familie Lebenstein Lembeck," private document handed to author, August 1987, 1.

33 1840 census: "Wissenswertes über Lembeck," Lembeck von A bis Z.

33 "without land ownership": Diethard Aschoff, "Juden und Christen in Westfalen im Alten Reich," in Iris Nölle-Hornkamp, ed., *Heimatkunde—Westfälische Juden und ihre Nachbarn* (Jüdisches Museum Westfalen, 2014), 28.

33 first appears: Schulte-Huxel, "Chronik de Familie Lebenstein," 3.

34 many names: Cosanne-Schulte-Huxel, "Im Schatten der Lembecker Kirche Die jüdischen Familien in Lembeck," in *1000 Jahre Lembeck in einem Buch Dreifachjubiläum* (1000 Jahre Lembeck e.V., 2017), 130, https://www.lembeck.de/lembeck-von-a-bis-z/geschichten-erinnerungen-aus-lembeck/juedische-familien-in-lembeck/.

34 an account from 1853: Cosanne-Schulte-Huxel, "Im Schatten der Lembecker," 127.

35 Marking XXX: Cosanne-Schulte-Huxel, "Im Schatten der Lembecker," 129.

35 "insignificant business": archive of the Jewish Museum Westphalia Dorsten, cited in Cosanne-Schulte-Huxel, "Im Schatten der Lembecker," 128.

36 the village's residents: Christine Cosanne, interview with Elisabeth Cosanne Schulte-Huxel, 1984, as cited in "Im Schatten der Lembecker," 128.

38 "a pear tree": Cosanne-Schulte-Huxel, "Im Schatten der Lembecker," 127–128.

38 "dressed in dark clothes": Elisabeth Schulte-Huxel, "Lebenstein/Katz Family," 10.

39 "went to Lembeck": Cosanne-Schulte-Huxel, "Im Schatten der Lembecker," 131–132.

39 my father told me: Rudy Katz, interview with author, 1990.

39 several of them by name: Cosanne-Schulte-Huxel, "Im Schatten der Lembecker," 131.

40 "It was too rich": Rudy Katz, interview with author, 1990.

40 There's a receipt: Cosanne-Schulte-Huxel, "Im Schatten der Lembecker," 131.

40 *Warum Rassenkunde*: Stegemann, "Rassenkunde 1934 warum?" published January 26, 2021, http://www.dorsten-lexikon.de/rassenkunde-1934-warum/.

40 "Nonsense about the Nordic": Stegemann, "Rassenkunde 1934 warum?"

41 The official persecution: "Boycott of Jewish Businesses," United States Holocaust Memorial Museum Encyclopedia, accessed July 24, 2024, https://encyclopedia.ushmm.org/content/en/article/boycott-of-jewish-businesses.

41 Nuremberg Race Laws: "The Nuremberg Race Laws," USHMM Encyclopedia, accessed July 24, 2024, https://encyclopedia.ushmm.org/content/en/article/the-nuremberg-race-laws.

41 Encouraged to Aryanize: "Aryanization," USHMM Encyclopedia, last modified October 24, 2017, https://encyclopedia.ushmm.org/content/en/article/aryanization.

41 swastika flags first flew: Stegemann, "Nationalsozialismus in Dorsten—ein allgemeiner Überblick," *Dorsten unterm Hakenkreuz*, accessed July 25, 2024, http://www.dorsten-unterm-hakenkreuz.de/2012/05/28/nationalsozialismus-in-dorsten-ein-allgemeiner-uberblick/#more-48.

41 troops were posted: Josef Ulfkotte, "Jewish Life in a Small Westphalian Town 200 Years Ago," in *From Dorsten to Chicago: Lectures and Contributions of the Eisendrath Family Reunion in Dorsten/Germany*, ed. Cosanne-Schulte-Huxel (privately published, 2012), 35–36.

41 ordered to perform: Stegemann, "1933 Machtübernahme der Nazis in Dorsten—Verhaftungen und Verbote, Gleichschaltung und Wettlauf in die NSDAP," *Dorsten unterm Hakenkreuz*, accessed July 25, 2024, http://www.dorsten-unterm-hakenkreuz.de/2012/05/28/1933-machtubernahme-der-nazis-in-dorsten-verbote-verhaftungen-gleichschaltung-und-wettlauf-in-die-nsdap/.

43 "I don't know what we have done": Bernhard Cosanne, interview with author, November 1986.

Chapter 4 A MOTHER'S TOUCH

45 more than 70 percent: "Germany: Jewish Population in 1933," USHMM Encyclopedia, accessed November 19, 2024, https://encyclopedia.ushmm.org/content/en/article/germany-jewish-population-in-1933.

45 *All the Light We Cannot See*: Anthony Doerr, *All the Light We Cannot See* (Scribner, 2014).

45 Essen benefited: Michael Meng, *Shattered Spaces: Encountering Jewish Ruins in Postwar Germany and Poland* (Harvard University Press, 2011), 113.

46 "Armorer of the Reich": William Tuohy, "Shedding Grimy Image: Ruhr—Air, Waters Are Clean Again," *Los Angeles Times*, February 19, 1986, https://www.latimes.com/archives/la-xpm-1986-02-19-mn-9423-story.html.

46 "very lighthearted man": Rudy Katz, interview with author, December 1990.

46 "I feel certain": Rudy Katz, letter to the author, June 1994. Much of the information in this chapter is based on this letter.

47 where she attended: Schulte-Huxel, "Lebenstein/Katz Family," Schulte-Huxel, June 2011, 14.

Chapter 5 THE TEXTILE ENTREPRENEUR

51 average life expectancy: Aaron O'Neill, "Life Expectancy (from Birth) in Germany, from 1875 to 2020," Statista, August 9, 2024, https://www.statista.com/statistics/1041098/life-expectancy-germany-all-time/.

51 *"ein erstaunlicher Mann":* Gernot Römer, Schwäbische Juden (Presse-Druck- und Verlags-GmbH, 1990), 98.

52 four Jewish families: "Hürben-Krumbach/Schwaben (Bayern)," Aus der Geschichte der jüdischen Gemeinden im deutschen Sprachraum, accessed July 23, 2024, https://www.xn—jdische-gemeinden-22b.de/index.php/gemeinden/h-j/970-huerben-krumbach-schwaben-bayern.

52 notorious *Matrikel*: Richard A. Hawkins, "Lynchburg's Swabian Jewish Entrepreneurs in War and Peace," in Southern Jewish History, Volume 3, ed. Mark K. Bauman (Southern Journal Historical Society, 2000), 46–47.
52 "Their physical condition": "Hürben-Krumbach/Schwaben (Bayern)."
53 A synagogue built in 1675: Ibid.
53 "All the inhabitants": Hürben und Krumbach, Alemannia Judaica, last modified June 7, 2014, https://www.alemannia-judaica.de/huerben_texte.htm.
53 written for its centennial: Otto Landauer, *100 Jahre Firma M.S. Landauer 1833–1933* (privately published, 1934).
53 two twelve-hour walks: Römer, *Schwäbische Juden*, 98.
53 "The stagecoach": Landauer, *100 Jahre Firma M.S. Landauer.*
54 "she worked every free minute": Römer, *Schwäbische Juden*, 100.
56 he obtained the rights: Ibid.
56 Lazarus Morgenthau: "Hürben-Krumbach/Schwaben (Bayern)."
56 "May the beautiful church": "Hürben-Krumbach/Schwaben (Bayern)."
56 Gögginger Gate: Gögginger Tor, Wikiwand, accessed July 23, 2024, https://www.wikiwand.com/de/G%C3%B6gginger_Tor.
56 harnessed power: Römer, *Schwäbische Juden*, 102.
57 first cotton manufacturer: "Bavarian Textile Industry Museum Augsburg," MunichFound.com, accessed April 15, 2025, https://web.archive.org/web/20241005184822if_/http://munichfound.com/sightseeing/around_bavaria/id/215/.
57 one remaining: "About Us," Bimatex, accessed July 25, 2024, https://https://www.bimatex.de/en/about-us.
57 "The availability of cheap cotton": Karl Borromäus Murr, interview with author, October 18, 2022.
57 "No evidence has survived": Murr, "The Local Face of Global Trade: Augsburg Cotton Imports from the United States in the Long Nineteenth Century," trans. Andrew Godfrey and Ellen Yutzy Glebe, *Bavarian Studies in History and Culture*, December 28, 2020, https://www.bavarian-studies.org/2020-murr/.
58 "With this, the relationship": Landauer, *100 Jahre Firma M.S. Landauer.*

Chapter 6 DARING ESCAPE

63 "come home immediately": Rudy Katz, interview with author, December 1990.
64 They were first mentioned: *City of Essen: Old Synagogue Essen, House of Jewish Culture* (Klartext Verlag, 2016), 196.
64 then expelled: "'*Alte Synagoge' Essen Haus jüdischer Kultur*," Stiftung Denkmal für die ermordeten Juden Europas, accessed July 25, 2024, https://www.memorialmuseums.org/memorialmuseum/alte-synagoge-essen-haus-judischer-kultur.
64 roughly 4,500 Jews: *City of Essen: Old Synagogue Essen,* 198.
64 "The new building incorporates": *Persecution and Resistance in Essen 1933–1945: Documentation of the Exhibition* (Published for Alte Synagoge Essen, English edition, 1984), 102.
64 "beginning of the twentieth century": Michael Meng, *Shattered Spaces*, 114.
65 Storm troopers stood outside: *Persecution and Resistance in Essen 1933–1945*, 107–108.

65 Haus Berta: Harald Lordick, "eine richtige Hachschara: Das jüdische Ferienheim 'Haus Berta' bei Schermbeck 1934/35," *Kalonymos: Beiträge zurdeutsch-jüdischenGeschichte aus demSalomon LudwigSteinheim-Institutan der UniversitätDuisburg-Essen,* 20–24, https://steinheim-institut.org/sti_files/files/kalonymos-2022_2-4-online.pdf.

65 The camp was visited: Schulte-Huxel, "An Lembeck erinnert," Schalom, March 2000, 4.

65 "a small hardware store": Rudy Katz, interview with author, December 1990.

65 He spoke to thousands: "Remaining Nazi Sites in Westphalia," Traces of Evil, accessed July 25, 2024, https://www.tracesofevil.com/search/label/Essen.

66 includes a small ad: *Gemeindezeitung for den Synagogenbezirk Essen*, November 27, 1936, 7.

67 changed the name: "Pogromnacht: Die Zerstörung der Synagogen in Essen am 9/10 November 1938," Historisches Portal Essen, accessed July 25, 2024, https://geschichte.essen.de/startseite_7/ereignisse_1/pogromnacht.de.html.

67 destroyed the iron gate: "Pogromnacht: Die Zerstörung der Synagogen in Essen."

67 forced the Heidts: Christina Wandt, "Essen: Jüdische Gäste aus aller Welt feiern neue Torarolle," *Westdeutsche Allgemeine Zeitung*, June 14, 2022, https://www.waz.de/staedte/essen/article235620651/Essen-Juedische-Gaeste-aus-aller-Welt-feiern-neue-Torarolle.html.

68 "two people from the SS": Rudy Katz, interview with author, December 1990.

69 "It is most regrettable": Schulte-Huxel, "Lebenstein/Katz Family," 16.

71 jumped out of the car: Schulte-Huxel, "An Lembeck erinnert," Schalom, March 2000, 4.

71 which had formed: "Aid for Hebrew Immigrants: Forming a Society to Assist Jewish Refugees from Russia," *New York Times*, November 28, 1881, 8, https://timesmachine.nytimes.com/timesmachine/1881/11/28/98920719.pdf?pdf_redirect=true&ip=0.

71 Its mission has broadened: "Our History," Hebrew Immigrant Aid Society, accessed July 25, 2024, https://hias.org/who/our-history/.

72 The Belgian government: Stefan Wunsch, speech for the opening of the exhibition, "Gerettet—auf Zeit. Kindertransporte nach Belgien 1938/1939," accessed July 25, 2024, https://auschwitz.be/images/vogelsang-transcriptions.pdf.

72 named Bochner: Rudy Katz, letter to Elisabeth Schulte-Huxel, July 26, 1986.

73 Quotas were part: "How did the United States government and American people respond to Nazism?" USHMM Encyclopedia, accessed August 15, 2024, https://encyclopedia.ushmm.org/content/en/question/how-did-the-united-states-government-and-american-people-respond-to-nazism.

74 the SS *Westernland*: "Westernland," Arnold Hague Ports Database, Port Arrivals/Departures, accessed June 20, 2024, http://www.convoyweb.org.uk/ports/index.html?search.php?vessel=WESTERNLAND~armain.

74 It was built in 1917: "Regina/Westernland," RedStarLineEU, accessed June 20, 2024, http://www.redstarline.eu/regina.html.

74 beginning in 1939: "Regina," Harland and Wolff, accessed June 20, 2024, https://www.theyard.info/ships/ships.asp?entryid=454.

74 a bronze plaque: "Emma Lazarus," National Park Service Statue of Liberty, last modified March 29, 2024, https://www.nps.gov/stli/learn/historyculture/emma-lazarus.htm.

75 arrived in the Port of New York: "Westernland," Arnold Hague Ports Database.
75 a seasonably cold day: "New York City Weather in 1940," Extreme Weather Watch, accessed January 29, 2025, https://www.extremeweatherwatch.com/cities/new-york/year-1940#march.
75 lists Rudi Katz: "New York City, New York, United States records," images, FamilySearch, United States National Archives and Records Administration, accessed January 29, 2025, https://www.familysearch.org/ark:/61903/3:1:33SQ-G5NZ-9MRK?view=index.
75 with the help of a photograph: Schulte-Huxel, "An Lembeck erinnert," Schalom, 4.
76 It sailed once more: "Regina/Westernland 1917," The Ships List, accessed June 20, 2024, https://www.theshipslist.com/ships/descriptions/ShipsR.shtml#regina.
76 Dutch Government in Exile: "Regina/Westernland," RedStarLineEU, accessed June 20, 2024, http://www.redstarline.eu/regina.html.
76 There's a photograph: "Dakar Operations, September 1940, on Board SS Westernland, During Voyage," Imperial War Museums, accessed June 20, 2024, https://www.iwm.org.uk/collections/item/object/205135857.
76 a boyhood friend: My dad didn't mention his friend's name. But the 1940 U.S. Census lists two other boarders at the Schulman home, besides my dad. One of them was Martin Leeds (Levy), previously of Essen. https://www.archives.com/imageviewer/censusimage?dbId=2442&mediaId=M-T0627-03755-00059&recordId=20878456:2442:892&recordType=Census&mediaIdOriginal=M-T0627-03755-00059&returnUrl=%2F1940-census%2Frecord%3FRecordType%3DCensus%26UniqueId%3D20878456:2442:892%26resultsurl%3D%252F1940-census%252Frecord%253FUniqueId%253D20878456:2442:892.
76 Abraham and Carrie Schulmann: "1940 U.S. Federal Population Census," https://www.archives.com/imageviewer/censusimage?dbId=2442&mediaId=M-T0627-03755-00058&recordId=20878444:2442:892&recordType=Census&mediaIdOriginal=M-T0627-03755-00058&returnUrl=%2F1940-census%2Fabraham-schulmann-pa-71593577.
77 turned up a letter: Joseph Savoretti, Acting Commissioner, T. B. Shoemaker, Assistant Commissioner, letter to J. W. Pehle, November 29, 1944, http://www.fdrlibrary.marist.edu/_resources/images/wrb/wrb0274.pdf.

Chapter 7 MARCHING IN THE STREETS

79 When Jewish blood: Schmidt, "Eine Rückkehr."
80 the factory operated: Römer, *Schwäbische Juden*, 104.
80 "did outstanding work": Römer, *Schwäbische Juden*, 102.
80 awarded an iron cross: Kay Graham, email to Bettina Kaplan, June 26, 2023.
80 one of the architects: "The Great Synagogue in Halderstraße," Jüdisches Museum Augsburg Schwaben, accessed July 30, 2024, https://jmaugsburg.de/en/museum/about/synagoge/.
80 "a good reputation": Römer, *Schwäbische Juden*, 102.
80 "very respected citizens": Murr, email to Jaime Landauer, January 10, 2020.
81 first documented appearance: Fritz Flater, "Augsburg unterm Hakenkreuz," pdf, accessed July 30, 2024, https://kipdf.com/augsburg-unterm-hakenkreuz_5acdff847f8b9afc8d8b4587.html. Also "Remaining Nazi Sites in Augsburg," Traces of Evil, accessed July 31, 2024, https://www.tracesofevil.com/2007/01/more-nazi-sites-in-bavaria.html.

81 he spoke there: "Adolf Hitler Speeches," Hitler Archive: A Biography in Pictures, accessed July 31, 2024, https://www.hitler-archive.com/speeches.php.
81 his first two speeches: "Adolf Hitler Speeches," Hitler Archive.
81 founded in Augsburg: "Remaining Nazi Sites in Augsburg," Traces of Evil.
81 Hitler returned triumphantly: "Remaining Nazi Sites in Swabia," Traces of Evil, accessed February 20, 2024.
81 TracesOfEvil.com: "Remaining Nazi Sites in Augsburg," Traces of Evil.
81 second largest local party: "Augsburg unterm Hakenkreuz," Fritz Flater, accessed October 4, 2024, https://kipdf.com/augsburg-unterm-hakenkreuz_5acdff847f8b9afc8d8b4587.html.
81 an oil lamp: "Augsburg (Schwaben/Bayern)," Aus der Geschichte der jüdischen Gemeinden im deutschen Sprachraum, accessed July 31, 2024, https://www.xn—jdische-gemeinden-22b.de/index.php/gemeinden/a-b/283-augsburg-bayern.
81 the thirteenth century: "Augsburg (Schwaben/Bayern)," Aus der Geschichte der jüdischen Gemeinden im deutschen Sprachraum.
81 A synagogue opened: "Augsburg: Jüdische Geschichte im 19./20. Jahrhundert / Betsäle und Synagogen," *Alemannia Judaica*, accessed July 31, 2024, https://www.alemannia-judaica.de/augsburg_synagoge.htm.
82 sell his business: "Oral History Interview with Paul Rosenau," USHMM Collection, December 11, 1997, https://collections.ushmm.org/search/catalog/irn566494. Transcript at https://collections.ushmm.org/oh_findingaids/RG-50.462.0871_trs_en.pdf.
82 "I had a feeling": Schmidt, "Eine Rückkehr ohne Groll im Herzen."
83 sold under duress: "Forced sale of a cotton mill," March 19, 1938: Aryanization, Leo Baeck Institute 1938 Projekt, https://www.lbi.org/1938projekt/detail/aryanization/.
83 "I will never forget": Schmidt, "Eine Rückkehr ohne Groll im Herzen."
83 urging congregants: "Geschichte. Zweite Gemeinde," IKG Schwaben Augsburg, accessed July 31, 2024, https://www.ikg-augsburg.com/zweite-gemeinde%20/.
83 forcibly entered the synagogue: "Geschichte. Zweite Gemeinde," IKG Schwaben Augsburg.
83 presence of a gas station: "Geschichte. Zweite Gemeinde," IKG Schwaben Augsburg.
83 confining the blaze: Rick Landman, "Kristallnacht Reichspogramnaht—November 1938," *InfoTrue*, accessed July 31, 2024, https://www.infotrue.com/k.html.
84 "They tried to get father": "Oral History Interview with Paul Rosenau," USHMM Collection.
84 "were rounded up": "Hürben," *Alemannia Judaica*, accessed June 10, 2024, https://www.alemannia-judaica.de/huerben_synagoge.htm.
84 "On entering the synagogue": Barbara Sallinger, "Zum Schicksal der jüdischen Gemeinde in Krumbach im Dritten Reich," *Krumbacher Heimatblätter,* No. 4/5 (1988), 19–62. As quoted in "Hürben," *Alemannia Judaica*, accessed June 10, 2024, https://www.alemannia-judaica.de/huerben_synagoge.htm.

Chapter 8 BROKEN BRANCHES FROM THE FAMILY TREE

86 "*Suche meine Eltern*": Classified ad, Aufbau, November 16, 1945, 26, https://archive.org/details/aufbau111945germ/page/n784/mode/1up?view=theater.

86 ordered to be transported: Schulte-Huxel, *Chronik der Familie Lebenstein,* 4.
87 a farm near Asperden: Schulte-Huxel, *Lebenstein/Katz Family,* 16.
87 My aunt and uncle pleaded: Rudy Katz, interview with author, December 1990.
87 "taken to an extermination camp": Jeffrey Katz, "Gestapo Escape: And Faint Welcome in America," *Commercial Appeal*, May 8, 1981, 7.
87 a ghetto in Łódź: Łódź, USHMM Encyclopedia, last modified August 9, 2021, https://encyclopedia.ushmm.org/content/en/article/lodz.
88 "to say goodbye": Schulte-Huxel, *Chronik der Familie Lebenstein,* 5.
88 a soldier from Lembeck: Schulte-Huxel, *Chronik der Familie Lebenstein,* 5.
88 "It was hard to imagine": Daniel Mendelsohn, *The Lost: A Search for Six of Six Million* (HarperCollins, 2006), 9.
88 "they'd been killed": Mendelsohn, *The Lost,* 91.
88 About three-quarters: Peter Hayes, *Why? Explaining the Holocaust* (W.W. Norton: 2017), 114–115.
89 An astounding average: Lewi Stone, "Quantifying the Holocaust: Hyperintense Kill Rates During the Nazi Genocide," *Science Advances*, 5 no. 1, January 2, 2019, https://www.science.org/doi/10.1126/sciadv.aau7292.
89 the senior Nazi official: "Heinrich Himmler," USHMM Encyclopedia, accessed July 29, 2024, https://encyclopedia.ushmm.org/content/en/article/heinrich-himmler.
89 The first wave: Saul Friedländer, *Nazi Germany and the Jews 1933–1945* (Harper Collins, 2009), 261.
89 The second phase: Friedländer, *Nazi Germany and the Jews,* 262.
89 occupying Minsk: "Minsk," USHMM Encyclopedia, accessed July 29, 2024, https://encyclopedia.ushmm.org/content/en/article/minsk.
89 "wrote a postcard": Schulte-Huxel, *Chronik der Familie Lebenstein,* 5.
89 a typewritten list: Thomas Freier, "Düsseldorf nach Minsk: Abfahrtsdatum: 10.11.41, Deportierte: 997," 260, accessed July 29, 2024, Statistik und Deportation, https://www.statistik-des-holocaust.de/OT411110-Essen3.jpg.
90 herded into the cattle hall: "Transport, Train Da 52 from Düsseldorf, Rhine Province, Germany to Minsk, Ghetto, Belorussia (USSR) on 10/11/1941," Yad Vashem, accessed July 29, 2024, https://collections.yadvashem.org/en/deportations/9437926.
90 The synagogue was ordered: Bastian Fleermann, "Deportiert von Düsseldorf in das Ghetto Minsk. Der Transportbericht des Schutzpolizisten Wilhelm Meurin vom Herbst 1941," in *Düsseldorfer Jahrbuch 83* (Klartext-Verlag, 2013), 269.
91 several advantages: "Alter Schlachthof Memorial Centre," Foundation Memorial to the Murdered Jews of Europe, accessed July 29, 2024, https://www.memorialmuseums.org/memorialmuseum/erinnerungsort-alter-schlachthof.
91 relatively well concealed: "Transport, Train Da 52 from Düsseldorf," Yad Vashem.
91 A deportee from a train: "Transport from Düsseldorf, Rhine Province, Germany to Lodz, Ghetto, Poland on 27/10/1941, accessed July 29, 2024, https://collections.yadvashem.org/en/deportations/9437857.
91 A report marked "*Vertraulich!*": Wilhelm Meurin, "Betr. Evakuierung von Juden nach Minsk Transportbegleitung vom 10.11. – 18.11.41." Document located by Bastian Fleermann in 2012 at Wiener Holocaust Library, London, ref 1113/1; scan in my possession per permission of the Wiener Holocaust Library.

92 "city lying in ruins": Petra Rentrop, *Tatorte der "Endlösung": das Ghetto Minsk und die Vernichtungsstätte von Maly Trostinez* (Metropol, 2011), 177. Accessed in Barbara Schuchard (Ed.) *"Liebster Iziu," Erlebte Judenverfolgung in den Briefen einer Mutter an ihren Sohn* (Friedrich-Ebert-Stiftung, 2018), 152.

92 "appalling" living conditions: Rentrop, *Tatorte der 'Endlösung*, accessed in Schuchard, *"Liebster Iziu,"* 152.

92 "Hunger, hunger, hunger!": Peter Christoffersen, *"Es war ein einziges Grauen," Die Deportation der Bremer Juden in das Ghetto Minsk und ihre Vernichtung*, in Christoffersen, Peter and Barbara Johr (eds.), *Stolpersteine in Bremen, Schwachhausen/Horn-Lehe*, Book 5 (Sujet Verlag Bremen, 2017 and updated 2023), 11.

92 shot or gassed: "Minsk," USHMM Encyclopedia.

93 destroyed the Minsk ghetto: Ibid.

93 *"Bitte rede"*: Schulte-Huxel, "Katz, Karl-Heinz und Manfred," Historisches Portal Essen, Gedenkbuch Alte Synagoge, last modified May 1988, https://media.essen.de/media/histiorisches_portal/historischesportal_dokumente/startseite_5/Gedenkbuch_Alte_Synagoge.pdf.

93 the same year: Ernst Brunzel, *Nie gehört–Schicksal einer jüdischen Gemeinde* (privately published, 1989), 23, http://www.heimatverein-suedlohn.de/wp-content/uploads/2022/04/nie_gehoert-Ernst-Brunzel.pdf.

93 according to a history: Brunzel, *Nie gehörtt*, 23.

93 Led by the paramilitary: "Stadtlohn," Geschichte der jüdischen Gemeinden im deutschen Sprachraum, accessed June 10, 2024, https://www-xn——jdische—gemeinden—22b-de.translate.goog/index.php/gemeinden/s-t/1854-stadtlohn-nordrhein-westfalen?_x_tr_sl=de&_x_tr_tl=en&_x_tr_hl=en&_x_tr_pto=sc.

93 Thugs first destroyed: "Südlohn," Destroyed German Synagogues and Communities, accessed July 29, 2024, http://germansynagogues.com/index.php/synagogues-and-communities?pid=63&sid=1248:suedlohn.

94 they rushed outside: Brunzel, *Nie gehört,* 32–33.

95 The timeline gets more frightening: Franz-Josef Wittstamm, "Lebenstein Sonja," Spuren im Vest Juden im Vest Recklinghausen, updated March 31, 2021, https://spurenimvest.de/2021/03/31/lebenstein-sonja/.

95 the Šķirotava freight station: Brunzel, *Nie gehört,* 34.

95 that made more room: Riga, USHMM Encyclopedia, accessed July 6, 2025, https://encyclopedia.ushmm.org/content/en/article/riga.

95 An eyewitness: Brunzel, *Nie gehört,* 35.

95 approached a corporal: Brunzel, *Nie gehört*, 33–34.

95 captured and deported: Cosanne-Schulte-Huxel, "Im Schatten der Lembecker Kirche Die jüdischen Familien in Lembeck," 132.

96 recalled the day: Schulte-Huxel, *Lebenstein/Katz Family,* 11.

96 two daughters deported: "Selma, Berta und Hugo Lebenstein," Eine Verbeugung vor den Opfern, accessed July 29, 2024, https://stolpersteine-dorsten.de/wulfener-str-16-lembeck/.

96 suffering many casualties: "Profile: Clinton M. Hedrick's Medal of Honor," National World War 2 Museum, March 22, 2023, https://www.nationalww2museum.org/war/articles/clinton-m-hedricks-medal-honor.

96 largest airborne operation: "Operation Varsity," The U.S. Army Airborne & Special Operations Museum, accessed January 17, 2025, https://www.asomf.org/operation-varsity/.

97 "fearless through two days": "Profile: Clinton M. Hedrick's Medal of Honor," National WW2 Museum.

97 His Medal of Honor: "Clinton M. Hedrick," Congressional Medal of Honor Society, accessed January 17, 2025, https://www.cmohs.org/recipients/clinton-m-hedrick; also, "World War II (G–L Index), Full-Text Citations," Medal of Honor, U.S. Army, accessed January 17, 2025, https://www.army.mil/medalofhonor/citations21.html#H.

97 last of its kind: Joshua Skovlund, "The First and Last Medals of Honor of World War II," *Task & Purpose*, December 6, 2024, https://taskandpurpose.com/history/first-last-medal-honor-wwii/.

97 a memorial plaque: Michael Menzebach, "In Gedenken an Sergeant Clinton M. Hedrick," *Lokalkompass.de Dorsten*, November 10, 2021, accessed April 5, 2025, https://www.lokalkompass.de/dorsten/c-kultur/in-gedenken-an-sergeant-clinton-m-hedrick_a1654648.

97 ninety-seven-year-old veterans: They were Gilbert Herrera, who was part of the 194th Glider Infantry Regiment, and Richard Weaver, who served at headquarters for the 17th Airborne Division. Another forty descendants made a pilgrimage to the castle in March 2025. "Memorial Day Services Planned in the Lakeland," *Pine Cone Press-Citizen*, May 20, 2022, https://www.pineconepress-citizen.com/news/2022/may/20/memorial-day-services-planned-in-the-lakeland/. Also, 17th Airborne Division Scions (Descendants), "Today, our traveling group of Scions visited Lembeck Castle," Facebook, March 21, 2025, https://www.facebook.com/share/p/18wQfxqMF4/.

98 wrote a letter: Private records of Franz Stutzinger and main state archive in Düsseldorf, dated Duisburg, July 14, 1946. Image reproduced in Cosanne-Schulte-Huxel, "Im Schatten der Lembecker," 134.

98 hiding with a family: Manfred Tietz, "Hanna und Herta, Martha und Anna … : Frauen im Duisburger Widerstand," in *Von Griet zu Emma: Beiträge zur Geschichte von Frauen in Duisburg vom Mittelalter bis heute*, ed. Doris Freer (Frauenbüro, 2000), 60, https://www.duisburg.de/microsites/rgc/von_Griet_zu_Emma.pdf.

98 they dug up: Schulte-Huxel, *Lebenstein/Katz Family*, 21.

98 finally returned to them: Schulte-Huxel, *Lebenstein/Katz Family*, 21.

99 Archival records: State Archives of North Rhine-Westphalia, Westphalia Department K 204, Münster Government.

99 *While Six Million Died:* Arthur D. Morse, *While Six Million Died: A Chronicle of American Apathy* (Random House, 1968).

99 "I feel very bitter": Jeffrey Katz, "Gestapo Escape/and Faint Welcome in America," *Commercial Appeal*, May 8, 1981, 7.

Chapter 9 NEW COUNTRIES, NEW LIVES

101 refugees turned to countries: Patrick von zur Mühlen, "The 1930s: The End of the Latin American Open-Door Policy," in *Refugees from Nazi Germany and the Liberal European States*, Frank Caestecker and Bob Moore, eds. (Berghahn Books, 2010), 107.

101 a liberal policy: Michele Migliori, "The Forgotten Emigration Government Policies Towards European Jewish Refugees in Ecuador and Colombia (1933–1945)," *Cuadernos Judaicos*, no. 37 (2020): 376–389, https://cuadernosjudaicos.uchile.cl/index.php/CJ/article/view/60645.

102 the SS *Orbita*: Shmidt, "Eine Rückkehr."
102 built in 1914: SS Orbita, Military Wiki, accessed July 8, 2025, https://military-history.fandom.com/wiki/SS_Orbita.
102 "It is a life": Michel (Mikhl) Radzinski, *The Scroll Of My Life (Siemiatycze, Poland)*, privately published, accessed August 16, 2024, https://www.jewishgen.org/yizkor/Siemiatycze/Siemiatycze.html?.
103 It only made: Alberto Dorfzaun, WhatsApp message to author, July 9, 2023.
104 imprisoned in the Dachau: Römer, *An meine Gemeinde in der Zerstreuung: Die Rundbriefe des Augsburger Rabbiners Ernst Jacob 1941–1949* (Wissner-Verlag, 2007), 12.
104 "colony of Augsburgers": Römer, *An meine Gemeinde in der Zerstreuung*, 50.
104 "Our house is particularly large": Römer, *An meine Gemeinde in der Zerstreuung*, 127.
106 "like being transported": Jaime Landauer, email to author, September 14, 2022.
106 Grünkern soup: Jeffrey L. Katz, "An Ancient, Humble Grain with the Taste of Bavaria," Connections: The Newsletter of the Descendants of the Jewish Community of Augsburg, June 2024, https://jmaugsburg.de/files/2024/06/2024_06_june_newsletter_connections_djca.pdf.
107 "pushed, shoved, spat upon": Margot Marx, "Margot Marx's History," document shared with the author, June 6, 2014.
107 "We only had ten dollars": John Nathan, interview with author, October 20, 2002.

Chapter 10 BUILDING BLOCKS

111 Daniel Pearl's final words: Larry Derfner, "Rattling the Cage: Daniel Pearl's last words, uncensored," *Jerusalem Post*, May 6, 2008, https://www.jpost.com/opinion/columnists/rattling-the-cage-daniel-pearls-last-words-uncensored.
113 ritual at age thirteen: Some branches of Judaism celebrate a girl's bat mitzvah at age twelve.
114 on the story: Katz, "School Becomes Oasis in a High-Crime Area," *Commercial Appeal*, November 19, 1978, 21.
116 "A Son Looks for a Home": Katz, "A Son Looks for a Home That's Not the Same," *Commercial Appeal*, May 16, 1980, 7.
116 his own experiences: Katz, "Gestapo Escape."
116 shot and killed: "Manuel Pardo Jr.," Clark County Prosecuting Attorney, accessed July 31, 2024, http://www.clarkprosecutor.org/html/death/US/pardo1320.htm.

Chapter 11 UNCOMFORTABLE HOMECOMINGS

121 he never went back: Rudy Katz, letter to Schulte-Huxel, June 27, 1985.
122 born in 1912: Stegemann, "Internationaler Auschwitz-Gedenktag: Der Dorstener Ernst Metzger hat die Hölle von Auschwitz überlebt—1983 besuchte er seine Heimatstadt, der er sich nicht mehr annähern konnte," last modified January 27, 2017, http://www.dorsten-transparent.de/2017/01/internationaler-auschwitz-gedenktag-der-dorstener-ernst-metzger-hat-die-holle-von-auschwitz-uberlebt-1983-besuchte-er-seine-heimatstadt-der-er-sich-nicht-mehr-annahern-konnte/.

122 *Dorsten unterm Hakenkreuz:* Ernst Metzger, "Sie warfen Menschen in die Flammen," in *Dorsten unterm Hakenkreuz: Die jüdische Gemeinde Book 1* (privately published, 1983), 54–56, http://www.dorsten-unterm-hakenkreuz.de/2012/05/28/ernst-metzger-ich-habe-die-holle-der-konzentrationslager-uberlebt-sie-warfen-menschen-in-die-flammen/.

123 He accepted an invitation: Stegemann, "Der Weg nach Auschwitz, Synonym für Vernichtung und Ermordung jüdischer Menschen, begann auch in Dorsten—Wege zurück gab es nach1945 kaum; wenn, dann nur besuchsweise," Dorsten Transparent, published February 2, 2020, http://www.dorsten-transparent.de/2020/02/der-weg-nach-auschwitz-synonym-fuer-vernichtung-und-ermordung-juedischer-menschen-begann-auch-in-dorsten-wege-zurueck-gab-es-nach1945-kaum-wenn-dann-nur-besuchsweise/.

123 collected money: Stegemann, "Der Weg nach Auschwitz."

123 "Not everyone he met": Stegemann, "Der Weg nach Auschwitz."

123 He wrote to Elisabeth: Metzger letter to Schulte-Huxel, June 23, 1985.

124 Alexander Lebenstein: My great-great-grandfather Nathan Lebenstein was Alexander Lebenstein's great-grandfather.

124 the only survivor: Ellen Robertson, "Holocaust Survivor Alexander Lebenstein Dies at 82," *Richmond Times-Dispatch*, January 29, 2010, updated September 19, 2019, https://richmond.com/news/holocaust-survivor-alexander-lebenstein-dies-at-82/article_ac04b267-14e8-55e9-a42a-7a52781ae304.html.

124 deported to Riga: Alexander Lebenstein, *The Gazebo*, ed. Don Levin (Author House, 2008), 63–70, 81–92.

124 "Germany was no longer": Lebenstein, *The Gazebo*, 133.

124 "insult to injury": Lebenstein, *The Gazebo*, 191.

124 "It is your grandfather": Lebenstein, *The Gazebo,* 195.

125 "Get the hell:" Lebenstein, *The Gazebo,* 197–198.

125 one of his many letters: Lebenstein, email/letter, January 14, 2003.

Chapter 12 STANDING WHERE MY RELATIVES DID

128 a spritely politician: "Ritter, Heinz," Dorsten Lexicon, October 26, 2014, http://www.dorsten-lexikon.de/ritter-heinz/.

128 Experienced chess player: Gerd Kathstede, "Ein Leben für den Schachsport," *Westdeutsche Allgemeine Zeitung,* April 18, 2008, https://www.waz.de/sport/lokalsport/vest-sport/article1855630/ein-leben-fuer-den-schachsport.html.

129 The mayor wanted to know: Ritter, interview with author, November 20, 1986.

130 two local newspapers: "U.S.-Redakteur besucht Land seiner Vorfahren," *Ruth-Nachrichten*, November 21, 1986, and "Das Schlimmste wäre, diesem Land den Rücken zu kehren," *Westdeutsche Allgemeine Zeitung (WAZ)*, November 21, 1986 .

130 "fine, elegant woman": Bernhard Cosanne, interview with author, November 1986.

132 "more than 2,500 Jews": Edna Brocke, *Gestern Synagoge—Haus jüdischer Kultur heute; Yesterday a Synagogue—House of Jewish culture today*, (Schrörs-Druck GmbH, 2011), 32.

132 soulless interior: Brocke, *Gestern Synagoge,* 37–40.

132 little awareness: Brocke, *Gestern Synagoge,* 37.
132 "For the first time": Brocke, *Gestern Synagoge,* 32.
132 Jews were rarely given: Edna Brocke, "On commemoration and its changes in Essen and in Germany," in *Persecution and Resistance in Essen 1933–1945*, ed. Angela Genger (Cultural Office of the City of Essen, English edition, 1984), 36.
132 permanent exhibit: *Persecution and Resistance in Essen 1933–1945.*
135 a bastion of fascism: "Holocaust Memory at Risk. The Distortion of Holocaust History Across Europe," Amadeu Antonio Stiftung, February 2, 2022, https://www.amadeu-antonio-stiftung.de/en/holocaust-memory-at-risk-80759/.
135 the communist resistance: Inka Bertz, "Jewish Museums in the Federal Republic of Germany," trans. Sharon Neeman, in *Visualizing and Exhibiting Jewish Space and History,* ed. Richard L. Cohen (Oxford University Press, 2012), 97.
135 "The GDR emphasized": Thomas Haury, "Current Anti-Semitism in East Germany," *Post-Holocaust and Anti-Semitism*, 59, August 1, 2007, https://jcpa.org/article/current-anti-semitism-in-east-germany/.
135 "a day of liberation": "Speech by Federal President Richard von Weizsäcker."
135 Obviously false: Max Czollek, *De-Integrate! A Jewish Survival Guide for the 21st Century,* trans. Jon Cho-Polizzi (Restless Books, 2023), 4.
136 Palestinian terrorists: "Munich massacre," Encyclopedia Britannica, August 29, 2024, https://www.britannica.com/event/Munich-Massacre.
136 "What I have heard": Ellen Lentz, "West German Youth Found to Be Ignorant About Hitler Period," *New York Times*, April 7, 1977, 13, https://www.nytimes.com/1977/04/07/archives/west-german-youth-found-to-be-ignorant-about-hitler-period.html.
136 "nothing short of a thunderbolt": Kati Marton, *Chancellor* (Simon & Schuster, 2021), 36.
137 "The History Movement emerged": Wüstenberg, Civil Society, 130.
137 Widen the Circle: "Fighting Bigotry. Starting with History," Widen the Circle, https://widenthecircle.org/.
137 straightforward question: Joel Obermayer, interview with author, October 4, 2022.
137 uncomfortable questions: Hartwich, email to author, September 2022.
138 letter to the editor: Dirk Hartwich, "Offene Fragen zu Nazis in Dorsten," *Ruhr Nachrichten*, November 16, 1982.
138 "Acknowledging that one's grandparents": Jacob S. Eder, "Germany Is Often Praised for Facing Up to Its Nazi Past. But Even There, the Memory of the Holocaust Is Still Up for Debate," *Time*, January 27, 2020, https://time.com/5772360/german-holocaust-memory/.
138 "When we started": Hartwich, email to author, September 2022.
139 "die gnade der späten geburt": Michael Borchard, "Deutsch-Israelische Beziehungen—die Rolle von Helmut," Bundeskanzler Helmut Kohl Stiftung, accessed August 7, 2024, https://www.bundeskanzler-helmut-kohl.de/seite/deutsch-israelische-beziehungen-die-rolle-von-helmut-kohl/.
140 Sister Johanna Eichmann: Norbert Reichling, "Johanna (Ruth) Eichmann / 1926: 'Unser Rüthchen bleibt ein Jüdchen,'" Frauen/Ruhr/Geschichte, accessed August 7, 2024, https://www.frauenruhrgeschichte.de/frg_biografie/johanna-ruth-eichmann-1926-2019/#.
140 "She was the face": Hartwich, email to author, September 2022.

140 attended a Protestant school: Andreas Jordan, "Rolf Abrahamsohn," GELSENZENTRUM, August 2008, http://www.gelsenzentrum.de/rolf_abrahamson.htm.
141 "I am in the right place": Rolf Abrahamsohn, interview with author, November 1986.
141 "In every encounter": Schulte-Huxel, email to author, December 7, 2023.
142 wrote about my visit: Katz, "Holocaust's Shadow: A Son Finds New Perspective," *Milwaukee Journal's Wisconsin Magazine*, April 17, 1988, 7–9, 31.
142 "I must confess": Schulte-Huxel, letter to author, May 1988.

Chapter 13 STUMBLING INTO HISTORY

143 raised fears: Volker Witting and Rina Goldenberg, "Germany and Nuclear Weapons: A Difficult History," Deutsche Welle, February 17, 2024, https://www.dw.com/en/germany-and-nuclear-weapons-a-difficult-history/a-68279838#:~:text=The%20West%20German%20and%20European,range%20missiles%20in%20the%20country.
143 built in 1937: "History of Dorsten—Station 27: Wulfen," Lions Club Dorsten-Hanse, accessed August 9, 2024, https://www.lions-dorsten-hanse.de/geschichtsstation.php?gsnr=27&lan=en&back=gs-radkarten.php&rundgang=&radtour=1.
143 fell into British hands: Jürgen Dreifke, "British Forces at Dülmen—a short summary," Bundeswehr in Westphalia, November 2019, accessed August 9, 2024, https://bw-duelmen.de/data/documents/BFG-Duelmen.pdf.
144 "biggest ammunition site": Dreifke, "British Forces at Dülmen," 4.
144 "the right thing to do": Birget Lapke, interview with author, October 13, 2022.
144 *Stern* magazine: Jochen Siemens, "Bückt euch und lest!" *Stern*, no. 42, October 9, 2003, 58–59.
144 "At first": Ulrike Matthäus-Robbert, interview with author, October 13, 2022.
144 1,200 locations: "Home," Stolpersteine.de, accessed August 9, 2024, https://www.stolpersteine.eu/en/home/.
144 100,000th block: "Stolpersteine: Holocaust Project Marks 100,000-Plaque Milestone in Germany," *Local.de*, June 1, 2023, https://www.thelocal.de/20230601/stolpersteine-holocaust-project-marks-100000-plaque-milestone-in-germany.
145 personally installed: "FAQ," Stolpersteine.de, accessed August 9, 2024, https://www.stolpersteine.eu/en/faq.
145 "You don't trip": Peter Bradley, "Stumbling Towards a Way to Remember Lost Family," *Jewish Chronicle*, August 25, 2022, https://www.thejc.com/life-and-culture/stumbling-towards-a-way-to-remember-lost-family-asp85ovm.
147 "I told the attendees": Schulte-Huxel, email to author, September 28, 2007.
147 began the invitation: "Wir erinnern an unsere Dorstener jüdischen Bürger, die von den Nationalsozialisten brutal ermordet wurden," brochure from October 2007, a facsimile in author's possession.
148 "We don't really like": "Unbequem, aber notwendig," Lembeck von A bis Z, October 13, 2007, https://www.lembeck.de/unbequem-aber-notwendig/.
148 "Well, Gunter": Gunter Demnig, interview with author, December 21, 2022.
148 he painted a U.S. flag: Suzanne Cords, "'Stolperstein' Holocaust Memorial Gets New App," Deutsche Welle, November 9, 2022, https://www.dw.com/en/stolperstein-holocaust-memorial-gets-new-app/a-41107926.

149 "tension between the stones'": Miriam Volmert, "Landscape, Boundaries, and the Limits of Representation: The Stolpersteine as a Commemorative Space," *Nordisk judaistik/Scandinavian Jewish Studies 28, no. 1 (2017),*, 8, https://doi.org/10.30752/nj.65910.

149 "It is my firm belief": Eliza Apperly, "'Stumbling Stones': A Different Vision of Holocaust Remembrance," *Guardian,* February 18, 2019, https://www.theguardian.com/cities/2019/feb/18/stumbling-stones-a-different-vision-of-holocaust-remembrance.

149 an international conference: World Federation of Jewish Holocaust Survivors and Descendants 2023 Conference, Washington, D.C., August 27, 2023.

153 bear the names: Tom Bailey, "Photographer Spends Year Capturing the Seasons in Historic Cemetery," *Daily Memphian*, October 30, 2019, https://dailymemphian.com/article/8490/Photographer-spends-year-capturing-the-seasons-in-historic-cemetery.

154 a condolence note: Elisabeth Schulte-Huxel, letter to author, July 30, 2002.

Chapter 14 RETURNING WITH MY FAMILY

159 a handy booklet: Jüdisches Museum Westfalen, *Stolpersteine in Dorsten*, (Gymnasium St. Ursula Dorsten, 2021), https://www.jmw-dorsten.de/wp-content/uploads/2022/02/Stolpersteine-Broschuere_JMW.pdf.

159 website: "Eine Verbeugung vor den Opfern," Stolpersteine Dorsten, accessed August 9, 2024, https://stolpersteine-dorsten.de/.

159 Lembeck's oldest families: Stegemann, "Langenhorst, Familie," Dorsten Lexikon, updated January 21, 2015, http://www.dorsten-lexikon.de/langenhorst-familie/.

159 he frequently visited: Josef Langenhorst, interview with author, June 25, 2011.

160 Germany takes responsibility: Heinz Denninger, interview with author, June 25, 2011.

160 "We have to be active": Barbara Seppi, "Versprechen der Generationen," *Westdeutsche Allgemeine Zeitung*, June 26, 2011, https://www.waz.de/daten-archiv/article4805316/versprechen-der-generationen.html

160 "Just what reminds you": Schulte-Huxel, letter to Dorsten Mayor Lambert Lütkenhorst, July 19, 2007.

161 purchased by my ancestors: Schulte-Huxel, "Lebenstein/Katz Family," 26.

165 he learned "really nothing": Gerd Gutschow, interview with author, October 11, 2022.

167 "Since I was fourteen": Gaby Springer, interview with author, October 14, 2022.

167 were sponsored by: "Stolpersteine erinnern/Stolpersteine in Essen," Historisches Portal Essen, accessed August 9, 2024, https://geschichte.essen.de/historisches-portal_namen/stolpersteine_2.de.html.

167 423 *Stolpersteine*: "Stolpersteine_sortiert_Namen.pdf," Historischer Verein für Stadt und Stift Essen e.V., updated April 28, 2024, https://media.essen.de/media/histiorisches_portal/historischesportal_dokumente/stolpersteine/pdf_listen/Stolpersteine_sortiert_Namen.pdf.

167 installed on July 1, 2005: "Stolperstein 'Rosalie Katz née Lebenstein,'" Historisches Portal Essen, accessed August 9, 2024, https://geschichte.essen.de/historischesportal_namen/stolpersteine_1/stolpersteine_detailseite_1011199.de.html.

167 she couldn't tell me: Birgit Hartings, email to author, June 5, 2024.

Chapter 15 FOUR HUNDRED YEARS IN HÜRBEN

177 "This is a place to remember": Wilhelm Fischer, interview with author, October 16, 2024.
177 "The corner of the old synagogue": Fischer, email to author, November 22, 2022.
178 activists' primary goal: Wüstenberg, "Germany as a Model for Confronting the Past?" *Zeitgeister, the Cultural Magazine of the Goethe-Institut,* February 2021, republished as https://www.goethe.de/ins/us/en/kul/art/stp/22106958.html.
179 elected museum director: Fischer, email to author.
179 "the self-confidence": "Jüdische Geschichte," Heimatverein Krumbach e.V., accessed August 1, 2024, https://www.heimatverein-krumbach.de/aktivitaeten/Juedische-Geschichte.html.
180 634-page book: Herbert Auer, *Ihre Seelen seien eingebunden im Bündel des Lebens* (Heimatverein Krumbach e.V., 2010).
180 built in 1833: "Krumbach incorp. Hürben," International Jewish Cemetery Project, updated September 2013, https://iajgscemetery.org/germany/bayern-bavaria/krumbach-incorp-huerben.
181 "The first concentration camp": Schulte-Huxel, email to author, September 22, 2023.
182 More than two hundred thousand people: Stephanie Pilzweger-Steiner, *Dachau Concentration Camp Memorial Site: A Tour* (utzverlag GmbH, 2017), 4.
182 "evasive answers": Harold Marcuse, *Legacies of Dachau: The Uses and Abuses of a Concentration Camp, 1933–2001* (Cambridge University Press, 2001), https://marcuse.faculty.history.ucsb.edu/publications/legdach/bookintro.99v.htm.
182 "Postwar society": Pilzweger-Steiner, *Dachau Concentration Camp Memorial Site*, 18–20.

Chapter 16 VISITING AUGSBURG

185 "My heart laughed": Schmidt, "Eine Rückkehr ohne Groll im Herzen."
188 a life-or-death decision: Michael Bernheim, "Wolfgang Bernheim—Not Forgotten at Last," *Connections: The Newsletter of the Jewish Descendants of Augsburg*, December 2021, 1, https://jmaugsburg.de/files/2022/01/2021-december-connections-vol-4-num-2-final-updated.pdf.
188 "In these times": Bernheim, interview with author, September 11, 2022.
188 "There are some conflicts": Bernheim, interview with author, October 17, 2022.
189 committed suicide: Deborah Rausch, emails to author, June 7 and 15, 2023.
189 A farewell note: "Farewell Letters from Paul and Hedwig Englaender and Hugo and Lina Steinfeld, 1941, 1943," John L. Englander Family Collection, AR 25170, Leo Baeck Institute, Box: 1, Folder: 269, https://archive.org/details/johnlenglanderfa01engl/page/n268/mode/1up?view=theater.
189 Sixteen months later: Benigna Schönhagen, Paul Englaender, in Benigna Schönhagen and Michael Spotka, *Augsburg's jüdische Ärzte im Nationalsozialismus ein Stadtrundgang* (Jüdisches Kulturmuseum Augsburg Schwaben, 2016). Appears in trans. Cynthia Byrne, "Paul Englaender," Erinnerungs Werkstatt Augsburg, https://gedenkbuch-augsburg.de/en/biografien/dr-paul-englaender.

190 survived the attempt: Rolf Hofmann and Herbert Immenkötter, *Jewish Cemetery Augsburg Gravelist Based on Original Vital Records 1867–1940s* (privately printed, 2018), 102, https://www.alemannia-judaica.de/images/Images%20427/AUGSBURG-EBOOK.pdf.

190 dated March 5: "Translation of Red Cross Cable dated March 5, 1943 (received here in October 1943) from my parents bidding my sister and myself farewell," John L. Englander Family Collection, AR 25170, Leo Baeck Institute, Box: 1, Folder, 255, https://archive.org/details/johnlenglanderfa01engl/page/n254/mode/1up?view=theater.

191 Thomas Keneally's book: Thomas Keneally, *Schindler's List* (Simon & Schuster, 1992).

191 a composite character: Douglas Martin, "Mietek Pemper, 91, Camp Inmate Who Compiled Schindler's List," *New York Times*, June 18, 2011 (appeared in print June 19, 2011, section A, page 24), https://www.nytimes.com/2011/06/19/world/europe/19pemper.html.

191 number 655: "The Jews of Kraków and Its Surrounding Towns: Schindler's List," JewishGen KehaliaLinks, source material from USHMM Archives, accessed August 1, 2024, https://kehilalinks.jewishgen.org/krakow/kra_schindler.htm.

191 told his employees: Mietek Pemper, *The Road to Rescue: The Untold Story of Schindler's List,* trans. David Dollenmayer (Other Press, 2008, originally published in German, 2005), 166.

192 "I always find": Pemper, *The Road to Rescue,* 192.

Chapter 17 SALVAGING A SYNAGOGUE

193 "you can't judge": Carmen Reichert, interview with author, October 18, 2022.

194 "After the first": Reichert, "Letter from JMAS Director Carmen Reichert," *Connections: The Newsletter of the Descendants of the Jewish Community of Augsburg*, June 2022, 3, https://jmaugsburg.de/files/2022/06/2022-june-connections-newsletter-final-final.pdf.

196 "You can see": Schillinger, interview with author, July 14, 2022.

196 a nearby Jewish cemetery: Schillinger, interview with author, July 14, 2022.

198 about 1,400 members: Bernheim, "Meet Alexander Mazo, President of Augsburg's Jewish Community," *Connections: The Newsletter of the Descendants of the Jewish Community of Augsburg*, June 2023, 3, https://jmaugsburg.de/files/2023/06/june-2023-final-updated-links-3.pdf.

198 prewar peak in 1925: "Geschichte. Zweite Gemeinde," IKG Schwaben Augsburg.

198 moved to Augsburg: Alexander Mazo, email with author, July 3, 2023.

198 "is not as integrated": Bernheim, "Meet Alexander Mazo."

199 nearly 20 percent: "Germany Update: Bavaria Grants Nearly €4.7 Million Toward the Ongoing Restoration of the Synagogue in Augsburg," *Jewish Heritage Europe*, March 24, 2023, https://jewish-heritage-europe.eu/2023/03/24/germany-update-augsburg/.

199 "preserving the traditions": Mazo, email, July 3, 2023.

199 Gögginger Gate: "Gögginger Tor Augsburg," Jüdisch Historischer Verein Augsburg, updated August 12, 2011, https://jhva.wordpress.com/tag/gogginger-tor/.

199 opened in 1725: Ayleen Winkler, interview with author, October 18, 2022.
200 they opened again: Winkler, interview.
200 "first public Sabbath": Sel Hubert, *Out of Broken Glass* (Xlibris, Corp., 2010), 41–42.

Chapter 18 WHO TELLS YOUR STORY

207 Two out of three: "Jewish Population of Europe," USHMM Encyclopedia, accessed August 1, 2024, https://encyclopedia.ushmm.org/content/en/gallery/jewish-population-of-europe.
208 vast majority of Jews: Shani Rozanes, "How German Jews Rebuilt After the Holocaust," Deutsche Welle, last modified February 22, 2021, https://www.dw.com/en/how-jewish-life-developed-in-germany-after-the-holocaust/a-56604526.
208 only a small portion: Bertz, "Jewish Museums in the Federal Republic of Germany," 80.
208 "Running a Jewish museum": Reichling, "An Introduction to the Jewish Museum of Westphalia," in *From Dorsten to Chicago: Lectures and Contributions of the Eisendrath Family Reunion 2020 in Dorsten/Germany*, ed. Elisabeth Cosanne-Schulte-Huxel (privately published, 2012), 19, http://www.eisendrath-stories.net/files/eisendrathbook-02102012.pdf.
209 The most prominent: "Members," Association of European Jewish Museums, accessed August 1, 2024, https://www.aejm.org/member-group/organisations/.
209 "For decades": Gruber, *Virtually Jewish,* 5.
209 "an apparent longing": Gruber, *Virtually Jewish,* 4.
209 "show more interest": Brocke, "On Commemoration and Its Changes in Essen and in Germany," 34.
209 *People Love Dead Jews*: Dara Horn, *People Love Dead Jews* (W.W. Norton, 2021), 191.
210 Jewish museum in Brussels: "Brussels Jewish Museum Murders: Mehdi Nemmouche Jailed for Life," BBC, March 11, 2019, https://www.bbc.com/news/world-europe-47533533.
210 Copenhagen's main synagogue: "Copenhagen Attacks: Danish Police Charge Two Men," *Guardian*, February 16, 2015, https://www.theguardian.com/world/2015/feb/16/copenhagen-attacks-danish-police-charge-two-men.
210 a heavy, bolted door: "Halle Synagogue Attack: Germany Far-Right Gunman Jailed for Life," BBC, December 21, 2020, https://www.bbc.com/news/world-europe-55395682.
210 shots were fired: "NRW-Antisemitismusbeauftragte: Angriffe lassen sich nie ganz verhindern," WDR, November 23, 2022, https://www1.wdr.de/nachrichten/nrw-antisemitismusbeauftragte-angriffe-auf-juedische-einrichtungen-essen-100.html; also "Nach Schüssen auf Synagoge in Essen: Debatte im Landtag mit klaren Worten," Radio Essen, November 24, 2022, https://www.radioessen.de/artikel/nach-schuessen-auf-synagoge-in-essen-debatte-im-landtag-mit-klaren-worten-1494058.html.
210 fewer visitors: "American and European Jewish Museums Since October 7—Survey Report," Association of Jewish Museums, December 27, 2024, https://www.aejm.org/aejm-cajm-survey-2024-download-the-survey-results/.

210 "It's hard": Melissa Eddy, "What and Whom Are Jewish Museums For?" *New York Times*, last modified July 10, 2019, appeared in print July 15, 2019, section C, page 2, https://www.nytimes.com/2019/07/09/arts/.design/jewish-museums-germany-berlin-europe.html.

210 "Guilt is not": Eddy, "What and Whom Are Jewish Museums For?"

210 "Crying doesn't educate": Felix Bohr, "Klima der Angst," *Spiegel Panorama*, October 17, 2019, https://www.spiegel.de/panorama/justiz/volkhard-knigge-mobbingvorwuerfe-gegen-leiter-von-ns-gedenkstaette-a-1291996.html.

211 assigned a role: Bertz, "Jewish Museums in the Federal Republic of Germany," 106.

211 "What should Jewish museums": Gruber, *Virtually Jewish*, 130.

211 The first was in Vienna: Gruber, *Virtually Jewish*, 159.

211 "the museum bolstered": Bertz, "The First Jewish Museum in Berlin," Jüdisches Museum Berlin, accessed August 1, 2024, https://www.jmberlin.de/en/first-jewish-museum-berlin.

211 plundered and lost: Eve M. Duffy, "Duffy on Rauschenberger, 'Jüdische Tradition im Kaiserreich und in der Weimarer Republik: Zur Geschichte des jüdischen Museumswesens in Deutschland,'" *H-German, H-Net Reviews,* September, 2004, https://www.h-net.org/reviews/showrev.php?id=9835.

212 "nonreligious Jewish shrines": Gruber, *Virtually Jewish*, 160.

212 private, independent museum: "Jewish Museum Augsburg Swabia," Association of European Jewish Museums, accessed August 1, 2024, https://www.aejm.org/members/jewish-museum-augsburg-schwabia/.

212 rare such initiative: Bertz, "Jewish Museums in the Federal Republic of Germany," 90.

212 Cesia and David Blitzer: "Wolf Blitzer's 'Roots,'" CNN, updated October 14, 2014, https://www.cnn.com/2014/10/10/world/gallery/roots-wolf-blitzer/index.html.

212 Many were assigned: "Survivors and the Displaced Persons era," The Holocaust Explained, The Wiener Holocaust Library, accessed August 1, 2024, https://www.theholocaustexplained.org/survival-and-legacy/survivors-and-dp-era/dp-camps/.

213 Spokojny was born: Sarah König, "Between Rite and Musealization. Judaica in the Jewish Communities of Southern Germany After the Shoah, Using the Example of Augsburg and the Person of Julius Spokojny," *Jewish Life and Culture in Germany after 1945: Sacred Spaces, Objects and Musical Traditions*, ed. Katrin Keßler, et al. (De Gruyter Oldenbourg, 2022), 149–162, https://doi.org/10.1515/9783110750812-010.

213 "the main exhibit": König, "Between Rite and Musealization," 156.

213 "Spokojny wanted to fill": König, "Between Rite and Musealization," 157.

213 opened in 2006: Bertz, "Jewish Museums."

214 "a good soul": "Oral History Interview with Paul Rosenau," USHMM Collection.

214 "the first person outside": "A Tribute to Gernot Römer," *Connections, The Newsletter of the Descendants of the Jewish Community of Augsburg,* December 2020, 1, https://jmaugsburg.de/files/2021/01/2020-december-connections-newsletter-final-12-2020-2.pdf.

214 "not an easy boss": Rudy Wais, "Gernot Römer hat der Zeitung Gesicht und Profil gegeben," Augsburger Allgemeine, July 5, 2022, https://www.augsburger-allgemeine.de/bayern/nachruf-gernot-roemer-hat-der-zeitung-gesicht-und-profil-gegeben-id63201386.html.

214 "I admire him still": Angela Bachmair, interview with author, November 18, 2022.

214 *Schwäbishe Juden*: Römer, *Schwäbishe Juden: Leben und Leistungen aus zwei Jahrhunderten* (Presse-Druck- und Verlags-GmbH, 1990).

214 postwar newsletters: Römer, *An meine Gemeinde in der Zerstreuung*.

214 "Some of my colleagues": Bachmaier, interview with author.

215 another incident: George Sturm, *An Early Life: Remembrances and Stories* (privately published, 2017), as excerpted in *Connections: The Newsletter of the Descendants of the Jewish Community of Augsburg*, December 2020, 13, https://jmaugsburg.de/files/2021/01/2020-december-connections-newsletter-final-12-2020-2.pdf.

215 "it took me much courage": Schönhagen, interview with author, September 17, 2022.

216 to the perpetrators: "Forum: Ian Kershaw: Beware the Moral High Ground," *H-Soz-Kult*, February 24, 2004, www.hsozkult.de/debate/id/fddebate-132084.

216 purposely played down: Nicolas Berg, *Der Holocaust und die westdeutschen Historiker* (Wallstein Verlag, 2003). Published in English as Nicolas Berg, *The Holocaust and the West German Historians*, trans. Joel Golb (University of Wisconsin Press, 2015).

216 "There are many reasons": Schönhagen, interview with author, September 17, 2022.

216 "the Jews vanished": Schönhagen, interview with author, September 24, 2022.

217 "I *want* to know it": Schönhagen, interview with author, September 17, 2022.

217 an impressive collection: Obermayer German Jewish History Award, Distinguished Service: "You Have to Defend Democracy, Which Gives You the Right to Be Different," Widen the Circle, accessed August 5, 2024, https://widenthe-circle.org/benigna-schonhagen.

217 renowned local silversmiths: Benigna Schönhagen, "Ort der Begegnung und des Lernens. Das Jüdische Kulturmuseum Augsburg-Schwaben," *Museum Today: Landesstelle für die nichtstaatlichen Museen in Bayern*, Museum 32, August 2007, 27–30, https://museumsberatung-bayern.de/fileadmin/Veroeffentlichungen_vor_Relaunch/Mh_32.pdf.

217 the last twelve Jews: "The First Jews of Dorsten," Eisendrath Stories, accessed August 5, 2024, http://www.eisendrath-stories.net/cont_19thcenturystories_the_first_jews_of_dorsten.php.

218 "We could hardly believe": Schulte-Huxel, Christel Winkel, Anke Klapsing-Reich, email to author, April 30, 2022.

218 "baldly declared": Gruber, *Virtually Jewish*, 31.

218 "an expression of modesty": Reichling, interview with author, March 23, 2023.

218 "He was perplexed": Kathrin Pieren, interview with author, October 12, 2022.

219 "the deeds of perpetrators": Pieren, email to author, October 14, 2022.

219 "we cannot reach": Pieren, interview with author.

219 mini exhibition: Reichert, email to author, March 30, 2025. Also in "A Major Milestone for the Renovation of Augsburg's Synagogue," Jüdisches Museum Augsburg Schwaben, accessed May 8, 2025, https://jmaugsburg.de/en/a-major-milestone-in-the-renovation-of-augsburgs-synagogue/.

219 "Jews lived in Westphalia": Principle, Jüdisches Museum Westphalen, accessed August 5, 2024, https://www.jmw-dorsten.de/en/building-history-and-principle/.

221 The story appeared: Petra Berkenbusch, "Jeffrey Katz aus den USA erforscht Spuren seiner jüdischen Familie," *Dorstener Zeitung,* October 14, 2022, DNL04, https://www.dorstenerzeitung.de/dorsten/us-journalist-sucht-in-dorsten-spuren-seiner-juedischen-familie-w1800906-4000633013/.

221 *Lebenslinien*: "Lebenslinien: Deutsch-jüdische Familiengeschichten," Jüdisches Museum Augsburg Schwaben, accessed August 8, 2024, https://jmaugsburg.de/publikationen/lebenslinien-reihe/.

221 "They were very old": Schönhagen, interview with author, September 24, 2022.

Chapter 19 DESCENDANTS DILEMMA

225 "antisemitism destroys home": Frank-Walter Steinmeier, "Festakt '100 Jahre Synagoge Augsburg,'" Der Bundespräsident, June 28, 2017, https://www.bundespraesident.de/SharedDocs/Downloads/DE/Reden/2017/06/170628-Augsburg-Synagoge-Englisch.pdf?__blob=publicationFile&v=3.

225 remembered the day vividly: Henry Stern, "Saying Goodbye to My Teddy Bear on My Last Day in Augsburg, 1939," *Connections: The Newsletter of the Jewish Descendants of Augsburg,* June 2019, 7, https://jmaugsburg.de/files/2021/01/2019-june-newsletter-connections-djca-volume-2-number-final.pdf.

225 "It was a hard time": Pola Sell, "Finding Memories," filmed June 25–29, 2017, in Augsburg, https://vimeo.com/242238631.

226 called out to him: Stern, "Saying Goodbye to My Teddy Bear," 1.

226 Helma Landherr: Diane Castiglione, email to author, July 29, 2023.

227 even easier to claim: Ian Bateson, "German Citizenship for Descendants of Nazi Victims," Deutsche Welle, June 25, 2021, https://www.dw.com/en/germany-lifts-restrictions-for-descendants-of-nazi-victimsto-get-citizenship/a-58046004.

227 An overwhelming majority: "Reflections on German Citizenship," *Connections: The Newsletter of the Descendants of the Jewish Community of Augsburg,* December 2021, 13, 17–19, https://jmaugsburg.de/files/2022/01/2021-december-connections-vol-4-num-2-final-updated.pdf.

228 monthlong voyage: "These Readers Survived the Holocaust. This Is What Worries Them About America Today," *Los Angeles Times*, January 21, 2022, https://www.latimes.com/opinion/story/2022-01-21/holocaust-survivors-what-worries-them-about-today.

228 her bedroom crying: Bettina Kaplan, interview with author, October 20, 2022.

228 "kicked my parents out": Ibid.

229 "reclaiming a home": Jonah Landor-Yamagata, interview with author, July 12, 2023.

230 "lost their German citizenship": Diane Castiglione, interview with author, May 19, 2023.

230 felt this acutely: Lawrence Kahn and Beth Handler, interview with author, September 29, 2022.

230 bombing of their Augsburg apartment: Lawrence S. Kahn, "Eva H. Eckert Remembered (1927–2022)," *Connections: The Newsletter of the Descendants of the Jewish Community of Augsburg*, June 2022, 9, https://jmaugsburg.de/files/2021/01/2020-december-connections-newsletter-final-12-2020-2.pdf.

231 "I am an American": Kahn and Beth Handler, letter, September 27, 2022.

231 "There was no hiding": Kahn and Handler, interview.

231 a story about her life: Eva Maria Knab, "Amerikanische Holocaust-Überlebende findet letzte Ruhe in Augsburg," *Augsburger Allgemeine*, September 9, 2022, 31, https://www.augsburger-allgemeine.de/augsburg/augsburg-us-nachfahrin-der-verfolgten-familie-kahn-laesst-sich-in-augsburg-beerdigen-id63861796.html.

232 a growing number: Knab, "Warum immer mehr Nachfahren von NS-Opfern nach Augsburg kommen," *Augsburger Allgemeine*, September 20, 2022, 40, https://www.augsburger-allgemeine.de/augsburg/augsburg-warum-immer-mehr-nachfahren-von-ns-opfern-nach-augsburg-kommen-id63870296.html.

Chapter 20 UNFINISHED BUSINESS

233 increasingly objected: For instance, a survey conducted February 13–25 found only two-thirds of American Jewish adults ages fifty or older thought Israel's military response was acceptable. Younger people were even less supportive; only about half of Jewish adults under age thirty-five approved of the military actions. Becka A. Alper, "How U.S. Jews Are Experiencing the Israel-Hamas War," Pew Research Center, April 2, 2024, https://www.pewresearch.org/short-reads/2024/04/02/how-us-jews-are-experiencing-the-israel-hamas-war/.

234 "No one should spend": "Reform Movement Statement on Starvation in Gaza," Union for Reform Judaism, July 27, 2025, https://urj.org/press-room/reform-movement-statement-starvation-gaza.

234 hurled Molotov cocktails: Ashifa Kassam, "Rise in Antisemitism 'Brings Germans Back to Most Horrific Times,'" *Guardian*, October 24, 2003, https://www.theguardian.com/world/2023/oct/24/rise-in-antisemitism-brings-germans-back-to-most-horrific-times.

234 inverted red triangles: Zeev Avrahami, "Pro-Palestinian Activists in Berlin Use New Symbol to Show Hamas Support," *Ynetnews*, June 15, 2024, https://www.ynetnews.com/article/rklj4msrr.

234 "All this really deep": Reichling, email to author, November 29, 2023.

234 "Schools represent": Reichert, email to author, March 30, 2025.

235 "anti-Semitism has grown rapidly": Mazo, email to author, February 21, 2024.

235 scrawled in pen: Pieren, interview with author, February 19, 2024.

235 they typically mentioned: Pieren, February 19, 2024.

235 a new reluctance: Wüstenberg, interview with author, February 6, 2024.

236 "the great lie": Max Czollek (@rubenmcloop), Twitter, September 14, 2023, https://x.com/rubenmcloop/status/1702260378552459377.

236 "Did we, for this process": Schönhagen, interview with author, September 24, 2022.

237 paid for the cost: "reparations," Encyclopedia Britannica, accessed May 8, 2025, https://www.britannica.com/topic/international-law/Historical-development.

237 "*Staatsräson*": William Noah Glucroft, "Germany's Unique Relationship with Israel," Deutsche Welle, October 15, 2023, https://www.dw.com/en/israel-and-germanys-reason-of-state-its-complicated/a-67094861.

237 "an unprecedented landmark:" Ariel Colonomos and Andrea Armstrong, "German Reparations to the Jews after World War II: A Turning Point in the History of Reparations," in Pablo de Greiff, ed., *The Handbook of Reparations* (Oxford, 2006) 390–419.
238 more than $90 billion: History, Conference on Jewish Material Claims Against Germany (Claims Conference), accessed July 14, 2025, https://www.claimscon.org/about/history/.
238 sixteen thousand valuable artifacts: "Justice for Uncompensated Survivors Today (JUST) Act Report: Germany," U.S. Department of State, accessed July 13, 2024, https://www.state.gov/reports/just-act-report-to-congress/germany/.
238 "instructive" for America: Ta-Nehisi Coates, "The Case for Reparations," *Atlantic*, June 2014, https://www.theatlantic.com/magazine/archive/2014/06/the-case-for-reparations/361631/.
238 *Learning from the Germans:* Susan Neiman, *Learning from the Germans* (Farrar, Straus and Giroux, 2019).
238 What can we learn from Germany?: Clint Smith, "Monuments to the Unthinkable: America Still Can't Figure Out How to Memorialize the Sins of Our History. What Can We Learn from Germany?" *Atlantic*, December 2022, 22–41.
238 Germany faced its horrible past: Michele L. Norris, "Germany Faced Its Horrible Past. Can We Do the Same?" *Washington Post*, June 3, 2021, https://www.washingtonpost.com/opinions/2021/06/03/slavery-us-germany-holocaust-reckoning/.
238 "'Germans & Jews'" and Americans: Andrew O'Hehir, "'Germans & Jews' and Americans: What Can We Learn from Germany's Reckoning with History?" *Salon*, June 9, 2016, https://www.salon.com/2016/06/09/germans_jews_and_americans_what_can_we_learn_from_germanys_reckoning_with_history/.
239 an ironic connotation: Chunjie Zhang, "Identity Freedom or on Choosing Who We Are," in *On Being Adjacent to Historical Violence*, ed. Irene Kacandes (De Gruyter, 2022), 69–88.
239 The term was coined: Y. Michal Bodemann, *Gedächtnistheater: Die jüdische Gemeinde und ihre deutsche Erfindung* (Robuch, 1996).
239 Jews are ascribed roles: Czollek, *De-Integrate!* 192.
239 the "Bear Jew,": Sanders Isaac Bernstein, "Shall We Not Revenge?" *Jewish Currents,* March 3, 2023, https://jewishcurrents.org/shall-we-not-revenge.
239 assigned a specific role: Jella Mehringer, "'Reconciliation Theater:' Max Czollek on One-Sided German Culture of Remembrance," *Das Ereste,* February 5, 2023, accessed August 30, 2023, https://www.daserste.de/information/wissen-kultur/ttt/sendung/ttt-titel-thesen-temperamente-2894.html.
240 primarily know one thing: Czollek, *De-Integrate!* 14.
240 "conception of Jewishness": Czollek, *De-Integrate!* 154.
240 to be expected: Czollek, *De-Integrate!* 192.
240 can be rebuilt: Czollek, *De-Integrate!* 11.
240 "a charming thing": Czollek, *De-Integrate!* 31.

240 "I am especially impressed": Helmut Walker Smith, "It Takes a Village to Create a Nation's Memory: Returning Jews and Local Communities Worked Together to Lead Germany Toward Historical Reckoning," *Zocalo Public Square*, January 11, 2021, https://www.zocalopublicsquare.org/2021/01/11/post-war-germany-jewish-return-memory-national-reckoning/ideas/essay/.

241 nearly 21 percent: Kristin Zeier and Gianna-Carina Grün, "German Election Results Explained in Graphics," February 27, 2025, Deutsche Welle, https://www.dw.com/en/german-election-results-explained-in-graphics/a-71724186.

241 strong base in the east: "Germany: AfD a Growing Threat to Democracy, Says Minister," Deutsche Welle, December 28, 2023, https://www.dw.com/en/germany-afd-a-growing-threat-to-democracy-says-minister/a-67839373.

241 criticized Germany's: Srinivas Mazumdaru, "US Criticizes Germany for Labeling AfD 'Extremist,'" Deutsche Welle, May 3, 2025, https://www.dw.com/en/us-criticizes-germany-for-labeling-afd-extremist/a-72423560.

241 withdrew cosponsorship: Laura Wagner, "Masha Gessen Won a 'Political Thought' Prize. Then They Wrote on Gaza," *Washington Post*, December 14, 2023, https://www.washingtonpost.com/style/media/2023/12/14/masha-gessen-hannah-arendt-prize/.

241 published an essay: Masha Gessen, "In the Shadow of the Holocaust: How the Politics of Memory in Europe Obscures What We See in Israel and Gaza Today," *New Yorker,* December 9, 2023, https://www.newyorker.com/news/the-weekend-essay/in-the-shadow-of-the-holocaust.

241 "terribly awry": Manuel Schwab, "Germany Pledged 'Never Again.' Here's How It's Grappling with Israel's Bombing of Gaza," *Los Angeles Times*, December 17, 2023, https://www.latimes.com/opinion/story/2023-12-17/germany-israel-gaza-antisemitism-holocaust-genocide-palestinians-solidarity#.

242 hadn't sufficiently condemned: Catherine Hickley, "Candice Breitz Exhibition in Germany Is Cancelled over Her Middle East Views," *Art Newspaper*, November 29, 2023, https://www.theartnewspaper.com/2023/11/29/candice-breitz-exhibition-in-germany-is-cancelled-over-her-middle-east-views.

242 "Need I point out": Philip Oltermann, "'A Frenzy of Judgement': Artist Candice Breitz on Her German Show Being Pulled over Gaza," *Guardian*, December 7, 2023, https://www.theguardian.com/artanddesign/2023/dec/07/a-frenzy-of-judgement-artist-candice-breitz-on-her-german-show-being-pulled-over-gaza.

242 "This country is not coping": Ilana Hammerman, "A Picturesque Bavarian Town Shows That Germany Isn't Confronting Its Nazi Past," *Haaretz*, December 6, 2019, https://www.haaretz.com/israel-news/2019-12-06/ty-article-magazine/.premium/a-picturesque-bavarian-town-shows-that-germany-isnt-confronting-its-nazi-past/0000017f-eef8-da6f-a77f-fefeac610000.

242 "the mosques": Czollek, *De-Integrate!* 192.

242 "Those who dream": Czollek, *De-Integrate!* 69.

243 "in voiding itself of Jews": James E. Young, *At Memory's Edge: After-Images of the Holocaust in Contemporary Art and Architecture* (Yale University Press, 2000), 208.

243 "just bird shit": "AfD Chief Downplays Nazi Era as 'Bird Shit,'" Deutsche Welle, February 6, 2018, https://www.dw.com/en/afds-gauland-plays-down-nazi-era-as-a-bird-shit-in-german-history/a-44055213.

243 "a 180-degree reversal": Jörg Diehl et al., "A New Wave of Anti-Semitism Sweeps Across Germany," *Spiegel International,* October 27, 2023, https://www.spiegel.de/international/germany/absolutely-appalling-a-new-wave-of-anti-semitism-sweeps-across-germany-a-50e18e6a-03ae-4ea5-99ec-6d0c8753558a.

243 "Collective shame": Ben Sales, "What a New Memorial for Black Lynching Victims Learned from Holocaust Commemoration," Jewish Telegraphic Agency, April 26, 2018, https://www.jta.org/2018/04/26/united-states/new-memorial-black-lynching-victims-learned-holocaust-commemoration.

243 "too much of a focus": Jim Tankersley and Christopher F. Schuetze, "Musk Says Germany Has 'Too Much of a Focus on Past Guilt,'" *New York Times*, January 27, 2025, https://www.nytimes.com/2025/01/27/world/europe/musk-germany-afd-auschwitz.html.

244 "the historical burden": "Holocaust Memory at Risk," Amadeu Antonio Stiftung.

244 adjusting their approach: Pieren, interview with author, February 19, 2024.

244 "something becomes doctrinaire": Obermayer, interview with author, March 5, 2024.

244 began to cry: "Did You Ever Tell This? She Said No, No One Ever Asked," Widen the Circle's 2020 Obermayer Award to Sabeth Schmidthals, https://widenthecircle.org/profiles/sabeth-schmidthals.

245 "You can't ask students": Obermayer, interview, March 5, 2024.

245 "not solely the product": Joseph Cronin, "Germany's Holocaust Memory Problems," *Georgetown Journal of International Affairs*, April 20, 2022, https://gjia.georgetown.edu/2022/04/20/germanys-holocaust-memory-problems%EF%BF%BC/.

245 "It was brief": Paul Scraton, "Can the German Path to Truth and Reconciliation Work in America?" *Literary Hub*, July 15, 2020, https://lithub.com/can-the-german-path-to-truth-and-reconciliation-work-in-america/.

245 Herero and Nama people: "What Is Genocide: The Herero and Namaqua Genocide," The Wiener Holocaust Library, accessed July 14, 2024, https://www.theholocaustexplained.org/what-was-the-holocaust/what-was-genocide/the-herero-and-namaqua-genocide/. Also, "Herero Revolt 1904–1907," South African History Online, accessed July 14, 2024, https://www.sahistory.org.za/article/herero-revolt-1904-1907#:~:text=In%201904%2C%20the%20Herero%20and,genocide%20of%20the%2020th%20century.

245 Maji-Maji Rebellion: "Germany's President Has Apologized for Colonial Era Killings in Tanzania over a Century Ago," AP News, last modified November 1, 2023, https://apnews.com/article/germany-tanzania-maji-maji-killings-apology-9ae1ec66a0b0fe2c75e0d6890e247f6a.

245 "people will read books": Christoph Hasselbach, "Holocaust Remembrance in Germany: A Changing Culture," January 27, 2019, Deutsche Welle, https://www.dw.com/en/holocaust-remembrance-in-germany-a-changing-culture/a-47203540.

245 a pdf online: "'Dort, wo unsere Schule steht, gab es früher eine jüdische Volksschule–was ist aus ihr geworden?'—Geschichte und Geschichten," February 2020, https://ebbk-essen.de/assets/files/2020_11_05_Infomaterial_Unsere_Schule_war_einmal_j_dische_Volksschule_1.pdf.

246 created by students: The project was inspired by a visit to the school in November 2019 by Solomon (Sally) Perel, a Jew who survived after he was captured by the German army by assuming a non-Jewish identity. Perel challenged the students to "report on the injustice that citizens have done to their fellow citizens." "'Jupp Has Remained Inside Me'—Identity in the Story of Shlomo Perel," Yad Vashem, accessed February 7, 2025, https://www.yadvashem.org/education/educational-materials/lesson-plans/shlomo-perel.html. His story also appears in "'Because You Must Live:' The Story of Shlomo (Solly) Perel," Yad Vashem, accessed February 7, 2025, https://www.yadvashem.org/education/testimony-films/shlomo-perel-story.html.

246 got a response: Laura Renell, emails to author, February 24 and April 28, 2025.

246 postwar rallying cry: Emily Burack, "How 'Never Again' Evolved from Holocaust Commemoration Slogan to Universal Call," *Times of Israel*, March 9, 2018, https://www.timesofisrael.com/how-never-again-evolved-from-holocaust-commemoration-slogan-to-universal-call/.

246 "The last few generations": Horn, *People Love Dead Jews*, 217–218.

246 "The claim that rounding": Neiman, *Learning from the Germans,* 31.

247 "exit the Theater of Memory": Sanders Isaac Bernstein, "Shall We Not Revenge?" *Jewish Currents,* March 3, 2023, https://jewishcurrents.org/shall-we-not-revenge.

247 "get to know Jews": Reichert, email to author, March 30, 2025.

247 other attempts to destroy: "About the Genocide Convention," United Nations Office on Genocide Prevention and the Responsibility to Protect, accessed July 14, 2024, https://www.un.org/en/genocideprevention/documents/Genocide%20Convention-FactSheet-ENG.pdf.

248 "This isn't only": Pieren, interview, February 19, 2024.

248 "standard of measurement": Adam Eisendrath, email to author, July 9, 2023.

248 "For those Jews": Julia Rymer Brucker, email to Descendants of the Jewish Community of Augsburg, September 21, 2023. Appears in Jeffrey L. Katz, "Descendants Confront Fading Memories of the Holocaust," *Connections: The Newsletter of the Descendants of the Jewish Community of Augsburg,* 12, https://jmaugsburg.de/files/2024/01/2023_12_december_newsletter-connections_djca.pdf.

249 retrieve the Torah scrolls: Christina Wandt, "Jüdische Gäste aus aller Welt feiern neue Torarolle," *Westdeutsche Allgemeine Zeitung,* June 14, 2022, https://www.waz.de/staedte/essen/article235620651/Essen-Juedische-Gaeste-aus-aller-Welt-feiern-neue-Torarolle.html.

249 Panama Hat business: Alberto Dorfzaun, "My Story: Rescue Through Emigration in the Nazi Era," JDC Archives, accessed July 14, 2024, https://archives.jdc.org/rescue-through-emigration-in-the-nazi-era-2/.

249 the flatware business: Dorfzaun, WhatsApp message to author, July 8, 2023.

249 "Every time I spoke": Dorfzaun, interview with author, July 31, 2023.

250 inscribing the last: Stefan Laurin, "Albertos Buchstabe: Eine Torarolle wurde in der Alten Synagoge fertiggestellt—von einem Urenkel des einstigen Gabbais," *Jüdische Allgemeine,* June 16, 2022, https://www.juedische-allgemeine.de/unsere-woche/albertos-buchstabe/.

250 "if the remembrance stuff": Castiglione, interview with author, May 19, 2023.

250 "They're acknowledging": Kaplan, interview with author, October 20, 2022.

250 a Lebenstein relative: Isaac Lebenstein's first wife, Helene, died in childbirth. Their daughter, Regina, married Max Bendix and had three children in nearby Dülmen. Her two sons emigrated to South Africa in 1936. Regina (who was widowed by then) and her daughter tried unsuccessfully to follow them in 1940; both were murdered in Auschwitz. Mark Bendix's visit to Lembeck is noted in "Family Trace Search 2015," Heimatkunde: Westfälische Juden und ihre Nachbarn, accessed July 14, 2024, http://heimatkunde-jmw.de/familien-spuren-suche-2015/.

250 "Clueless": Mark Bendix, interview with author, July 10, 2023.

251 A public opinion survey: "Israelis Have a Positive View of Germany—Germans Are Increasingly Critical of Israel," Bertelsmann Stiftung, May 9, 2025, https://www.bertelsmann-stiftung.de/en/our-projects/german-israeli-young-leaders-exchange/project-news/israelis-have-a-positive-view-of-germany-germans-are-increasingly-critical-of-israel.

251 "It is wrong": Stephan Vopel, Bertelsmann Stiftung, ed., "Germany and Israel Today: Between Stability and Tension," May 28, 2025, 11, https://www.bertelsmann-stiftung.de/fileadmin/files/BSt/Publikationen/GrauePublikationen/Germany_and_Israel_today_Between_stability_and_tension.pdf.

251 "I object always": Hartwich, email to author, November 25, 2023.

251 "It's not like": Obermayer, interview with author, March 5, 2024.

Chapter 21 IMAGINING A HOME

253 "have a long tradition": Schulte-Huxel, letter to author, May 1988.

253 "It was not easy": Schulte-Huxel, letter to author, September 22, 2023.

254 culminated in a book: *From Dorsten to Chicago: Lectures and contributions of the Eisendrath Family Reunion in Dorsten/Germany*, ed. Cosanne-Schulte-Huxel (privately published, 2012).

254 Elise Hallin-Reifeisen: Cosanne-Schulte-Huxel, *Mein liebes Ilsekind: Mit dem Kindertransport nach Schweden—Briefe an eine gerettete Tochter* (Klartext-Verlag 2013).

258 on the same train: Richard Aronowitz, "Broken Inheritance," *London Magazine*, December 2020/January 2021, https://thelondonmagazine.org/essay-broken-inheritance-by-richard-aronowitz/.

259 "Hate gets us nowhere": Pemper, *The Road to Rescue*, 195.

260 several different groups: "What Groups of People Did the Nazis Target?" USHMM Encyclopedia, last modified April 4, 2024, https://encyclopedia.ushmm.org/content/en/article/what-groups-of-people-did-the-nazis-target.

ABOUT THE AUTHOR

Veteran journalist Jeffrey L. Katz has traveled to Germany several times to explore his family's roots and meet with local members of the country's remembrance movement. He has written and spoken frequently about Germany's reconciliation efforts and his connections to a new generation there. His stories about these experiences have been featured by NPR, *Moment Magazine*, and various newspapers.

For more than four decades, Katz reported, edited, and managed at local and national news organizations in print, broadcast, and online. His editing experience included fifteen years at NPR. He also worked as a reporter and staff writer at *Congressional Quarterly* and *Governing* magazines and *The Milwaukee Journal* and *The (Memphis) Commercial Appeal* newspapers. More recently, Katz has indulged his love of books by working as a part-time bookseller. He's a graduate of the University of Illinois. He and his wife, Mollie, have two grown children.